The Invention

·····································

# of Women

The Invention of Women

MAKING AN AFRICAN SENSE OF
WESTERN GENDER DISCOURSES

Oyèrónké Oyěwùmí

University of Minnesota Press
Minneapolis
London

Published by the University of Minnesota Press
111 Third Avenue South, Suite 290, Minneapolis, MN 55401-2520
http://www.upress.umn.edu
Printed in the United States of America on acid-free paper
Fourth Printing 2003

Library of Congress Cataloging-in-Publication Data

Oyěwùmí, Oyèrónké.
    The invention of women : making an African sense of western gender
discourses / Oyèrónké Oyěwùmí.
        p.   cm.
    Includes bibliographical references and index.
    ISBN 0-8166-2440-2 (hc : alk. paper). – ISBN 0-8166-2441-0 (pb :
alk. paper)
    1. Women, Yoruba – Social conditions.   2. Women, Yoruba – History.
3. Philosophy, Yoruba.   4. Sex role – Nigeria.   5. Sex differences –
Nigeria.   6. Body, Human – Social aspects – Nigeria.   I. Title.
DT515.45.Y67094   1997
305.48'896333 – dc21   97–36162

For my children,
the source of life and its inspiration:

Ọlásǔnbọ̀
Akínbóyè
and
Mapaté

Ọmọlayọ̀
Ọmọlasọ
Ọmọniyì
Ọmọnidẹ

Contents

•••

Preface

•••

THIS BOOK is about the epistemological shift occasioned by the imposition of Western gender categories on Yorùbá discourse. Since there is a clear epistemological foundation to cultural knowledge, the first task of the study is to understand the epistemological basis of both Yorùbá and Western cultures. This endeavor is best described as archaeological, in that it is concerned with revealing the most basic but hidden assumptions, making explicit what has been merely implicit, and unearthing the taken-for-granted assumptions underlying research concepts and theories. Only when such assumptions are exposed can they be debated and challenged.

This book is not about the so-called woman question. The woman question is a Western-derived issue — a legacy of the age-old somato-centricity in Western thought. It is an imported problem, and it is not indigenous to the Yorùbá. If it has become relevant in Yorùbá studies, the history of that process needs to be told. This study has become part of that history. When I started the research, I believed that it was possible for me to do a study on gender in a contemporary Yorùbá community that would primarily address the question from a local perspective. It soon became clear to me that because of the academic practice of relying on disciplinary theories and conceptual debates originating in and dominated by the West, many of the questions that informed the initial research project were not (and could not be) generated from local conditions. But I continued to believe that the problem could be surmounted in the process.

As the work and my thinking progressed, I came to realize that the fundamental category "woman" — which is foundational in Western gender discourses — simply did not exist in Yorùbáland prior to its sustained contact with the West. There was no such preexisting group characterized by shared interests, desires, or social position. The cultural logic of Western social categories is based on an ideology of biological determinism: the conception that biology provides the rationale for the organization of the social world. Thus this cultural logic is actually a "bio-logic." Social categories like "woman" are based on body-type

ix

and are elaborated in relation to and in opposition to another category: man; the presence or absence of certain organs determines social position. It is not surprising, then, that feminist sociologist Dorothy Smith notes that in Western societies "a man's body gives credibility to his utterance, whereas a woman's body takes it away from hers."[1] Judith Lorber also notes the depth and ubiquity of notions of biology in the social realm when she writes that "gender is so pervasive in our [Western] society we assume it is bred into our genes."[2] Given this, it is obvious that if one wanted to apply this Western "bio-logic" to the Yorùbá social world (i.e., use biology as an ideology for organizing that social world), one would have first to invent the category "woman" in Yorùbá discourse. *because Yoruba does not have a biologic*

The assertion that "woman" as a social category did not exist in Yorùbá communities should not be read as antimaterialist hermeneutics, a kind of poststructuralist deconstructing of the body into dissolution. Far from it — the body was (and still is) very corporeal in Yorùbá communities. But, prior to the infusion of Western notions into Yorùbá culture, the body was not the basis of social roles, inclusions, or exclusions; it was not the foundation of social thought and identity. Most academic studies on the Yorùbá have, however, assumed that "body-reasoning" was present in the Yorùbá indigenous culture. They have assumed the Western constructions as universal, which has led to the uncritical usage of these body-based categories for interpreting Yorùbá society historically and in the contemporary period.

Consequently, in order to analyze how and why gender is constructed in Yorùbá society (and indeed in other contemporary African societies), the role and impact of the West are of utmost importance, not only because most African societies came under European rule by the end of the nineteenth century but also because of the continued dominance of the West in the production of knowledge. In African studies, historically and currently, the creation, constitution, and production of knowledge have remained the privilege of the West. Therefore, body-reasoning and the bio-logic that derives from the biological determinism inherent in Western thought have been imposed on African societies. The presence of gender constructs cannot be separated from the ideology of biological determinism. Western conceptual schemes and theories have become so widespread that almost all scholarship, even by Africans, utilizes them unquestioningly.

This book grew out of the realization of Western dominance in African studies. That realization made it necessary to undertake a reexamination of the concepts underpinning discourse in African studies, consciously taking into account African experiences. Clearly, all concepts come with their own cultural and philosophical baggage, much of which becomes alien distortion when applied to cultures other than those from which they derive. Thus, as a first step toward mapping the cultural logic of an African society like that of the Yorùbá, conceptual categories and theoretical formulations that derive from Western experiences had to be unpacked.

After all these considerations, I found that it was no longer possible for me to do a study of "gender" (a biologically conceived category) in a Yorùbá locality; I first had to write a history of gender discourses in Yorùbá studies. It became clear to me that, to make an analogy with Michel Foucault's explication of the history of sexuality, the history of gender — that is, the history of what functions in academic discourse as a specific field of truth — must first be written from the viewpoint of a history of discourses.[3] Further, an analysis of some of the material reorganization that took place as a result of British colonization had to be undertaken. My explication of colonization, however, does not rest on the period of formal colonization. I assume the period of the Atlantic slave trade as an integral part of this process. In Yorùbá history, there is no logical way of separating these two periods. They were logically one process unfolding over many centuries. Without attention to the global material dominance of the West, there can be no comprehensive accounting for its continued hegemony in ideas and knowledge-production. Because of that, this study is also about the sociology of knowledge.

This study, then, seeks to document why and how gender came to be constructed in the Yorùbá society of southwestern Nigeria (Yorùbáland was formally colonized by the British from 1862 to 1960) and how gender is constituted as a fundamental category in academic scholarship on the Yorùbá. The major question addressed is this: What are the relationships between, on the one hand, bio-anatomical distinctions and gender differences as a part of social reality and, on the other hand, gender constructs as something that the observer brings to a particular situation?

I interrogate the ways in which Western assumptions about sex differences are used to interpret Yorùbá society and, in the process, create a local gender system. My analysis challenges a number of ideas, some mentioned above, common in many Western feminist writings:

1. Gender categories are universal and timeless and have been present in every society at all times. This idea is often expressed in a biblical tone, as if to suggest that "in the beginning there was gender."

2. Gender is a fundamental organizing principle in all societies and is therefore always salient. In any given society, gender is everywhere.

3. There is an essential, universal category "woman" that is characterized by the social uniformity of its members.

4. The subordination of women is a universal.

5. The category "woman" is precultural, fixed in historical time and cultural space in antithesis to another fixed category — "man."

I posit that these assumptions are a result of the fact that in Western societies, physical bodies are *always* social bodies. As a consequence, there is really no distinction between sex and gender, despite the many attempts by feminists to distinguish the two. In the West, social categories have a long history of being embodied and therefore gendered. According to anthropologist Shelly Errington, "Sex (with a capital 'S') is the gender system of the West." She continues: "But Sex is not the only way to sort out human bodies, not the only way to make sense of sex. One can easily imagine different cultural classifications and rationales for gender categories, different scenarios that equally take into account the evidence our bodies provide."[4]

The Yorùbá case provides one such different scenario; and more than that, it shows that the human body need not be constituted as gendered or be seen as evidence for social classification at all times. In precolonial Yorùbá society, body-type was not the basis of social hierarchy: males and females were not ranked according to anatomic distinction. The social order required a different kind of map, not a gender map that assumed biology as the foundation for social ranking.

I use the concepts "sex" and "gender" as synonyms. With regard to Yorùbá society in the precolonial period, however, I have coined the terms "anatomic sex," "anatomic male," and "anatomic female" to emphasize the nongendered attitude toward the relation between the human body and social roles, positions, and hierarchies. In some places I have shortened those terms to "anasex," "anamale," and "anafemale." My purpose in qualifying these terms with "anatomic" (or "ana-") is to show that the Yorùbá distinctions were superficial and did not assume any social hierarchical dimensions, as they do in the West (Western social categories derive essentially from a perceived sexual dimorphism of the human body). Gender was simply not inherent in human social organization.

Although precolonial Yorùbá cultural logic did not use the human body as the basis for social ranking (in no situation in Yorùbá society was a male, by virtue of his body-type, inherently superior to a *organ-ization*

female), Yorùbá society was hierarchically organized, from slaves to
rulers. The ranking of individuals depended first and foremost on seniority, which was usually defined by relative age. Another fundamental
difference between Yorùbá and Western social categories involves the
highly situational nature of Yorùbá social identity. In Yorùbá society
before the sustained infusion of Western categories, social positions of
people shifted constantly in relation to those with whom they were
interacting; consequently, social identity was relational and was not essentialized. In many European societies, in contrast, males and females
have gender identities deriving from the elaboration of anatomic types;
therefore, man and woman are essentialized. These essential gender
identities in Western cultures attach to all social engagements no matter how far from the issues of reproduction such undertakings may be.
The classic example is that for many years women could not vote solely
because they were women. Another example is the genderization of professions to the extent that professional lexicons contain phrases such
as "woman pilot," "woman president," and "professor emerita," as if
whatever these women do in these occupations is different from what
men do in the same professions.

In light of the foregoing, I will argue that the concentration of feminist scholars on the status of women — an emphasis that presupposes
the existence of "woman" as a social category always understood to
be powerless, disadvantaged, and controlled and defined by men — can
lead to serious misconceptions when applied to Ọ̀yọ́-Yorùbá society.[5] In
fact, my central argument is that there were no *women* — defined in
strictly gendered terms — in that society. Again, the concept "woman"
as it is used and as it is invoked in the scholarship is derived from
Western experience and history, a history rooted in philosophical discourses about the distinctions among body, mind, and soul and in ideas
about biological determinism and the linkages between the body and
the "social."[6]

central argument

Western social forces influence social org

Yorùbáland covers a vast area, and despite homogenizing factors like
language and recent historical experiences, one can discern some significant institutional, cultural specificities in given locales. For example,
Ondo and a number of polities in eastern Yorùbáland manifest cultural
specificities different from those present in Ọ̀yọ́-Yorùbá culture. For my
purposes, then, it was necessary to limit somewhat the area to be studied. My primary unit of analysis is Ọ̀yọ́-Yorùbá culture. That said, it
should be noted that those local cultural specificities were more pro-
nounced before the sweeping changes that occurred in the civil war and
colonial and post-nineteenth-century periods. Because the goal of my research was to capture the broad, sweeping institutional changes brought

about by European domination, it made sense, in places, to open my perspective beyond Ọ̀yọ́-Yorùbá culture. I should add here that language is central to my study, and my engagement is with the Yorùbá language as spoken by the Ọ̀yọ́.[7]

Although it is clear that the findings of this study are applicable to some other African societies, I hesitate to apply them broadly, primarily because I do not want to fall into the common trap of erasing a multitude of African cultures by making facile generalizations, a process that results in unwarranted homogenization. The erasure of African cultures, a major defect of many studies on Africa, motivates my efforts not to make a simplistic general case about Africa from the Yorùbá example. There are two common ways in which African cultures are discounted, even in studies that are purportedly about African societies. The first is through the uncritical imposition on African cultures of supposedly objective conceptual categories and theories that are in origin and constitution bound to Western culture. The second is what I call the mishmash theory of Africa — the result of which is unbridled homogenization of African cultures even when it is clear that these cultures do not share identical institutions or histories. There is no question that Africans have many things in common and that some generalizations are possible. But care must be taken in deciding how these claims are to be made and at what level they are to be applied given the paucity of detailed, historically grounded, and culturally informed studies of many African societies.

Another concern of this work is to historicize and account for androcentrism in the study of Yorùbá history and culture. The assumption of male privilege in many of these writings and in parts of Yorùbá life today is questioned because there is evidence that this has not always been the case. Additionally, I posit that although male dominance is present in scholarship and popular writing on the Yorùbá, such dominance in Yorùbá life both historically and today cannot be taken for granted to the same degree in all places, institutions, and situations. For example, in 1996 there were two female *baálẹ̀* (village heads) in Ògbómọ̀sọ́. These women were the torchbearers of their family heritage of rulership. I was privileged to conduct a series of interviews with one of them — Baálẹ̀ Máyà (see chap. 3). What is remarkable is that such women are not given the prominence that they deserve, even in the era of international women's conferences — the emphasis, erroneously, is on how tradition victimizes women.

The degree to which gender hierarchy manifests itself today in state institutions is different from the degree to which it shows up in the family or indigenous religions. How widespread it is, how deep, among

which social groupings, and when and where it is manif
cal issues that call for research, not unquestioned assun
issue is that scholars have assumed that present-day "c
encounter are always rooted in ancient traditions. I
timelessness should not be taken for granted; some of them are "new
traditions."

Another theme, which has been mentioned above, is the role of
scholars in the process of gender-formation. I argue that concepts and
theoretical formulations are culture-bound and that scholars themselves
are not merely recorders or observers in the research process; they are
also participants. I posit, therefore, that even when African scholarship seeks to validate the specificity of the African experience, it does
so within the frameworks of European-derived categories of knowledge.
Hence, although the origins of body-reasoning may be locatable in European thought, its influences are everywhere, including the variety of
disciplines in African studies. Merely by analyzing a particular society
with gender constructs, scholars create gender categories. To put this another way: by writing about any society through a gendered perspective,
scholars necessarily write gender into that society. Gender, like beauty,
is often in the eye of the beholder. The idea that in dealing with gender
constructs one necessarily contributes to their creation is apparent in Judith Lorber's claim that "the prime paradox of gender is that in order
to dismantle the institution, you must first make it very visible."[8] In ac-
tuality, the process of making gender visible is also a process of creating
gender.

Thus, scholarship is implicated in the process of gender-formation.
In a historical study of Zulu society in southern Africa, Keletso Atkins
objected to the theoretical fashion in scholarship of imposing gender constructs acontextually. Summarizing a number of Zulu historical
texts, Atkins notes:

> So far as one is able to tell, these incidents cannot be made intel-
> ligible by relating them to fashionable concepts of the present day.
> There are no allusions to gender relations in the aforementioned
> texts; nowhere is there a discussion delineating jobs that fell within
> the purview of women's work. To insist, then, that these incidents
> somehow linked to gender issues would grossly misinterpret the
> passages, assigning to them a meaning never intended.[9]

The present study draws attention to the pitfalls of interpreting "biological facts" and "statistical evidence" outside of the cultural frame of
reference from which they derive. It cannot be overstated that in African
studies a careful evaluation of the genealogy of concepts and theoret-

ıcal formulation must be integral to research. Ultimately, in research endeavors, I argue for a cultural, context-dependent interpretation of social reality. The context includes the social identity of the researcher, the spatial and temporal location of the research, and the debates in the academic literature. There is, of course, the fundamental question of the relationship between research and social reality, an important question given the policy bent of research — particularly in women's studies.

The connections between social identity, personal experiences, and the nature of one's research and perspective are complex; often the linkages are unpredictable and nonlinear. Nevertheless, despite the many postmodernist treatises deconstructing social identities, I would assert that I am Yorùbá. I was born into a large family, and the comings and goings of my many relations constituted an important introduction into Yorùbá lifeways. In 1973, my father ascended the throne and became the Ṣòún (monarch) of Ògbómòṣó, a major Òyó-Yorùbá polity of some historical significance. Since then and up to the present, ààfin Ṣòún (the palace) has been the place I call home. Daily, I have listened to the drummers and heard the oríkì (praise poetry) of my forebears recited as the royal mothers rendered the poems to family members as greetings as we passed through the saarè — the courtyard in which the departed monarchs are buried. Our ancestors are still very much with us.

The palace anchors the old town, which is surrounded on all sides by the two marketplaces (Ojà Igbó and Ojà Jagun), markets that come into their full glory at night. The ààfin Ṣòún is the center of daily rituals and of a constant stream of townspeople coming to pay homage and bringing their various stories to my father and mother. Spending time with my mother, Ìgbàyílolá (the olorì [senior royal wife]), whose "court" is the first port of call for many of the ará ìlú (townspeople), added yet another vantage point from which to view this dynamic world. All these happenings provided ample opportunity for me to observe and reflect on the personal and public aspects of living culture.

The annual festivals, such as the Egúngún, Ọ̀ọ̀lè, and Ìgbé, taught me to recognize cultural continuity and made me appreciate indigenous institutions, even in the midst of phenomenal changes. During the Ọ̀ọ̀lè festival, the Egúngún (masquerade) of the five branches of the royal family would perform. I want to believe that all these events and processes have been significant in shaping my views and some of the questions I deal with in this book. On this count I cannot overemphasize the contributions of the conversations I had with my parents, older and younger siblings, the many mothers and fathers in the palace, and the family in general in the course of the many years of this research.

•

Chapter 1 of this study reviews how Western social thought is rooted in biology, using the body as the bedrock of the social order. It also looks at the dominance of the West in the constitution of knowledge about Africa and the implications of this privileged position as the reference point in African studies. Chapter 2 examines Ọ̀yọ́-Yorùbá society on its own terms — that is, with an awareness that viewing that society through the gendered lens of the West is a cause of distorted perception. Chapter 3 discusses how scholars apply Western paradigms on gender in their own work on Africa, and it uses the received history of the Old Ọ̀yọ́ state as a point of entry into the question of reconstructing the past and the problem of engendering history. Chapter 4 analyzes colonization as a multifaceted process that stimulated the institutionalization of gender categories in Yorùbáland. Chapter 5 interrogates the impact of Yorùbá/English bilingualism on Yorùbá society and the translation of Yorùbá orature into English, given that English is a gender-specific language and Yorùbá is not. The world we live in today — that is, by turns, both multicultural and monocultural — is thus problematized. In a sense, this book intends to raise many questions, while answering only some — some of the empirical questions can only be resolved by future research. It is my hope that the claims made and the questions raised will generate debate and research on African societies that will consciously interrogate embedded scholarly assumptions.

Acknowledgments

American sociology is unaware of Africa. In the dark ages, Africa was ceded over to anthropology as "the front lawn" of the discipline. Thus, "African sociology" is considered an oxymoron. But some of us sociologists insist that there is much sociology to be done in Africa; and we just do it. Against this background, I am grateful to Troy Duster and Robert Blauner, who as members of my dissertation committee (this book originated from my dissertation) guided me through the sociology department at Berkeley. Barbara Christian was the third member of the committee; I thank her for unstinting intellectual support and more throughout my time in graduate school. David Lloyd of the English department, as a friend, read the dissertation and provided generous comments that goaded me to refine my ideas. Lula Fragd and Pauline Wynter, members of a dissertation group, provided valuable comments that were indispensable for the progress of the work.

Unlike sociology, feminist discourse is not impervious to Africa. The problem, however, is that Africa constitutes a part of what Marnia Lazreg (in *The Eloquence of Silence: Algerian Women in Question*) calls the "doom and gloom of the discursive domination" of the West. In light of the "more liberated than thou attitude" of Western feminists toward African women and indeed women from other parts of the world, Nkiru Nzegwu's painting *Mirror on the Wall* (reproduced on the cover of this book) is most appropriate and appreciated. "Mirror, mirror on the wall, who is the most liberated of them all?" is a constant refrain in feminist discourse. I am grateful to Nkiru Nzegwu, friend, philosopher, art historian, and artist, for drawing my attention to the painting, for allowing me to use it, and for her many contributions, intellectual and otherwise, to this project.

My heartfelt thanks go to my friends Naheed Islam, Thokozani Xaba, and Hyun Ok Park for all those stimulating intellectual exchanges and for making the Berkeley sociology department less provincial.

To my friends Leonie Hermantin, Zita Nunes, and Adhiambo Odaga: thanks for being a positive part of my personal, political, and intellectual life.

This project had a long gestation period. Consequently, the list of institutions and persons who supported me at various points is a long one. My most extended trip to Nigeria was paid for by a Ford Foundation grant. I received a Population Council Fellowship in the Social Sciences, an American Association of University Women (AAUW) International Fellowship, and a postdoctoral Rockefeller Humanities Fellowship at the Center for Advanced Feminist Study (CAFS) at the University of Minnesota. Much appreciation goes to CAFS for providing access to a feminist community from which my work benefited; my special thanks go to Shirley Nelson Garner, who was the director at the time. The Institute for African Studies at the University of Ibadan provided office space and an intellectual community that was indispensable to my work. Professors S. O. Babayemi and C. O. Adepegba were especially generous with their time. My heartfelt gratitude goes to Professor Bolanle Awe, the director of the institute; her work in history and Yorùbá studies continues to inspire me.

To my perpetual friends Olufunke Okome and Ọ̀jọ̀gbọn Olufemi Taiwo: I say thank you for being good "local informants"; the view of the native is always indispensable. The help of my "country woman" Ify Iweriebor was invaluable in making the manuscript more readable. I deeply appreciate the help of Yetunde Laniran, friend and linguist, who brought her expertise to my Yorùbá language texts.

A number of scholars were willing to take my phone calls whenever I needed to make a Yorùbá sense of one thing or another. In this regard, I especially value the contribution of Olabiyi Yai, professor of comparative literature, and Jacob Olupona, professor of religion.

At the University of California–Santa Barbara, my present place of work, both Cedric Robinson and Gerald Horne read and commented on parts of the manuscript. Mimi Navarro, Carolyn Grapard, and Rachel Bargiel, staff in the black studies department, have all contributed in one way or another to the project. My deeply felt appreciation goes to them all. I also express my deep appreciation to the University of California–Santa Barbara for extraordinary support for my work in general. The award of numerous Regent Junior Faculty Fellowships for the summer months in the last few years has been especially important for oiling the wheels of progress.

I cannot thank enough Janaki Bakhle, my original editor at the University of Minnesota Press. Her enthusiasm for the project, even before the dissertation was completed, constituted real encouragement. With appreciation, I also mention Carrie Mullen, my present editor, who finally brought the project to a close after Janaki left the press.

Finally, to my family and friends upon whom I continuously imposed strange and sometimes "unintelligible" questions: thank you for your endurance. I have dedicated the book to my children, who endured much and have managed to be born and to grow up in the midst of the process of the writing of this endless book.

I must thank the many people (family and friends) in Ìbàdàn, Ọ̀yọ́, and Ògbómọ̀ṣọ́ who shared their thoughts and parts of their lives with me. Ẹ ṣeé o, Ọlọrun yíò ṣe nínú ti yín náà. Aṣẹ o.

Of course I, and I alone, am responsible for "the bad" and "the ugly," if ever such things are found in this book.

A Note on Orthography

Yorùbá is a tonal language, with three underlying pitch levels for vowels and syllabic nasals: the low tone is marked with a grave accent; the mid tone is unmarked; and the high tone is indicated with an acute accent. I have used tonal accents and subscript marks (e.g., ẹ, ọ, ṣ). Some syllables require two diacritics, as in my last name: Oyěwùmí, where an acute accent joins with a grave accent over the e to form a ˇ. As to the subscript marks: the ẹ is approximately equivalent to the e in the English word "yet"; the ọ is close to the o sound in "dog"; and the ṣ is close to the English *sh* sound. I have used tonal marks on the Yorùbá words and names that are part of my text. However, there are many Yorùbá names, especially of scholars, that remain unmarked because up to this point, the tendency has been to discount the diacritics in African languages. Yet without the diacritics, those words do not make sense.

Chapter 1

Visualizing the Body

WESTERN THEORIES AND AFRICAN SUBJECTS

•••

biology is destiny

T HE IDEA that biology is destiny — or, better still, destiny is biology — has been a staple of Western thought for centuries.[1] Whether the issue is who is who in Aristotle's polis[2] or who is poor in the late twentieth-century United States, the notion that difference and hierarchy in society are biologically determined continues to enjoy credence even among social scientists who purport to explain human society in other than genetic terms. In the West, biological explanations appear to be especially privileged over other ways of explaining differences of gender, race, or class. Difference is expressed as degeneration. In tracing the genealogy of the idea of degeneration in European thought, J. Edward Chamberlain and Sander Gilman noted the way it was used to define certain kinds of difference, in the nineteenth century in particular. "Initially, degeneration brought together two notions of difference, one scientific — a deviation from an original type — and the other moral, a deviation from a norm of behavior. But they were essentially the same notion, of a fall from grace, *a deviation from the original type.*"[3] Consequently, those in positions of power find it imperative to establish their superior biology as a way of affirming their privilege and dominance over "Others." Those who are different are seen as genetically inferior, and this, in turn, is used to account for their disadvantaged social positions.

The notion of society that emerges from this conception is that society is constituted by bodies and as bodies — male bodies, female bodies, Jewish bodies, Aryan bodies, black bodies, white bodies, rich bodies, poor bodies. I am using the word "body" in two ways: first, as a metonymy for biology and, second, to draw attention to the sheer physicality that seems to attend being in Western culture. I refer to the corporeal body as well as to metaphors of the body.

The body is given a logic of its own. It is believed that just by looking at it one can tell a person's beliefs and social position or lack thereof.

1

As Naomi Scheman puts it in her discussion of the body politic in premodern Europe:

> The ways people knew their places in the world had to do with their bodies and the histories of those bodies, and when they violated the prescriptions for those places, their bodies were punished, often spectacularly. One's place in the body politic was as natural as the places of the organs in one's body, and political disorder [was] as unnatural as the shifting and displacement of those organs.[4]

Similarly, Elizabeth Grosz remarks on what she calls the "depth" of the body in modern Western societies:

> Our [Western] body forms are considered expressions of an interior, not inscriptions on a flat surface. By constructing a soul or psyche for itself, the "civilized body" forms libidinal flows, sensations, experiences, and intensities into needs, wants.... *The body becomes a text, a system of signs to be deciphered, read, and read into. Social law is incarnated, "corporealized"[;] correlatively, bodies are textualized, read by others as expressive of a subject's psychic interior.* A storehouse of inscriptions and messages between [the body's] external and internal boundaries...generates or constructs the body's movements into "behavior," which then [has] interpersonally and socially identifiable meanings and functions within a social system.[5]

Consequently, since the body is the bedrock on which the social order is founded, the body is always *in* view and *on* view. As such, it invites a *gaze,* a gaze of difference, a gaze of differentiation — the most historically constant being the gendered gaze. There is a sense in which phrases such as "the social body" or "the body politic" are not just metaphors but can be read literally. It is not surprising, then, that when the body politic needed to be purified in Nazi Germany, certain kinds of bodies had to be eliminated.[6]

The reason that the body has so much presence in the West is that the world is primarily perceived by sight.[7] The differentiation of human bodies in terms of sex, skin color, and cranium size is a testament to the powers attributed to "seeing." The gaze is an invitation to differentiate. Different approaches to comprehending reality, then, suggest epistemological differences between societies. Relative to Yorùbá society, which is the focus of this book, the body has an exaggerated presence in the Western conceptualization of society. The term "worldview," which is used in the West to sum up the cultural logic of a society, captures the

West's privileging of the visual. It is Eurocentric to use it to describe cultures that may privilege other senses. The term "world-sense" is a more inclusive way of describing the conception of the world by different cultural groups. In this study, therefore, "worldview" will only be applied to describe the Western cultural sense, and "world-sense" will be used when describing the Yorùbá or other cultures that may privilege senses other than the visual or even a combination of senses.

The foregoing hardly represents the received view of Western history and social thought. Quite the contrary: until recently, the history of Western societies has been presented as a documentation of rational thought in which ideas are framed as the agents of history. If bodies appear at all, they are articulated as the debased side of human nature. The preferred focus has been on the mind, lofty and high above the foibles of the flesh. Early in Western discourse, a binary opposition between body and mind emerged. The much-vaunted Cartesian dualism was only an affirmation of a tradition[8] in which the body was seen as a trap from which any rational person had to escape. Ironically, even as the body remained at the center of both sociopolitical categories and discourse, many thinkers denied its existence for certain categories of people, most notably themselves. "Bodylessness" has been a precondition of rational thought. Women, primitives, Jews, Africans, the poor, and all those who qualified for the label "different" in varying historical epochs have been considered to be the embodied, dominated therefore by instinct and affect, reason being beyond them. They are the Other, and the Other is a body.[9]

In pointing out the centrality of the body in the construction of difference in Western culture, one does not necessarily deny that there have been certain traditions in the West that have attempted to explain differences according to criteria other than the presence or absence of certain organs: the possession of a penis, the size of the brain, the shape of the cranium, or the color of the skin. The Marxist tradition is especially noteworthy in this regard in that it emphasized social relations as an explanation for class inequality. However, the critique of Marxism as androcentric by numerous feminist writers suggests that this paradigm is also implicated in Western somatocentricity.[10] Similarly, the establishment of disciplines such as sociology and anthropology, which purport to explain society on the bases of human interactions, seems to suggest the relegation of biological determinism in social thought. On closer examination, however, one finds that the body has hardly been banished from social thought, not to mention its role in the constitution of social status. This can be illustrated in the discipline of sociology. In a monograph on the body and society, Bryan Turner laments what he perceives as the absence of the body in sociological inquiries. He attributes this phenomenon of "absent bodies"[11] to the fact that "sociology emerged as a discipline which took the social meaning of human interaction as its principal object of inquiry, claiming that the meaning of social actions can never be reduced to biology or physiology."[12]

One could agree with Turner about the need to separate sociology from eugenics and phrenology. However, to say that bodies have been absent from sociological theories is to discount the fact that the social groups that are the subject matter of the discipline are essentially understood as rooted in biology. They are categories based on perceptions of the different physical presence of various body-types. In the contemporary U.S., so long as sociologists deal with so-called social categories like the underclass, suburbanites, workers, farmers, voters, citizens, and criminals (to mention a few categories that are historically and in the cultural ethos understood as representing specific body-types), there is no escape from biology. If the social realm is determined by the kinds of bodies occupying it, then to what extent is there a social realm, given that it is conceived to be biologically determined? For example, no one hearing the term "corporate executives" would assume them to be women; and in the 1980s and 1990s, neither would anyone spontaneously associate whites with the terms "underclass" or "gangs"; indeed, if someone were to construct an association between the terms, their meanings would have to be shifted. Consequently, any sociologist who studies these categories cannot escape an underlying biological insidiousness.

This omnipresence of biologically deterministic explanations in the social sciences can be demonstrated with the category of the criminal or criminal type in contemporary American society. Troy Duster, in an excellent study of the resurgence of overt biological determinism in intellectual circles, berates the eagerness of many researchers to associate criminality with genetic inheritance; he goes on to argue that other interpretations of criminality are possible:

> The prevailing economic interpretation explains crime rates in terms of access to jobs and unemployment. A cultural interpretation tries to show differing cultural adjustments between the police and those apprehended for crimes. A political interpretation sees criminal activity as political interpretation, or pre-revolutionary. A conflict interpretation sees this as an interest conflict over scarce resources.[13]

Clearly, on the face of it, all these explanations of criminality are non-biological; however, as long as the "population" or the social group they are attempting to explain — in this case criminals who are black and/or poor — is seen to represent a genetic grouping, the underlying assumptions about the genetic predisposition of that population or group will structure the explanations proffered whether they are body-based or not. This is tied to the fact that because of the history of racism, the underlying research question (even if it is unstated) is not why certain individuals commit crimes: it is actually why black people have such a propensity to do so. The definition of what is criminal activity is very much tied up with who (black, white, rich, poor) is involved in the activity.[14] Likewise, the police, as a group, are assumed to be white. Similarly, when studies are done of leadership in American society, the researchers "discover" that most people in leadership positions are white males; no matter what account these researchers give for this result, their statements will be read as explaining the predisposition of this group to leadership.

The integrity of researchers is not being questioned here; my purpose is not to label any group of scholars as racist in their intentions. On the contrary, since the civil rights movement, social-scientific research has been used to formulate policies that would abate if not end discrimination against subordinated groups. What must be underscored, however, is how knowledge-production and dissemination in the United States are inevitably embedded in what Michael Omi and Howard Winant call the "everyday common sense of race — a way of comprehending, explaining and acting in the world."[15] Race, then, is a fundamental organizing principle in American society. It is institutionalized, and it functions irrespective of the action of individual actors.

In the West, social identities are all interpreted through the "prism of heritability,"[16] to borrow Duster's phrase. Biological determinism is a filter through which all knowledge about society is run. As mentioned in the preface, I refer to this kind of thinking as body-reasoning;[17] it is a biologic interpretation of the social world. The point, again, is that as long as social actors like managers, criminals, nurses, and the poor are presented as groups and not as individuals, and as long as such groupings are conceived to be genetically constituted, then there is no escape from biological determinism.

Against this background, the issue of gender difference is particularly interesting in regard to the history and the constitution of difference in European social practice and thought. The lengthy history of the embodiment of social categories is suggested by the myth fabricated by Socrates to convince citizens of different ranks to accept whatever status was imposed upon them. Socrates explained the myth to Glaucon in these terms:

Citizens, we shall say to them in our tale, you are brothers, yet God has framed you differently. Some of you have the power of command, and in the composition of these he has mingled gold, wherefore also they have the greatest honor; others he has made silver, to be auxiliaries; others again who are to be husbandmen and craftsmen he has composed of brass and iron; and the species will generally be preserved in the children. . . . An Oracle says that when a man of brass or iron guards the state, it will be destroyed. Such is the tale; is there any possibility of making our citizens believe in it?

Glaucon replies, "Not in the present generation; there is no way of accomplishing this; but their sons may be made to believe in the tale, and their sons' sons, and posterity after them."[18] Glaucon was mistaken that the acceptance of the myth could be accomplished only in the next generation: the myth of those born to rule was already in operation; mothers, sisters, and daughters — women — were already excluded from consideration in any of those ranks. In a context in which people were ranked according to association with certain metals, women were, so to speak, made of wood, and so were not even considered. Stephen Gould, a historian of science, calls Glaucon's observation a prophecy, since history shows that Socrates' tale has been promulgated and believed by subsequent generations.[19] The point, however, is that even in Glaucon's time, it was more than a prophecy: it was already a social practice to exclude women from the ranks of rulers.

Paradoxically, in European thought, despite the fact that society was seen to be inhabited by bodies, only women were perceived to be embodied; men had no bodies — they were walking minds. Two social categories that emanated from this construction were the "man of reason" (the thinker) and the "woman of the body," and they were oppositionally constructed. The idea that the man of reason often had the woman of the body on his mind was clearly not entertained. As Michel Foucault's *History of Sexuality* suggests, however, the man of ideas often had the woman and indeed other bodies on his mind.[20]

In recent times, thanks in part to feminist scholarship, the body is beginning to receive the attention it deserves as a site and as material for the explication of European history and thought.[21] The distinctive contribution of feminist discourse to our understanding of Western societies is that it makes explicit the gendered (therefore embodied) and male-dominant nature of all Western institutions and discourses. The feminist lens disrobes the man of ideas for all to see. Even discourses like science that were assumed to be objective have been shown to be male-biased.[22]

The extent to which the body is implicated in the construction of socio-political categories and epistemologies cannot be overemphasized. As noted earlier, Dorothy Smith has written that in Western societies "a man's body gives credibility to his utterance, whereas a woman's body takes it away from hers."[23] Writing on the construction of masculinity, R. W. Connell notes that the body is inescapable in its construction and that a stark physicalness underlies gender categories in the Western worldview: "In our [Western] culture, at least, the physical sense of maleness and femaleness is central to the cultural interpretation of gender. Masculine gender is (among other things) a certain feel to the skin, certain muscular shapes and tensions, certain postures and ways of moving, certain possibilities in sex."[24]

From the ancients to the moderns, gender has been a foundational category upon which social categories have been erected. Hence, gender has been ontologically conceptualized. The category of the citizen, which has been the cornerstone of much of Western political theory, was male, despite the much-acclaimed Western democratic traditions.[25] Elucidating Aristotle's categorization of the sexes, Elizabeth Spelman writes: "A woman is a female who is free; a man is a male who is a citizen."[26] Women were excluded from the category of citizens because "penis possession"[27] was one of the qualifications for citizenship. Lorna Schiebinger notes in a study of the origins of modern science and women's exclusion from European scientific institutions that "differences between the two sexes were reflections of a set of dualistic principles that penetrated the cosmos as well as the bodies of men and women."[28] Differences and hierarchy, then, are enshrined on bodies; and bodies enshrine differences and hierarchy. Hence, dualisms like nature/culture, public/private, and visible/invisible are variations on the theme of male/female bodies hierarchically ordered, differentially placed in relation to power, and spatially distanced one from the other.[29]

In the span of Western history, the justifications for the making of the categories "man" and "woman" have not remained the same. On the contrary, they have been dynamic. Although the boundaries are shifting and the content of each category may change, the two categories have remained hierarchical and in binary opposition. For Stephen Gould, "the justification for ranking groups by inborn worth has varied with the tide of Western history. Plato relied on dialectic, the church upon dogma. For the past two centuries, scientific claims have become the primary agent of validating Plato's myth."[30] The constant in this Western narrative is the centrality of the body: two bodies on display, two sexes, two categories persistently viewed — one in relation to the other. That narrative is about the unwavering elaboration of the body as the site and cause of differences and hierarchies in society. In the West, so long as the issue is difference and social hierarchy, then the body is constantly positioned, posed, exposed, and reexposed as their cause. Society, then, is seen as an accurate reflection of genetic endowment — those with a superior biology inevitably are those in superior social positions. No difference is elaborated without bodies that are positioned hierarchically. In his book *Making Sex*,[31] Thomas Laqueur gives a richly textured history of the construction of sex from classical Greece to the contemporary period, noting the changes in symbols and the shifts in meanings. The point, however, is the centrality and persistence of the body in the construction of social categories. In view of this history, Freud's dictum that anatomy is destiny was not original or exceptional; he was just more explicit than many of his predecessors.

Social Orders and Biology: Natural or Constructed?

The idea that gender is socially constructed — that differences between males and female are to be located in social practices, not in biological facts — was one important insight that emerged early in second-wave feminist scholarship. This finding was understandably taken to be radical in a culture in which difference, particularly gender difference, had always been articulated as natural and, therefore, biologically determined. Gender as a social construction became the cornerstone of much feminist discourse. The notion was particularly attractive because it was interpreted to mean that gender differences were not ordained by nature; they were mutable and therefore changeable. This in turn led to the opposition between social constructionism and biological determinism, as if they were mutually exclusive.

Such a dichotomous presentation is unwarranted, however, because the ubiquity of biologically rooted explanations for difference in Western social thought and practices is a reflection of the extent to which biological explanations are found compelling.[32] In other words, so long as the issue is difference (whether the issue is why women breast-feed babies or why they could not vote), old biologies will be found or new biologies will be constructed to explain women's disadvantage. The Western preoccupation with biology continues to generate constructions of "new biologies" even as some of the old biological assumptions are being dislodged. In fact, in the Western experience, social construction and biological determinism have been two sides of the same coin, since both ideas continue to reinforce each other. When social categories like gender are constructed, new biologies of difference can be invented.

When biological interpretations are found to be compelling, social categories do derive their legitimacy and power from biology. In short, the social and the biological feed on each other.

The biologization inherent in the Western articulation of social difference is, however, by no means universal. The debate in feminism about what roles and which identities are natural and what aspects are constructed only has meaning in a culture where social categories are conceived as having no independent logic of their own. This debate, of course, developed out of certain problems; therefore, it is logical that in societies where such problems do not exist, there should be no such debate. But then, due to imperialism, this debate has been universalized to other cultures, and its immediate effect is to inject Western problems where such issues originally did not exist. Even then, this debate does not take us very far in societies where social roles and identities are not conceived to be rooted in biology. By the same token, in cultures where the visual sense is not privileged, and the body is not read as a blueprint of society, invocations of biology are less likely to occur because such explanations do not carry much weight in the social realm. That many categories of difference are socially constructed in the West may well suggest the mutability of categories, but it is also an invitation to endless constructions of biology — in that there is no limit to what can be explained by the body-appeal. Thus biology is hardly mutable; it is much more a combination of the Hydra and the Phoenix of Greek mythology. Biology is forever mutating, not mutable. Ultimately, the most important point is not that gender is socially constructed but the extent to which biology itself is socially constructed and therefore inseparable from the social.

The way in which the conceptual categories sex and gender functioned in feminist discourse was based on the assumption that biological and social conceptions could be separated and applied universally. Thus sex was presented as the natural category and gender as the social construction of the natural. But, subsequently, it became apparent that even sex has elements of construction. In many feminist writings thereafter, sex has served as the base and gender as the superstructure.[33] In spite of all efforts to separate the two, the distinction between sex and gender is a red herring. In Western conceptualization, gender cannot exist without sex since the body sits squarely at the base of both categories. Despite the preeminence of feminist social constructionism, which claims a social deterministic approach to society, biological foundationalism,[34] if not reductionism, is still at the center of gender discourses, just as it is at the center of all other discussions of society in the West.

Nevertheless, the idea that gender is socially constructed is significant.

from a cross-cultural perspective. In one of the earliest feminist texts to assert the constructionist thesis and its need for cross-cultural grounding, Suzanne J. Kessler and Wendy McKenna wrote that "by viewing gender as a social construction, it is possible to see descriptions of other cultures as evidence for alternative but equally real conceptions of what it means to be woman or man."[35] Yet, paradoxically, a fundamental assumption of feminist theory is that women's subordination is universal. These two ideas are contradictory. The universality attributed to gender asymmetry suggests a biological basis rather than a cultural one, given that the human anatomy is universal whereas cultures speak in myriad voices. That gender is socially constructed is said to mean that the criteria that make up male and female categories vary in different cultures. If this is so, then it challenges the notion that there is a biological imperative at work. From this standpoint, then, gender categories are mutable, and as such, gender then is denaturalized.

In fact, the categorization of women in feminist discourses as a homogeneous, bio-anatomically determined group which is always constituted as powerless and victimized does not reflect the fact that gender relations are social relations and, therefore, historically grounded and culturally bound. If gender is socially constructed, then gender cannot behave in the same way across time and space. If gender is a social construction, then we must examine the various cultural/architectural sites where it was constructed, and we must acknowledge that variously located actors (aggregates, groups, interested parties) were part of the construction. We must further acknowledge that if gender is a social construction, then there was a specific time (in different cultural/architectural sites) when it was "constructed" and therefore a time before which it was not. Thus, gender, being a social construction, is also a historical and cultural phenomenon. Consequently, it is logical to assume that in some societies, gender construction need not have existed at all.

From a cross-cultural perspective, the significance of this observation is that one cannot assume the social organization of one culture (the dominant West included) as universal or the interpretations of the experiences of one culture as explaining another one. On the one hand, at a general, global level, the constructedness of gender does suggest its mutability. On the other hand, at the local level — that is, within the bounds of any particular culture — gender is mutable only if it is socially constructed as such. Because, in Western societies, gender categories, like all other social categories, are constructed with biological building blocks, their mutability is questionable. The cultural logic of Western social categories is founded on an ideology of biological determinism: the conception that biology provides the rationale for the organization of the social world. Thus, as pointed out earlier, this cultural logic is actually a "bio-logic."

The "Sisterarchy": Feminism and Its "Other"

From a cross-cultural perspective, the implications of Western bio-logic are far-reaching when one considers the fact that gender constructs in feminist theory originated in the West, where men and women are conceived oppositionally and projected as embodied, genetically derived social categories.[36] The question, then, is this: On what basis are Western conceptual categories exportable or transferable to other cultures that have a different cultural logic? This question is raised because despite the wonderful insight about the social construction of gender, the way cross-cultural data have been used by many feminist writers undermines the notion that differing cultures may construct social categories differently. For one thing, if different cultures necessarily always construct gender as feminism proposes that they *do and must,* then the idea that gender is socially constructed is not sustainable.

The potential value of Western feminist social constructionism remains, therefore, largely unfulfilled, because feminism, like most other Western theoretical frameworks for interpreting the social world, cannot get away from the prism of biology that necessarily perceives social hierarchies as natural. Consequently, in cross-cultural gender studies, theorists impose Western categories on non-Western cultures and then project such categories as natural. The way in which dissimilar constructions of the social world in other cultures are used as "evidence" for the constructedness of gender and the insistence that these cross-cultural constructions are gender categories as they operate in the West nullify the alternatives offered by the non-Western cultures and undermine the claim that gender is a social construction.

Western ideas are imposed when non-Western social categories are assimilated into the gender framework that emerged from a specific sociohistorical and philosophical tradition. An example is the "discovery" of what has been labeled "third gender"[37] or "alternative genders"[38] in a number of non-Western cultures. The fact that the African "woman marriage,"[39] the Native American "berdache,"[40] and the South Asian "hijra"[41] are presented as gender categories incorporates them into the Western bio-logic and gendered framework without explication of their own sociocultural histories and constructions. A number of questions are pertinent here. Are these social categories seen as gendered in the cultures in question? From whose perspective are they gendered? In fact, even the appropriateness of naming them "third gender" is questionable since the Western cultural system, which uses biology to map the social world, precludes the possibility of more than two genders because gender is the elaboration of the perceived sexual dimorphism of the human body into the social realm. The trajectory of feminist discourse in the last twenty-five years has been determined by the Western cultural environment of its founding and development.

Thus, in the beginning of second-wave feminism in Euro-America, sex was defined as the biological facts of male and female bodies, and gender was defined as the social consequences that flowed from these facts. In effect, each society was assumed to have a sex/gender system.[42] The most important point was that sex and gender are inextricably bound. Over time, sex tended to be understood as the base and gender as the superstructure. Subsequently, however, after much debate, even sex was interpreted as socially constructed. Kessler and McKenna, one of the earliest research teams in this area, wrote that they "use gender, rather than sex, even when referring to those aspects of being a woman (girl) or man (boy) that have been viewed as biological. This will serve to emphasize our position that the element of social construction is primary in all aspects of being male or female."[43] Judith Butler, writing almost fifteen years later, reiterates the interconnectedness of sex and gender even more strongly:

> It would make no sense, then, to define gender as the cultural interpretation of sex, if sex itself is a gendered category. Gender ought not to be conceived merely as a cultural inscription of meaning on a pregiven surface (a juridical conception); gender must also designate the very apparatus of production whereby the sexes themselves are established. As a result, gender is not to culture as sex is to nature; gender is also the discursive/cultural means by which "sexed nature" or "a natural sex" is produced.[44]

Given the inseparability of sex and gender in the West, which results from the use of biology as an ideology for mapping the social world, the terms "sex" and "gender," as noted earlier, are essentially synonyms. To put this another way: since in Western constructions, physical bodies are always social bodies, there is really no distinction between sex and gender.[45] In Yorùbá society, in contrast, social relations derive their legitimacy from social facts, not from biology. The bare biological facts of pregnancy and parturition count only in regard to procreation, where they must. Biological facts do not determine who can become the monarch or who can trade in the market. In indigenous Yorùbá conception, these questions were properly social questions, not biological ones; hence, the nature of one's anatomy did not define one's social position. Consequently, the Yorùbá social order requires a different kind of map, not a gender map that assumes biology as the foundation for the social.

The splitting of hairs over the relationship between gender and sex, the debate on essentialism, the debates about differences among women,[46] and the preoccupation with gender bending/blending[47] that have characterized feminism are actually feminist versions of the enduring debate on nature versus nurture that is inherent in Western thought and in the logic of its social hierarchies. These concerns are not necessarily inherent in the discourse of society as such but are a culture-specific concern and issue. From a cross-cultural perspective, the more interesting point is the degree to which feminism, despite its radical local stance, exhibits the same ethnocentric and imperialistic characteristics of the Western discourses it sought to subvert. This has placed serious limitations on its applicability outside of the culture that produced it. As Kathy Ferguson reminds us: "The questions we can ask about the world are enabled, and other questions disabled, by the frame that orders the questioning. *When we are busy arguing about the questions that appear within a certain frame, the frame itself becomes invisible; we become enframed within it.*"[48] Though feminism in origin, by definition, and by practice is a universalizing discourse, the concerns and questions that have informed it are Western (and its audience too is apparently assumed to be composed of just Westerners, given that many of the theorists tend to use the first-person plural "we" and "our culture" in their writings). As such, feminism remains enframed by the tunnel vision and the bio-logic of other Western discourses.

Yorùbá society of southwestern Nigeria suggests a different scenario, one in which the body is not always enlisted as the basis for social classification. From a Yorùbá stance, the body appears to have an exaggerated presence in Western thought and social practice, including feminist theories. In the Yorùbá world, particularly in pre-nineteenth-century[49] Ọ̀yọ́ culture, society was conceived to be inhabited by people in relation to one another. That is, the "physicality" of maleness or femaleness did not have social antecedents and therefore did not constitute social categories. Social hierarchy was determined by social relations. As noted earlier, how persons were situated in relationships shifted depending on those involved and the particular situation. The principle that determined social organization was seniority, which was based on chronological age. Yorùbá kinship terms did not denote gender, and other nonfamilial social categories were not gender-specific either. What these Yorùbá categories tell us is that the body is not always in view.

and on view for categorization. The classic example is the female who played the roles of *ọba* (ruler), *omo* (offspring), *ọkọ, aya, ìyá* (mother), and *aláwo* (diviner-priest) all in one body. None of these kinship and nonkinship social categories are gender-specific. One cannot place persons in the Yorùbá categories just by looking at them. What they are heard to say may be the most important cue. Seniority as the foundation of Yorùbá social intercourse is relational and dynamic; unlike gender, it is not focused on the body.[50]

If the human body is universal, why does the body appear to have an exaggerated presence in the West relative to Yorùbáland? A comparative research framework reveals that one major difference stems from which of the senses is privileged in the apprehension of reality — sight in the West and a multiplicity of senses anchored by hearing in Yorùbáland. The tonality of Yorùbá language predisposes one toward an apprehension of reality that cannot marginalize the auditory. Consequently, relative to Western societies, there is a stronger need for a broader contextualization in order to make sense of the world.[51] For example, Ifá divination, which is also a knowledge system in Yorùbáland, has both visual and oral components.[52] More fundamentally, the distinction between Yorùbá and the West symbolized by the focus on different senses in the apprehension of reality involves more than perception — for the Yorùbá, and indeed many other African societies, it is about "a particular presence in the world — a world conceived of as a whole in which all things are linked together."[53] It concerns the many worlds human beings inhabit; it does not privilege the physical world over the metaphysical. A concentration on vision as the primary mode of comprehending reality promotes what can be seen over that which is not apparent to the eye; it misses the other levels and the nuances of existence. David Lowe's comparison of sight and the sense of hearing encapsulates some of the issues to which I wish to draw attention. He writes:

> Of the five senses, hearing is the most pervasive and penetrating. I say this, although many, from Aristotle in *Metaphysics* to Hans Jonas in *Phenomenon of Life,* have said that sight is most noble. But sight is always directed at what is straight ahead. . . . And sight cannot turn a corner, at least without the aid of a mirror. On the other hand, sound comes to one, surrounds one for the time being with an acoustic space, full of timbre and nuances. It is more proximate and suggestive than sight. Sight is always the perception of the surface from a particular angle. But sound is that perception able to penetrate beneath the surface. . . . Speech is the communica-

tion connecting one person with another. Therefore, the quality of
sound is fundamentally more vital and moving than that of sight.[54]

Just as the West's privileging of the visual over other senses has been
clearly demonstrated, so too the dominance of the auditory in Yorùbáland can be shown.

In an interesting paper appropriately entitled "The Mind's Eye," feminist theorists Evelyn Fox Keller and Christine Grontkowski make the
following observation: "We [Euro-Americans] speak of knowledge as il-
lumination, knowing as seeing, truth as light. How is it, we might ask,
that vision came to seem so apt a model for knowledge? And having
accepted it as such, how has the metaphor colored our conceptions of
knowledge?"[55] These theorists go on to analyze the implications of the
privileging of sight over other senses for the conception of reality and
knowledge in the West. They examine the linkages between the privileging of vision and patriarchy, noting that the roots of Western thought in
the visual have yielded a dominant male logic.[56] Explicating Jonas's observation that "to get the proper view, we take the proper distance,"[57]
they note the passive nature of sight, in that the subject of the gaze is
passive. They link the distance that seeing entails to the concept of objectivity and the lack of engagement between the "I" and the subject —
the Self and the Other.[58] Indeed, the Other in the West is best described
as another body — separate and distant.

Feminism has not escaped the visual logic of Western thought.
The feminist focus on sexual difference, for instance, stems from this
legacy. Feminist theorist Nancy Chodorow has noted the primacy and
limitations of this feminist concentration on difference:

> For our part as feminists, even as we want to eliminate gender in-
> equality, hierarchy, and difference, we expect to find such features
> in most social settings. . . . We have begun from the assumption that
> gender is *always a salient* feature of social life, and we do not
> have theoretical approaches that emphasize sex similarities over
> differences.[59]

Consequently, the assumption and deployment of patriarchy and
"women" as universals in many feminist writings are ethnocentric and
demonstrate the hegemony of the West over other cultural groupings.[60]
The emergence of patriarchy as a form of social organization in Western history is a function of the differentiation between male and female
bodies, a difference rooted in the visual, a difference that cannot be
reduced to biology and that has to be understood as being constituted
within particular historical and social realities. I am not suggesting that

gender categories are necessarily limited to the West, particularly in the contemporary period. Rather, I am suggesting that discussions of social categories should be defined and grounded in the local milieu, rather than based on "universal" findings made in the West. A number of feminist scholars have questioned the assumption of universal patriarchy. For example, the editors of a volume on Hausa women of northern Nigeria write: "A preconceived assumption of gender asymmetry actually distorts many analyses, since it precludes the exploration of gender as a fundamental component of social relations, inequality, processes of production and reproduction, and ideology."[61] Beyond the question of asymmetry, however, a preconceived notion of gender as a universal social category is equally problematic. If the investigator assumes gender, then gender categories will be found whether they exist or not.

Feminism is one of the latest Western theoretical fashions to be applied to African societies. Following the one-size-fits-all (or better still, the Western-size-fits-all) approach to intellectual theorizing, it has taken its place in a long series of Western paradigms — including Marxism, functionalism, structuralism, and poststructuralism — imposed on African subjects. Academics have become one of the most effective international hegemonizing forces, producing not homogenous social experiences but a homogeny of hegemonic forces. Western theories become tools of hegemony as they are applied universally, on the assumption that Western experiences define the human. For example, a study of Gã residents of a neighborhood in Accra, Ghana, starts thus: "Improving our analysis of women and class formation is necessary to refine our perceptions."[62] Women? What women? Who qualifies to be women in this cultural setting, and on what bases are they to be identified? These questions are legitimate ones to raise if researchers take the constructedness of social categories seriously and take into account local conceptions of reality. The pitfalls of preconceived notions and ethnocentricity become obvious when the author of the study admits:

> Another bias I began with I was forced to change. Before starting fieldwork I was not particularly interested in economics, causal or otherwise. But by the time I had tried an initial presurvey, ... the overweening importance of trading activities in pervading every aspect of women's lives made a consideration of economics imperative. And when the time came to analyze the data in depth, the most cogent explanations often were economic ones. I started out to work with women; I ended by working with traders.[63]

Why, in the first place, did Claire Robertson, the author of this study, start with women, and what distortions were introduced as a result?

What if she had started with traders? Would she have ended up with women? Beginnings are important; adding other variables in midstream does not prevent or solve distortions and misapprehensions. Like many studies on Africans, half of Robertson's study seems to have been completed — and categories were already in place — before she met the Gã people. Robertson's monograph is not atypical in African studies; in fact, it is one of the better ones, particularly because unlike many scholars, she is aware of some of her biases. The fundamental bias that many Westerners, including Robertson, bring to the study of other societies is "body-reasoning," the assumption that biology determines social position. Because "women" is a body-based category, it tends to be privileged by Western researchers over "traders," which is non-body-based. Even when traders are taken seriously, they are embodied such that the trader category, which in many West African societies is non-gender-specific, is turned into "market women," as if the explanation for their involvement in this occupation is to be found in their breasts, or to put it more scientifically, in the X chromosome.[64] The more the Western bio-logic is adopted, the more this body-based framework is inscribed conceptually and into the social reality.

It is not clear that the body is a site of such elaboration of the social in the Gã world-sense or in other African cultures. This warrants investigation before one can draw conclusions that many studies are drawing on gender in African cultures. Why have African studies remained so dependent on Western theories, and what are the implications for the constitution of knowledge about African realities? Contrary to the most basic tenets of body-reasoning, all kinds of people, irrespective of body-type, are implicated in constructing this biologically deterministic discourse. Body-reasoning is a cultural approach. Its origins are easily locatable in European thought, but its tentacles have become all pervasive. Western hegemony appears in many different ways in African studies, but the focus here will be on the hand-me-down theories that are used to interpret African societies without any regard to fit or how ragged they have become.

Western Hegemony in African Studies

An assessment of African studies as an interdisciplinary field will reveal that it is by and large "reactionary."[65] Reaction, in essence, has been at once the driving force of African studies and its limitation in all its branches. It does not matter whether any particular scholar is reacting for or against the West; the point is that the West is at the center of

African knowledge-production. For instance, a whole generation of African historians have reconstructed African history, complete with kings, empires, and even wars, to disprove European claims that Africans are peoples without history.[66] In other fields, a lot of ink has been spilled (and trees felled) to refute or support assertions about whether some African peoples have states or are stateless peoples. Now, in the closing years of the twentieth century, arguably the hottest debate in African studies is whether Africans had philosophy before European contact or whether Africans are best described as "philosophyless" peoples.[67] This is perhaps the most recent phase in an old Western concern with the evolving status of African primitivism, where the indices have moved from historylessness to statelessness and now to philosophylessness.

Whether the discussion focuses on history or historylessness, on having a state or being stateless, it is clear that the West is the norm against which Africans continue to be measured by others and often by themselves. The questions that inform research are developed in the West, and the operative theories and concepts are derived from Western experiences. African experiences rarely inform theory in any field of study; at best such experiences are exceptionalized. Consequently, African studies continues to be "Westocentric," a term that reaches beyond "Eurocentric" to include North America. The presence of Africans in the academy is important in and of itself and has made possible some important changes. However, it has not brought about fundamental changes — despite the sociology-of-knowledge thesis and the politics of identity.[68] That the Euro-American scholar is Westocentric needs no comment. But what accounts for the persistent Westocentricity of a lot of African scholarship?

This question is posed against the background of a debate among African scholars about the inability of many studies conducted by Africans to grapple with the real issues facing African countries. A number of African thinkers have tried to explain why many studies conducted by Africans fail to deal with those issues. The argument has been put forward that many writings by Africans are too focused on exhibiting Africa as different from Europe, instead of dealing with those real issues. Africa is undoubtedly in the midst of a crisis of global proportions, and this fact has lent an urgency to self-examination by African intellectuals. I shall call one group of scholars the antinativists[69] because of their very critical stance toward any espousals of an African culture. The other group, who entertain a notion of an African way of being, are referred to as nativist[70] in their orientation. For the antinativist, the problem of the avoidance of central issues stems from the fact that many African thinkers are cultural nationalists; the charge is that these thinkers are unwilling to acknowledge Africa's failures and European technological superiority and thus focus simply on how different Africa is from the West. The antinativists argue further that the nativists set themselves apart from the West in order to shore up their self-esteem. Literary critic Abiola Irele sums up this antinativist viewpoint very well:

> The whole movement in modern African thought has been to define this identity (African id, located in traditional culture). The intellectual reaction to our humiliation under the colonial system and to our devaluation has consisted in *affirming our difference from the white man, the European. This conscious effort of differentiation has produced the well-known ideologies of African personality* and negritude. In Senghor's formulation of the latter, the idea of the African identity takes the form of an irreducible essence of the race whose objective correlative is the traditional culture. This essence is held to confer an estimable value upon our past and to justify our claim to a separate existence. The whole movement of mind in Black cultural nationalism, from Blyden to Senghor, leads to a mystique of traditional forms of life.[71]

In this article, "In Praise of Alienation," Irele suggests that African intellectuals are unduly holding on to their culture. His solution is to accept Africa's defeat and "alienation" and embrace Europe in all its grandeur and scientific capacity. Only then will Africa have the modern tools to confront its predicament. While no one can deny the myriad problems facing Africa today and the need for leadership, intellectual and otherwise, critical thinkers like Irele have misdiagnosed the source of Africa's problem. The solution they proffer, therefore, is suspect. The foundation of Africa's problem is its close identification with Europe, which is the source and the rationale for continued Western dominance of African peoples and African thought.

My point here, then, is that African thought (from Blyden to Senghor; through Kagame, Mbiti, and Idowu; to Irele, Hountondji, Bodunrin, Oruka, and Wiredu), whether nativist or antinativist, has always focused not on *difference* from the West but on *sameness* with the West. It is precisely because African intellectuals accept and identify so much with European thinking that they have created African versions of Western things. They seem to think that the European mind-set is universal and that, therefore, since Europeans have discovered the way the world works and have laid the foundations of thought, all that Africans need to do is to add their own "burnt" bricks on top of the foundation. Senghorian negritude, for example (one of the earliest modern African intellectual movements), far from being an exercise in difference, is actually a result of Senghor's acceptance of European categories of essence, race, and reason and the linkages among the three. Senghor asserts that since Africans are a race like Europeans, they must have their own brand of essence. The fact that these are European-derived categories is not given enough consideration. Body- or race-reasoning, after all, is not rational; it is not rational or reasonable to declare somebody a criminal just by looking at his face, something racists do relentlessly. Stanislaus Adotevi is correct when he writes that "negritude is the last-born child of an ideology of domination. . . . It is the *black way of being white.*"[72]

The problem of importing Western concepts and categories into African studies and societies takes a decisive turn in the work of a number of African feminist scholars. I find this development particularly unfortunate because this new generation of scholars has the potential to radically transform African studies, which has by and large mirrored the androcentrism of its European origins. Using all sorts of Western models, writers like Tola Pearce and Molara Ogundipe-Leslie have characterized Yorùbá society as patriarchal. Their mastery of Marxism, feminism, and structuralism is dazzling, but their understanding of Yorùbá culture is seriously lacking. Samuel Johnson, a pioneering Yorùbá intellectual, wrote of late nineteenth-century Yorùbáland that "educated natives of Yorùbá are well acquainted with the history of England and with that of Rome and Greece, but of the history of their own country they know nothing whatever!"[73] More than a century later, Johnson's lament remains relevant. More recently, philosopher and art historian Nkiru Nzegwu clearly framed the problem by asserting that when a number of African feminist scholars rushed to characterize indigenous society "as implicitly patriarchal, the question of the legitimacy of patriarchy as a valid transcultural category of analysis was never raised. . . . The problem of evaluating Igbó and Yorùbá cultures on the bases of their cultural other (the West) is that African societies are misrepresented without first presenting their positions."[74]

Pearce's description of the Yorùbá household as consisting of "a patriarch, his wives, his sons, and their wives"[75] sounds like a depiction of the *pater familias* of the Greeks or a description of Abraham's family in the Bible and makes me wonder whether she has ever observed an indigenous Yorùbá lineage or has read earlier accounts of the Yorùbá family by N. A. Fadipe[76] or Johnson.[77] Ogundipe-Leslie, in a 1994 collection of mostly outdated essays, defines the Yorùbá institution of *ilémosú* as one in which women are left on the marriage shelf (*ilémosú* is an institution whereby daughters return to their natal families after marriage and make the family home their lifelong residence). She says, metaphorically, that the institution leaves women "growing fungi

on their bodies in the house."[78] It is difficult to account for her interpretation of *ilémosú;* what it shows, however, is her flippant attitude
toward Yorùbá culture — she has not bothered to ascertain the nature
and the meaning of the institution. The major limitation of Ogundipe-
Leslie's collection of essays is that she provides no cultural context for
her claims. Because gender is preeminently a cultural construct, it cannot be theorized in a cultural vacuum, as many scholars tend to do.
Indeed, one of the useful things that African feminists can learn from
their Western "sisters" is the painstaking archaeological approach with
which many of them have conducted studies that have elucidated Western culture in previously unimaginable ways. African feminists can learn
a lot from the methods of feminist scholarship as they have been applied to the West, but they should scorn methods of Western, imperial,
feminist Africanists who impose feminism on the "colonies." African
scholars need to do serious work detailing and describing indigenous
African cultures from the inside out, not from the outside in. To date,
very little has been written about African societies in and of themselves;
rather, most scholarship is an exercise in propounding one newfangled
Western model or the other. The frame of reference of a culture has
to be identified and described on its own terms before one can make
the sort of gratuitous claims that are being made about patriarchy and
other social ills.

In Yorùbá studies, the manifestation of this preoccupation with finding African equivalents of European things did not originate with
feminists. It is apparent in the work of an earlier generation of scholars such as the theologian E. Bolaji Idowu. He writes on religion that
"if they [Europeans] have God, we have Olodumare; if they have Jesus
Christ, we have Ela the god of salvation, same as them."[79] The theme is
manifested in the work of the antinativists when they describe African
thought as prephilosophic and prescientific or claim that Africa is late
to philosophy. Whether the charge is that Africa was too early or too
late in doing philosophy, the idea is that the Western type of philosophy is a human universal. Such thinking suggests that Africa is the West
waiting to happen or that Africa is like the West, albeit a preformed
or deformed West. With this evolutionary bent, antinativists anthropol-
ogize Africa and deny its coevality with the West.[80] There is nothing
wrong with Africans affirming their humanity and a common humanity
with their nemeses (i.e., Westerners); this affirmation was, indeed, necessary. The problem is that many African writers have assumed Western
manifestations of the human condition to be the human condition itself. To put this in another way: they have misapprehended the nature
of human universals.

Many African scholars, then, have simply failed to distinguish between universals and Western particulars. That human groups have a remembered past is a universal; that the Sumerians developed writing and produced written history at a certain period in time is a particular manifestation of this. That people organize themselves is universal; that they do so under the structure of a state or some other specific form of organization is a particular. That they organize production and reproduction (marriage) is a universal; that in certain places or during certain epochs production and reproduction appear to be separated and separable are particulars. Exchange has always been the universal; sex, cowry shells, gold, money, and credit cards are a few of its particulars. Self-reflection is integral to the human condition, but it is wrong to assume that its Western manifestation — written philosophy — is the universal. In the era of global capitalism, Coca Cola is universal, but it is hardly inherent in the human condition. To help avoid this confusion, a linguistic distinction should be made between *"universal" as a metaphysical term* referring to an inherent truth and *"universal" as a descriptive term*.

Modern African studies has remained dominated by Western modes of apprehension of reality and knowledge-production for a number of reasons. From a materialist perspective, Western dominance in academics is only a reflection of Western global economic and cultural dominance. But that is not an adequate explanation because there are non-Western regions in the world beyond Africa where indigenously grounded studies and concerns have developed to a considerable degree.[81] In the case of Africa, explanations about this dependency on the West have focused on the colonial mentality of African intellectuals, the politics of research funding, and the common class interests or privileged position of intellectuals wherever they are found. These explanations have validity. There is, however, another reason that is rarely acknowledged, and even when it is highlighted, its effect is underestimated: that is, the nature of the academy, especially its logic, structure, and practices. At the core of the problem is the way in which business is conducted in the knowledge-producing institutions; the way in which the foundational questions that inform research are generated in the West; the way in which theories and concepts are generated from Western experiences; and the way in which scholars have to work within disciplines, many of which were constituted to establish dominance over Africa and all of which have logics of their own quite distinct from questions about the social identity of scholars. The point is that as long as Africans take Western categories, like universities, bounded disciplines, and theories, for granted and array themselves around them — for or against does not matter — there can be no fundamental difference in scholarship among these practitioners of knowledge, no matter what their points of origin.

My claim here can be illustrated with reference to the debate about African philosophy. In an anthology entitled *African Philosophy: The Essential Readings,* Tsenay Serequeberhan, the editor of the volume, notes that only African scholars are represented in the book; he goes on to defend what he calls the exclusionist policy:

> In my perception, this exclusionist approach is necessary — at least at this time in the development of African Philosophy — precisely because African philosophers need to formulate their differing positions in confrontation and in dialogue *on their own, that is minus foreign mediators/moderators or meddlers.* African Philosophers must engage in a theoretical threshing in confrontation and dialogue on their own.[82]

Looking at the papers in the collection, no matter their ideological bent, one finds that they quote Lévy-Bruhl, Descartes, Kant, Plato, and Tempels, to mention a few names. These authors are, obviously, not Africans. Europeans, in other words, were not excluded; they might be dead Europeans, but they are still setting the agenda and consequently the terms of discourse. In fact, the question should be asked as to who made these congregated Africans philosophers. How were they initiated? By the so-called mediators/moderators and meddlers?[83] These questions are pertinent since there were some real unnamed and unacknowledged exclusions being practiced in the assembling of the anthology. These other exclusions should be part of the discussion because they underscore very graphically the dilemmas of African scholarship.

This practice of excluding non-Africans as contributors while at the same time accepting the Western/academic terms of discourse as givens is problematic and unrealistic. It should be obvious that it is next to impossible to create an African theoretical space when the ground of discourse has been crowded by the DWEMs — dead, white, European males.[84] The "culture wars" over what should be included in the canon and indeed the curriculum in universities in the United States in the 1980s underscored this point. Let me be clear about what the concern is here. It is not that Africans should not read whatever they please — in fact we must read widely in order to be able to face the challenges posed by late twentieth-century global capitalism. The point is that the foundations of African thought cannot rest on Western intellectual traditions that have as one of their enduring features the projection of Africans as Other and our consequent domination.

At the level of intellectual production, we should recognize that theories are not mechanical tools; they affect (some will say determine) how we think, who we think about, what we think, and who thinks with us. Sometimes scholars seem to forget that intellectual tools are supposed to frame research and thinking. As long as the "ancestor worship"[85] of academic practice is not questioned, scholars in African studies are bound to produce scholarship that does not focus primarily on Africa — for those "ancestors" not only were non-Africans but were hostile to African interests. The foundational questions of research in many disciplines are generated in the West. A recent anthology entitled *Africa and the Disciplines* asks the very Westocentric and ridiculous question: What has Africa contributed to the disciplines?[86] (Following the logic of the question, consider what Africans contributed to craniometry — our heads; and to French *anthropologie* — our butts!)[87] The more important issue for Africa is what the disciplines and the practitioners of disciplines like anthropology have done *to* Africa.[88]

In general, African intellectuals seem to underestimate or fail to grasp the implications of academic practices for the production of knowledge. Research, teaching, and learning in academic institutions are not innocuous business practices. Kwame Anthony Appiah makes this point in an essay reflecting on the limitations of what he calls the nativist critique of the West in the field of African literature: "The Western emperor has ordered the natives to exchange their robes for trousers: their act of defiance is to insist on tailoring them from homespun material. Given their arguments, plainly, the cultural nationalists do not go far enough; they are blind to the fact that their nativist demands inhabit a Western architecture."[89] Appiah's own unabashed and uncritical acceptance of the West and his dismissal of Africa are understandable given his matrilineal descent lines,[90] but this is hardly the solution for other African scholars whose *abusua* (matrilineage) is located on African soil, not in England. It is remarkable that despite Appiah's antinativist stance in relation to African culture, he is an unapologetic nativist himself. Appiah is a Euro-nativist; what he opposes is African nativism. His privileging of European categories of thought and practice (such as patrilineality) over Akan matrilineality in his book *In My Father's House* attests to his erasure of the norms of his father's house (African norms) and the imposition of the values of his mother's house (Anglo-Saxon norms) on Africa.[91]

Appiah, however, makes a valid point when he notes that many African critics of the West fail to realize that acceptance of the Western "architecture" at one level necessarily means embracing the "furnishings" also. In short, certain things go with the territory — academic and otherwise. To think that one can inhabit the territory and then change the rules is a fallacy because the rules and the territory are not separable; they are mutually constituting. The one does not exist without the other.

That said, the position of Appiah and other antinativists is still deeply flawed, in part because of a huge oversight. The antinativist admonition that Africa should embrace the West as a new strategy for the future is flawed because this is actually what African leaders have done in the past and where we still are at present: that is, in the critical embrace of the West. Embracing the West is nothing new; it is actually a failed program of action. The idea that Africa can make a choice about whether it wants to embrace the West or not is a displaced metaphor. The point is that Africa is already locked in an embrace with the West; the challenge is how to extricate ourselves and how much. It is a fundamental problem because without this necessary loosening we continue to mistake the West for the Self and therefore see ourselves as the Other.

Appiah makes the claim that the nativist call for Afrocentricity in the reading and writing of African literature fails to appreciate the multiplicity of the heritage of modern African writers and hence fails to see that, for example, "Soyinka's reference to Euripides is as real as his appeal to Ògún."[92] Appiah himself, however, fails to understand the nature of Soyinka's references to Ògún and Euripides. The problem is not Soyinka's appeal to Euripides; the problem is Appiah's failure to grasp that Soyinka's appeals to Euripides and Ògún are not of the same order.[93] To take a cue from Yorùbá culture: in the practice of Yorùbá religion, despite the 401[94] òrìṣà (gods) to which anybody can appeal, all lineages and individuals have their own òrìṣà that they propitiate first before they appeal to the other gods. They secure their own base first, and it is only after this has been done that they can join in the worship of other gods. There is no question that people can and do change their gods; the fallacy here is the idea that one can start with multiple gods. There is always a privileging going on, whether this is acknowledged or not. Ògún and Euripides cannot be passed off as an expression of "on the one hand and on the other hand (otoh-botoh)" — one must be a foundational "god."

More fundamentally, Appiah fails to grasp that almost all institutionally privileged African scholars are being trained in the Western tradition; there is hardly any training at the academic level in African traditions and cultures. Because of this, it is rare if not impossible to find scholars who can discuss Ògún with the same sophistication and depth of knowledge with which they discuss Zeus. It is no wonder then that for many African intellectuals, Africa remains only an idea. Philosopher V. Y. Mudimbe's experience is telling enough. In his appraisal of anthropological texts on Luba peoples, Mudimbe poses the following question, "Whence comes my authority?" He answers:

> It is true that I am not an anthropologist and do not claim to be one. I spent at least ten years of my life studying ancient Greek and Latin for an average of twelve hours each week, with more than that amount of time devoted to French and European cultures, before being eligible for a doctorate in philology (Greek, Latin and French) at Louvain University. I do not know many anthropologists who could publicly demonstrate a similar experience about their specialty in order to found their authority in African studies.[95]

The more interesting question is this: What is Mudimbe's own claim to authority in African studies? He confesses that this authority rests on "my Luba-Lulua mother, my Songye father, the Swahili cultural context of my education in Katanga (Shaba), the Sanga milieu of my secondary education."[96] The contrast between his sources of knowledge about the West, on the one hand, and Africa, on the other, is striking. Knowledge about the West is cultivated over decades, but knowledge about Africa is supposed to be absorbed, so to speak, through the mother's breast milk. I have nothing against mothers (I am one myself). But while we as African scholars are busy developing the "mother of all canons," who do we suppose will develop the knowledge-base for transforming Africa? Of course, one cannot dismiss the knowledge of one's culture acquired during the crucial formative years. Neither can the possession of the mother tongue be overstated as a key to the understanding of a culture. Even so, many Western-educated Africans do not stay long enough with their mothers to absorb the essentials of an African education. Like Mudimbe, many enter European-derived boarding schools or monasteries at an early age, embarking on a life-long process of absorbing European cultures at the expense of their own. Like Appiah, they may have been tucked away behind "the hibiscus hedge" and subsequently sent to school in Europe while Africa unfolded in the march of history.

It is crucial that our knowledge of Africa be continuously cultivated and developed; it should not be reduced to the level of the instinctual or the primeval (primitive), as some antinativist/Euro-nativist would like. Too many Africans display a lack of knowledge of African cultures, while reveling in their knowledge of European classics and dead languages. Mudimbe himself noted that his European "codisciples" went through the same kind of training as he for the specialization in philology.[97] Apparently, their mothers' milk was not enough as a source of knowledge about their European culture; they still had to spend a lifetime studying it.

As a prologue to his acclaimed book *The Invention of Africa,* Mudimbe disseminates what he calls the "good news" — that the African now has "the freedom of thinking of himself or herself as the starting point of an absolute discourse."[98] His claim is surprising given that the content of his book does not derive epistemologically from Africa and is heavily dependent on European thought. This is hardly the multicultural heritage that Appiah wants us to believe obtains in African studies. It is clearly a Western heritage and explains why Ògún does not stand a chance against Zeus and why Africa remains merely an idea in the minds of many African scholars. Of course, in reality Africa continues to unfold in the march of history. The original human history at that!

Writing Yorùbá into English: Propagating the West

To demonstrate concretely the implications for scholarship of the uncritical acceptance of Western categories and questions in the study of African societies, I will now address a specific regional discourse, Yorùbá studies.[99] Yorùbá discourse in English is a particularly good place to examine the problems of Westocentricity in the determination of research questions, because scholars of Yorùbá origin are very well represented. As an anthropologist in a recent monograph put it, "Western scholars don't write *about* the Yorùbá; they write *with* the Yorùbá."[100] Prepositions aside, the reverse is more the case — Yorùbá scholars write with the West about Yorùbá. This is revealed in the failure to take Yorùbá language seriously in Yorùbá scholarship — the language is that of West. The lack of interest in the Yorùbá language beyond "fieldworkese" is not surprising, since African studies is one of the few areas in the academy where one can claim to be an expert without the benefit of language competence.[101] African nationalities are said to be based on language groups, but the marginalization of language in African studies belies this fact. One wonders whether the endurance of the nebulous category "Africa" as the unit of analysis in many studies is related to these facts. No doubt, there is some research that necessitates using Africa as the unit of analysis; however, at this point in the history of the scholarship, Africa, as Paulin J. Hountondji observes, is best used as a descriptive geographic term.[102]

Regional studies that are based on particular cultural groups are essentially exercises in translation at different levels: translation from oral to written; translation from one culture to another; and finally translation from one language to another. Each category — written, oral, culture, language — is permeated with all sorts of unstated assumptions, and each move is fraught with potentials for missteps. Language is crucial, and Marc Bloch's observation about the problem that discounting language poses for historians is relevant: "What an absurd illogicality that men who half the time can have access to their subject only through words, are permitted, among other deficiencies, to be ignorant of the fundamental attainments of linguistics!"[103] Another absurdity is that Yorùbá scholars continue to build knowledge about our society in the English language. This theater of the absurd expands with the realization that many Africans come to know their societies only through what Western anthropologists and missionaries have written about them.

Against this background, the lack of critical studies on Yorùbá language, despite the expansion of the corpus, is shocking. This is not a minor problem — the lack of appreciation that language carries with it the world-sense of a people has led to the assumption that Western categories are universal. In most studies of the Yorùbá, the indigenous categories are not examined but are assimilated into English. This practice has led to serious distortions and quite often to a total misapprehension of Yorùbá realities. The implications of this situation are not just semantic, however, but also epistemological, in that they have affected the type of knowledge that has been produced and who has done the producing in Yorùbá written discourse. A thorough analysis of the language is essential to the construction of knowledge about the Yorùbá in English. That this has never been done calls into question findings in various disciplines, and this shall be illustrated in subsequent chapters. Granted, linguists have done some studies on the Yorùbá language, but language study cannot be confined to linguists. All researchers, regardless of discipline, are translators in one way or another, and this must be borne in mind in the practice of research. In Yorùbá studies, historians translate the oral traditions of the arókin (royal bards); orature critics translate oríkì (praise poetry); and those in religion may translate Ifá divination, poetry, or the chants of Ṣàngó devotees. These are just a few examples that show the futility of imposing Western disciplinary boundaries on Yorùbá knowledge. Malian philosopher Amadou Hampate Ba underscores the holistic nature of African oral traditions: "Oral tradition is the great school of life, all aspects of which are covered and affected by it. It may seem chaos to those who do not penetrate its secret; *it may baffle the Cartesian mind accustomed to dividing everything into clear-cut categories*. In oral tradition, in fact, *spiritual and material are not dissociated*."[104] The problem of gender and its constructs in Yorùbá language, literature, and social practice calls for immediate attention. Yorùbá language is gender-free, which means that many categories taken for granted in English are absent. There are no gender-specific words denoting son, daughter, brother, or sister. Yorùbá names are not gender-specific; neither are oko and aya — two categories translated as the English husband and wife, respectively. Given that anatomic categories are not used as social categories, it is clear that apprehending the gender of particular individuals or personages in a different time period and across space is at best an ambiguous adventure. In the discipline of history, for example, how should dynastic lists popularly known as "kings' lists" (which have been generated by historians for different Yorùbá polities) be interpreted? Many contemporary historians have assumed that, with a couple of exceptions, all the rulers on the lists are male, but what is their basis for this assumption? At the very least, the basis of assigning sex to each ruler has to be explained for the period during which there were no written accounts. Given the gender-free terms oba (ruler) and aláàfin (ruler), historians should provide evidence for such gender assumptions.

Yorùbá scholar of religion Bolaji Idowu was forced to deal with the question of gender in his study of Yorùbá religion. He found that there were two different oral traditions about the sex of Òdùduwà, the Yorùbá progenitor; in one tradition s/he was said to be male, and in the other s/he was female.[105] Idowu suggests that the confusion about the sex identity of Òdùduwà may be due in part to language in that the liturgy that refers to Òdùduwà as mother also calls the progenitor "lord" and "husband." Idowu translates the beginning of this liturgy as follows:

> O mother, we beseech thee to deliver us;
> Look after us, look after (our) children;
> Thou who art established at Ado...

Idowu continues: "But yet, as the ritual ballad is recited, we hear phrases like 'my lord' and 'my husband,' and such phrases strongly indicate that a god is being addressed."[106] It is apparent that Idowu erred in thinking that the presence of the word "husband" constituted evidence of maleness, since the Yorùbá word oko, translated as the English "husband," is a non-gender-specific category encompassing both male and female. Thus Òdùduwà can be "husband," lord, and mother. This suggests that Idowu accepted the English category unquestioningly, despite his own awareness of Yorùbá culture. Idowu is not an exception; in fact, he typifies the process of patriarchalizing Yorùbá history and culture. In many intellectual writings, the male is assumed to be the norm, just as in the West. In the case of historical events and personages, the process has been achieved primarily through translation. That oba, which means "ruler" (non-gender-specific) in Yorùbá, has come to mean "king" in Yorùbá discourse (whatever the historical time period) is symptomatic. Ade Obayemi, another Yorùbá scholar, demonstrates this problem glaringly. In his discussion of the historical records regarding the person of Òdùduwà, he writes: "Taken together, existing genealogical or sex placings of Oduduwa do not and cannot on their own take us far in any attempt to definitively fix his position vis-à-vis other *heroes, kings,* or *legendary figures.*" Obviously, even as Obayemi declaims fixing gender identity, he does so with the help of the English language.[107]

Gender as an analytic category is now at the heart of contemporary Yorùbá discourse. Yet very little has been done to untangle this web of Yorùbá/English mistranslations. Gender has become important in Yorùbá studies not as an artifact of Yorùbá life but because Yorùbá life, past and present, has been translated into English to fit the Western pattern of body-reasoning. This pattern is one in which gender is omnipresent, the male is the norm, and the female is the exception; it is a pattern in which power is believed to inhere in maleness in and of itself. It is also a pattern that is not grounded on evidence. Based on a review of the existing literature, it does not appear that Yorùbá scholars have given much thought to the linguistic divergence of Yorùbá and English and its implications for knowledge-production. This is an issue that will be explored in subsequent chapters.

Different modes of apprehending knowledge yield dissimilar emphases on types and the nature of evidence for making knowledge-claims. Indeed, this also has implications for the organization of social structure, particularly the social hierarchy that undergirds who knows and who does not. I have argued that Western social hierarchies such as gender and race are a function of the privileging of the visual over other senses in Western culture. It has also been noted that the Yorùbá frame of reference was based more on a combination of senses anchored by the auditory. Consequently, the promotion in African studies of concepts and theories derived from the Western mode of thought at best makes it difficult to understand African realities. At worse, it hampers our ability to build knowledge about African societies.

Chapter 2

(Re)constituting the Cosmology and Sociocultural Institutions of Ọ̀yọ́-Yorùbá

ARTICULATING THE YORÙBÁ WORLD-SENSE

•••

INDISPUTABLY, gender has been a fundamental organizing principle in Western societies.[1] Intrinsic to the conceptualization of gender is a dichotomy in which male and female, man and woman, are constantly and binarily ranked, both in relationship to and against each other. It has been well documented that the categories of male and female in Western social practice are not free of hierarchical associations and binary oppositions in which the male implies privilege and the female subordination. It is a duality based on a perception of human sexual dimorphism inherent in the definition of gender. Yorùbá society, like many other societies worldwide, has been analyzed with Western concepts of gender on the assumption that gender is a timeless and universal category. But as Serge Tcherkézoff admonishes, "An analysis that starts from a male/female pairing simply produces further dichotomies."[2] It is not surprising, then, that researchers always find gender when they look for it.

Against this background, I will show that despite voluminous scholarship to the contrary, gender was not an organizing principle in Yorùbá society prior to colonization by the West. The social categories "men" and "women" were nonexistent, and hence no gender system[3] was in place. Rather, the primary principle of social organization was seniority, defined by relative age. The social categories "women" and "men" are social constructs deriving from the Western assumption that "physical bodies are social bodies,"[4] an assumption that in the previous chapter I named "body-reasoning" and a "bio-logic" interpretation of the so-

31

cial world. The original impulse to apply this assumption transculturally is rooted in the simplistic notion that gender is a natural and universal way of organizing society and that male privilege is its ultimate manifestation. But gender is socially constructed: it is historical and culture-bound. Consequently, the assumption that a gender system existed in Ọ̀yọ́ society prior to Western colonization is yet another case of Western dominance in the documentation and interpretation of the world, one that is facilitated by the West's global material dominance.

The goal of this chapter is to articulate the Yorùbá world-sense or cultural logic and to (re)map the Yorùbá social order. It challenges the received assumption that gender was a fundamental organizing principle in Old Ọ̀yọ́ society. To this effect, there will be an examination of social roles as they were articulated in a number of institutions, including language, lineage, marriage, and the market. The social categories of *ìyá* (mother), *bàbá* (father), *ọmọ, aya, ọkọ, àbúrò* (see below on the translation of these terms), *ẹ̀gbọ́n* (elder sibling or relation), *aláwo* (diviner), *àgbẹ̀* (farmer), and *onísòwò* (trader) are presented and analyzed. Acknowledging the dangers of mistranslation of key concepts, I will use Yorùbá terminology as much as possible. Using Yorùbá vocabularies of culture — my knowledge of Yorùbá society acquired through experience and research — I will interrogate a range of feminist, anthropological, sociological, and historical literatures, and in the process I will critically evaluate the notion that gender is a timeless and universal category.

Yorùbá language and oral traditions represent major sources of information in constituting world-sense, mapping historical changes, and interpreting the social structure. Documented accounts that I will refer to include the writings of the Reverend Samuel Johnson, a pioneering Yorùbá historian and ethnographer, and the memoirs and diaries of European travelers and missionaries of the nineteenth century. Finally, in conceptualizing the past, the present is not irrelevant. All of the institutions that I describe are not archaic — they are living traditions.

Putting Woman in Her Place

Gender as a dichotomous discourse is about two binarily opposed and hierarchical social categories — men and women. Given that, I should immediately point out that the usual gloss of the Yorùbá categories *obìnrin* and *ọkùnrin* as "female/woman" and "male/man," respectively, is a mistranslation. This error occurs because many Western and Western-influenced Yorùbá thinkers fail to recognize that in Yorùbá practice and thought, these categories are neither binarily opposed nor hierarchical. The word *obìnrin* does not derive etymologically from *okùnrin,* as "wo-man" does from "man." *Rin,* the common suffix of *okùnrin* and *obìnrin,* suggests a common humanity; the prefixes *obìn* and *okùn* specify which variety of anatomy. There is no conception here of an original human type against which the other variety had to be measured. *Ènìyàn* is the non-gender-specific word for humans. In contrast, "man," the word labeling humans in general in English that supposedly encompasses both males and females, actually privileges males. It has been well documented that in the West, women/females are the Other, being defined in antithesis to men/males, who represent the norm.[5] Feminist philosopher Marilyn Frye captures the essence of this privileging in Western thought when she writes, "The word 'woman' was supposed to mean *female of the species,* but the name of the species was 'Man.' "[6] In the Yorùbá conception, *okùnrin* is not posited as the norm, the essence of humanity, against which *obìnrin* is the Other. Nor is *okùnrin* a category of privilege. *Obìnrin* is not ranked in relation to *okùnrin;* it does not have negative connotations of subordination and powerlessness; and, above all, it does not in and of itself constitute any social ranking. Another reason *okùnrin* and *obìnrin* cannot be translated into the English "male" and "female" is that the Yorùbá categories only apply to adult human beings and are not normally used for *omodé* (children) or *eranko* (animals). The terms *ako* and *abo* are used for male and female animals, respectively. They are also applied to some fruit trees like the papaya and to the abstract idea of a period in time, that is, the year. Thus *ako ibépe* is a papaya tree that does not bear fruit; and *odún t'ó ya 'bo* is a fruitful (good) year. "May your year be fruitful [*yabo*]"[7] is a standard prayer and greeting at the beginning of the Yorùbá new year, which is signaled by the arrival of the "new yam." Because *ako* and *abo* are not oppositionally constructed, the opposite of a good (*abo*) year is not an *ako* year. An unproductive year is a year that is not *abo.* There is no conception of an *ako* year. A fruitless pawpaw tree is an *ako* tree. A fruitful pawpaw tree is not described as *abo;* rather, a fruitful tree is considered the norm; therefore, it is just referred to as a pawpaw tree. I cite these examples to show that these Yorùbá concepts, just like *okùnrin* and *obìnrin,* which are used for humans, are not equivalent to the English "male" and "female," respectively. Thus, in this study, the basic terms *okùnrin* and *obìnrin* are best translated as referring to the anatomic male and anatomic female, respectively; they refer only to physiologically marked differences and do not have hierarchical connotations like the English terms "male/men" and "female/women." The distinctions these Yorùbá terms signify are superficial. For ease of deployment, "anatomic" has been shortened to "ana" and added on to the words "male," "female," and "sex" to underscore the fact that in the Yorùbá world-sense it is possible to acknowledge these physiological distinctions without inherently projecting a hierarchy of the two social categories. Thus I propose the new concepts *anamale, anafemale,* and *anasex.* The need for a new set of constructs arose from the recognition that in Western thought, even the so-called biological concepts like male, female, and sex are not free of hierarchical connotations.[8]

Indeed, the Yorùbá term *obìnrin* is not equivalent to "woman" because the concept of woman or female conjures up a number of images, including the following:

1. those who do not have a penis (the Freudian concept of penis envy stems from this notion and has been elucidated at length in Western social thought and gender studies);[9]

2. those who do not have power; and

3. those who cannot participate in the public arena.

Hence, what females *are not* defines them as women, while the male is assumed to be the norm. The aforementioned images are derived from the Western experience and are not associated with the Yorùbá word *obìnrin.* Since the conceptual language of gender theories is derived from the West, it is necessary to view these theories as *vectors* of the issue they are designed to explain. Unlike "male" and "female" in the West, the categories of *obìnrin* and *okùnrin* are primarily categories of anatomy, suggesting no underlying assumptions about the personalities or psychologies deriving from such. Because they are not elaborated in relation and opposition to each other, they are not sexually dimorphic and therefore are not gendered. In Old Òyó, they did not connote social ranking; nor did they express masculinity or femininity, because those categories did not exist in Yorùbá life or thought.

Necessary Distinctions without Difference

The Yorùbá terms *obìnrin* and *okùnrin* do express a distinction. Reproduction is, obviously, the basis of human existence, and given its import, and the primacy of anafemale body-type, it is not surprising that the Yorùbá language describes the two types of anatomy. The terms *okùnrin* and *obìnrin,* however, merely indicate the physiological differences between the two anatomies as they have to do with procreation and intercourse. They refer, then, to the physically marked and physiologically apparent differences between the two anatomies. They do

not refer to gender categories that connote social privileges and disadvantages. Also, they do not express sexual dimorphism[10] because the
distinction they indicate is specific to issues of reproduction. To appreciate this point, it would be necessary to go back to the fundamental
difference between the conception of the Yorùbá social world and that
of Western societies.

In the previous chapter, I argued that the biological determinism in
much of Western thought stems from the application of biological explanations in accounting for social hierarchies. This in turn has led to the
construction of the social world with biological building blocks. Thus
the social and the biological are thoroughly intertwined. This worldview
is manifested in male-dominant gender discourses, discourses in which
female biological differences are used to explain female sociopolitical
disadvantages. The conception of biology as being "everywhere" makes
it possible to use it as an explanation in any realm, whether it is directly implicated or not.[11] Whether the question is why women should
not vote or why they breast-feed babies, the explanation is one and the
same: they are biologically predisposed.

The upshot of this cultural logic is that men and women are perceived as essentially different creatures. Each category is defined by
its own essence. Diane Fuss describes the notion that things have a
"true essence...as a belief in the real, the invariable and fixed properties which define the whatness of an entity."[12] Consequently, whether
women are in the labor room or in the boardroom, their essence is said
to determine their behavior. In both arenas, then, women's behavior is
by definition different from that of men. Essentialism makes it impossible to confine biology to one realm. The social world, therefore, cannot
truly be socially constructed.

The reaction of feminists to conservative, male-dominant discourse
was to reject it totally as a vehicle of oppression. Feminists then went
on to show that the existence of two sexes, which has been regarded
as an "irreducible fact,"[13] is actually a social construction. In the process of challenging the essentialism of male-dominant discourses, many
feminist writings treated all distinctions between men and women as
fabrications.[14] Thus the fact that women bear children is not given the
attention it deserves; instead it is located on a continuum of what are
called "gender differences." It is given the same degree of importance
as the fact that women have less body hair than men. Thus despite the
relentless feminist assault on mainstream essentialism, feminist constructionism contains within it the very problem it seeks to address. Like the
traditional male-dominant discourses, feminism does not entertain the
possibility that certain differences are more fundamental than others.

That women bear children calls for a distinctive assessment. If Western conservative discourses collapse the social world into biology by seeing all observed differences between men and women as natural, feminism maintains this lack of a boundary between the social and the biological by homogenizing men and women and insisting that all observed differences are social fabrications. This is the problem.

Undoubtedly, in a postchromosomal and posthormonal world in which genes are said to determine behavior, and science is the unassailable source of wisdom on all things, it is difficult to imagine that acceptance of distinctive reproductive roles for men and women would not lead to a creation of social hierarchies. The challenge that the Yorùbá conception presents is a social world based on social relations, not the body. It shows that it is possible to acknowledge the distinct reproductive roles for *obìnrin* and *ọkùnrin* without using them to create social ranking. In the Yorùbá cultural logic, biology is limited to issues like pregnancy that directly concern reproduction. The essential biological fact in Yorùbá society is that the *obìnrin* bears the baby. It does not lead to an essentializing of *obìnrin* because they remain *ènìyàn* (human beings), just as *ọkùnrin* are human too, in an ungendered sense.

Thus the distinction between *obìnrin* and *ọkùnrin* is actually one of reproduction, not one of sexuality or gender, the emphasis being on the fact that the two categories play distinct roles in the reproductive process. This distinction does not extend beyond issues directly related to reproduction and does not overflow to other realms such as the farm or the *ọba*'s (ruler's) palace. I have called this a distinction without social difference. The distinction in Yorùbáland between the way in which anatomic females pay obeisance to their superiors and the way in which anatomic males do is useful in elaborating the distinct but ungendered consideration of pregnancy. Any casual observer would notice that in the contemporary period, *obìnrin* usually *kúnlẹ̀* (kneel down, with both knees touching the floor) when greeting a superior. *Ọkùnrin* are seen to *dòbálẹ̀* (prostrate themselves, lying flat on the ground and then raising their torsos with arms holding them up in a push-up pose). Some might assume that these two distinct forms of greeting are constructions of gender, yielding social valuations and difference. However, a simple association of anatomic females with kneeling and anatomic males with prostrating will not elucidate the cultural meanings of these acts. What is required is a comprehensive examination of all other modes of greeting and address, how they are represented in a multiplicity of realms, and how they relate to one another.

When anatomic females pay obeisance to the *ọba* (ruler), they have to *yìká* — in which case they lie on their sides, propping themselves up with one elbow at a time. In practice, *iyîká* looks like an abbreviation of *ìdòbálè*. It appears that in the past, *ìyîká* was the primary mode of female obeisance to superiors. But over time, kneeling has become dominant. Thus, it would seem that the preferred position for paying obeisance for all persons, whether *obìnrin* or *okùnrin*, is for the "greeter" to prostrate to the "greetee." I would assert that the contingencies of pregnancy led to the *iyîká* modification for anatomic *obìnrin*. It is obvious that even pregnant *obìnrin* can *yîká*, but they cannot prostrate easily. Johnson lends historical background to this interpretation. In the late nineteenth century, he observed that the mode of saluting a superior involved "the men prostrating on the ground, and the women sitting on the ground and reclining on their left elbow."[15] The predominance of *obìnrin* kneeling is a more recent development. In fact, female prostration can be seen even today. I have observed *obìnrin* prostrating themselves in the *oba*'s palace in Ògbómòsó. Moreover, a common stance of worship of the deities is the *idòbálè*, irrespective of anatomic type.[16] Therefore, the disassociation of *obìnrin* from prostration is uncalled-for. Similarly, the disassociation of *okùnrin* from kneeling is unwarranted.[17] In Yorùbá cosmology, there is the conception of *àkúnlèyàn*, literally "kneeling to choose" — which is the position that all persons assume in front of Elèdá (the Maker) when choosing their fate before being born into the world. On closer examination, it is clear that kneeling is a position used not so much for paying homage as for addressing one's superior. All persons who choose to address the *oba*, for example, whether *okùnrin* or *obìnrin*, will of necessity end up on their knees. This is not difficult to understand, given that it is impractical to engage in long conversations in the *iyîká* or *idòbálè* positions. In fact, the saying *eni b'óba jiyàn ô yíò pé lórí ikúnlè* (someone who would argue with the *oba* must be prepared to spend a long time in the kneeling position) alludes to this fact. Further, we know from Johnson's writings that the *aláàfin* (ruler) of Òyó traditionally had to kneel down for only one person — an *obìnrin* official of the palace. In explicating the nature of the office and duties of this official — the *iyámode* (a high official who resides in the palace compound) — Johnson writes:

> Her office is to worship the spirits of the departed kings, calling out their Egúngúns in a room in her apartments set aside for that purpose. . . . The king looks upon her as his father, and addresses her as such, being the worshipper of the spirit of his ancestors. *He kneels in saluting her, and she also returns the salutation, kneeling, never reclining, on her elbow as is the custom of the women in saluting their superiors.* The king kneels for no one else but her,

and prostrates before the god Ṣàngó, and before those possessed with the deity, calling them "father."[18]

The propitiations and thank-offerings to the lineage ancestors during the first two days of the Egúngún (annual festival of ancestor veneration) are named ìkúnlè.[19] Finally, ìkúnlè was the preferred position of giving birth in traditional society and is central to the construction of motherhood. This position, ìkúnlè abiyamọ́ (the kneeling of a mother in labor), is elaborated as the ultimate moment of human submission to the will of the divine. Perhaps the fact that the mode and manner of acknowledging a superior does not depend on whether s/he is an anamale or anafemale indicates the nongendered cultural framework. A superior is a superior regardless of body-type.

It is significant that in Yorùbá cosmology, when a body part is singled out it is the orí (head), which is elaborated as the seat of individual fate (orí). The word orí thus has two closely intertwined meanings — fate and head. Orí has no gender. The preoccupation with choosing one's orí (fate, destiny) before one is born into the world is to choose a good one. In Ifá discourse,[20] there is a myth about three friends who went to Àjàlá, the potter, the maker of heads, to choose their orí (fate, heads) before making their journey to earth. The anasex of these three friends is not the issue in this myth, and it has nothing to do with who made a good choice and who did not. What is of importance is that due to impatience and carelessness, two of the friends chose a defective orí while only one of them chose a good orí:

They then took them to Àjàlá's [the Potter's] store-house of heads.
When Oriseeku entered,
He picked a newly made head
Which Àjàlá had not baked at all.
When Orileemere also entered,
He picked a very big head,
Not knowing it was broken.
The two of them put on their clay heads,
And they hurried off to earth.

They worked and worked, but they had no gain.
If they traded with one half-penny,
It led them
To a loss of one and one-half pennies.

The wise men told them that the fault was in the bad heads they
    had chosen.
When Afùwàpẹ́ arrived on earth,

He started to trade.
And he made plenty of profit.

When Oriseeku and Orileemere saw Afùwàpẹ́, they started to weep and said the following:

> "I don't know where the lucky ones chose their heads;
> I would have gone there to choose mine.
> I don't know where Afùwàpẹ́ chose his head.
> I would have gone there to choose mine."[21]

Afùwàpẹ́ answered them, saying in essence that even though we choose our heads from the same place, our destinies are not equal. Rowland Abiodun elaborates this distinction between orí-inú (inner head or destiny) and the physical orí (head), and in discussing the importance of orí-inú for each individual he makes a number of telling points:

> A person's Ori-Inu is so crucial to a successful life that it is propitiated frequently, and its support and guidance are sought before undertaking a new task. For this reason, personal Ori shrines are indispensable and are present in homes, *irrespective of sex*, religious belief, or cult affiliation, and in the performance of virtually all sacrifices, ancestral worship, and major and minor festivals, Ori features prominently, since it determines their favorable outcome.[22]

The purpose of the foregoing explorations of some apparent distinctions in Yorùbá social life is to problematize the idea that the distinction between *obìnrin* and *okùnrin* necessarily concerns gender. Gender is not a property of an individual or a body in and of itself by itself. Even the notion of a gender identity as part of the self rests on a cultural understanding. Gender is a construction of two categories in hierarchical relation to each other; and it is embedded in institutions. Gender is best understood as "an institution that establishes patterns of expectations for individuals [based on their body-type], orders the social processes of everyday life, and is built into major social organizations of society, such as the economy, ideology, the family, and politics."[23]

The frame of reference of any society is a function of the logic of its culture as a whole. It cannot be arrived at piecemeal, by looking at one institutional site or social practice at a time. The limitations of basing interpretations on observation without probing meanings contextually immediately become apparent. Next, attention will be turned to specific institutions in Ọ̀yọ́ society, explicating them to map cultural meanings and ultimately to understand the world-sense that emerges from the whole. In the final analysis, comprehension comes from totalizing and situating the particular into its self-referent context.

question

does language really carry cultural values in it?

Seniority: The Vocabulary of Culture and the Language of Status

Language is preeminently a social institution, and as such it constitutes and is constituted by culture. Because of the pervasiveness of language, it is legitimate to ask what a particular language tells us about the culture from which it derives. Language carries cultural values within it.[24] In this study, I am not so much interested in taking an inventory of words as in teasing out the world-sense that any particular language projects.

Seniority is the primary social categorization that is immediately apparent in Yorùbá language. Seniority is the social ranking of persons based on their chronological ages. The prevalence of age categorization in Yorùbá language is the first indication that age relativity is the pivotal principle of social organization. Most names and all pronouns are ungendered. The third-person pronouns ó and wón make a distinction between older and younger in social interactions. Thus the pronoun wón is used to refer to an older person, irrespective of anatomic sex. Like the old English "thou" or the French pronoun vous, wón is the pronoun of respect and formality. Ó is used in situations of familiarity and intimacy.[25]

In social interactions and conversations, it is necessary to establish who is older because that determines which pronoun to use and whether one can refer to a person by that person's given name. Only older persons can use another's name. It is possible to hold a long and detailed conversation about a person without indicating the gender of that person, unless the anatomy is central to the issue under discussion, as with conversations about sexual intercourse or pregnancy. There is, however, considerable anxiety about establishing seniority in any social interaction. It is almost sacrilegious to call someone who is older by name; it is regarded as uncultured. The etiquette is that in the initial meeting of two people, it is the older person who has the responsibility and privilege first of asking, S'álàfíà ni? (How are you?). Because who is older or younger is not always obvious, the pronoun of choice for all parties meeting for the first time is ẹ, the formal second-person pronoun, at least until the seniority order has been determined.

Kinship terms are also encoded by age relativity. The word àbúrò refers to all relatives born after a given person, encompassing sisters, brothers, and cousins. The distinction indicated is one of relative age. The word ègbón performs a similar function. Ọmọ, the word for "child," is best understood as "offspring." There are no single words for boy or girl. The terms ọmọkùnrin (boy) and ọmọbìnrin (girl) that have gained currency today indicate anasex for children (deriving from *ọmọ ọkùnrin* and *ọmọ obìnrin*, literally "child, anatomic male" and "child, anatomic female"); they show that what is privileged socially is the youth of the child, not its anatomy. These words are a recent attempt at gendering the language and reflect Johnson's observation of Yorùbáland in the nineteenth century. Commenting on the new vocabulary of the time, he noted that "our translators, in their desire to find a word expressing the English idea of sex rather than of age, coined the . . . words 'arakonrin,' i.e., the male relative; and 'arabinrin,' the female relative; these words have always to be explained to the pure but illiterate Yoruba man."[26]

Ìyá and *bàbá* can be glossed as the English categories "mother" and "father," respectively, and to English speakers they may appear to be gender categories. But the issue is more complicated. The concept of parenthood is closely intertwined with adulthood. It is expected that people of a certain age have had children because procreation is considered the raison d'être of human existence. It is the way things are and have to be for the group to survive. Although the uniqueness of the *ọkùnrin* and *obìnrin* roles in reproduction is coded in language, the most important attribute these categories indicate is not gender; rather, it is the expectation that persons of a certain age should have had children. Unlike the English concepts of mother and father, *bàbá* and *ìyá* are not just categories of parenthood. They are also categories of adulthood, since they are also used to refer to older people in general. More importantly, they are not binarily opposed and are not constructed in relation to each other.

The importance of the seniority principle in Yorùbá social organization has been acknowledged and analyzed variously by interpreters of the society. It is the cornerstone of social intercourse. The sociologist N. A. Fadipe captures the range and scope of this principle when he writes, "The principle of seniority applies in all walks of life and in practically all activities in which men and women are brought together. The custom cuts through the distinctions of wealth, of rank, and of sex."[27] He goes on to show that seniority is not just about civility; it confers some measure of social control and guarantees obedience to authority, which reinforces the idea of leadership.

It should also be stressed, however, that seniority is not just a matter of privilege in everyday life. It is also about responsibility. In the socialization of children, for example, the oldest in a group is the first to be served during meal times and is held responsible in cases of group infraction because this older child should have known better. The supreme insult is to call a person *àgbàyà* (senior for nothing). It is used to put people in their place if they are violating a code of seniority by not behaving as they should or are not taking responsibility. If a child starts eating from the common bowl first and fails to leave some of the food for the junior ones, s/he is chided with *àgbà'yà*. There is no notion of "sissy" or "tomboy."

Unlike European languages, Yorùbá does not "do gender";[28] it "does seniority" instead. Thus social categories — familial and nonfamilial — do not call attention to the body as English personal names, first-person pronouns, and kinship terms do (the English terms being both gender-specific/body-specific). Seniority is highly relational and situational in that no one is permanently in a senior or junior position; it all depends on who is present in any given situation. Seniority, unlike gender, is only comprehensible as part of relationships. Thus, it is neither rigidly fixated on the body nor dichotomized.

The importance of gender in English kinship terminology is reflected in the words "brother" (male sibling) and "sister" (female sibling), categories that require conscious qualifiers in Yorùbá conceptualization. There are no single words in Yorùbá denoting the English gendered kinship categories of son, daughter, brother, sister. Qualifiers have to be added to the primary categories in order to make the anasex of the relation apparent. The absence of gender-differentiated categories in Yorùbá language underscores the absence of gender conceptions.

The importance of seniority-ranking has attracted the attention of scholars of Yorùbá culture. American anthropologist William Bascom, who did ethnographic work in the 1930s, made the following observation: "Yorùbá kinship terminology stresses the factor of seniority including relative age as one of its manifestations, which is so important in relationships between members of the clan.... Sex is of relatively little importance, being used only to distinguish 'father' and 'mother.' "[29] Likewise, British ethnographer J. S. Eades, writing about fifty years later, underlined the importance of age in social interactions: "Many older Yorùbá do not know when they were born, but they do know precisely who is senior or junior to themselves because being older confers respect and deference. The junior members of the compound are expected to take on the 'dirtier' and more onerous tasks."[30] The absence of gender categories does not mean that the Yorùbá language cannot describe notions or convey information about male and female anatomic differences. The critical point is that those differences are not codified because they did not have much social significance and so do not project into the social realm.

The differences between the Yorùbá and English conceptualizations can be understood through the following examples. In English, to the question, "Who was with you when you went to the market?" one might answer, "My son." To the same question in Yorùbá, one would answer, Ọmọ mìi (My child or offspring). Only if the anatomy of the child was directly relevant to the topic at hand would the Yorùbá mother add a qualifier thus, "Ọmọ mìi ọkùnrin" (My child, the male). Otherwise, birth-order would be the more socially significant point of reference. In that case, the Yorùbá mother would say, Ọmọ mìi àkọ́bí (My child, the first born). Even when the name of the child is used, gender is still not indicated because most Yorùbá names are gender-free.

In contrast, in English-speaking, Euro-American cultures, one can hardly place any person in social context without first indicating gender. In fact, by merely mentioning gender, Euro-Americans immediately deduce many other things about people. In the English language, for example, it is difficult to keep referring to one's offspring with the non-gender-specific "child." It is not the norm to do this; it may be considered strange or suggest a deliberate withholding of information. Kathy Ferguson, a feminist mother and scholar, recognized this:

> When my son was born I began a determined campaign to speak to him in a non-stereotypical fashion. I told him often that he is a sweet boy, a gentle boy, a beautiful boy, as well as a smart and strong boy. The range of adjectives may have been impressive, but there was a predictability in the nouns: whatever variation existed, it rotated around that anchor word boy. The substitution of gender-neutral nouns ("you're such a terrific infant, such an adorable child, such a wonderful kid"), was unsustainable.[31]

A Yorùbá mother does not need to trouble herself about such things. The problem of constant gendering and gender-stereotyping does not arise in the Yorùbá language. The anchor word in Yorùbá is ọmọ, a non-gender-specific word denoting one's offspring, irrespective of age or sex. Ọmọdé is the more specific term for young child(ren). Though ọmọ is often translated as "child," it does not show any age restriction. A seventy-year-old mother would refer to her forty-year-old as ọmọ 'mì (my child).

Lineage Hierarchies: The *Ilé*, Junior Consorts, and Senior Siblings

The previous sections have focused on the sociocultural meaning of certain linguistic concepts in order to understand Yorùbá cosmology. In this and the following sections, my focus shifts somewhat to a number of

specific social institutions and practices, with the purpose of further documenting the Yorùbá social world and world-sense. Yorùbá have been
urbanized for centuries; we live in towns — settlements that are characterized by large populations engaged in farming, trade, and a number
of specialized craft occupations. Individual identity is reckoned in terms
of ancestral town of origin. In the 1820s, Hugh Clapperton, a European
traveler who passed through Ọ̀yọ́, identified by name thirty-five towns.[32]
The Reverend T. J. Bowen,[33] an American Baptist missionary, estimated
the population of some towns in 1855: Ọ̀yọ́ at eighty thousand; Ibadan
at seventy thousand; Ilorin at one hundred thousand; and Ede at fifty
thousand. Until its fall in 1829, Ọ̀yọ́ was dominant, being the center
of a thriving empire.[34] It is against this background that the following
discussion becomes clearer.

The primary social and political unit in Ọ̀yọ́-Yorùbá towns was the
agbo ilé — a compound housing the group of people who claimed a
common descent from a founding ancestor. It was a landholding and
titleholding sociopolitical unit that in some cases practiced specialized
occupations such as weaving, dyeing, or smithing. These units have been
described as corporate patrilineages in the anthropological literature.[35]
Most of the members of a lineage, including their conjugal partners
and their children, resided in these large compounds. Because marriage
residence was in general patrilocal, the presence in the compound of
anafemale members and some of their children has often been discounted in the literature. The labeling of these compounds as corporate
patrilineages is the most obvious example of this lack of acknowledgment. The implications of this reductionist labeling will be discussed
later.

All the members of the *idílé* (lineage) as a group were called *ọmọ-ilé*
and were ranked by birth-order. The in-marrying anafemales were as a
group called *aya ilé*[36] and were ranked by order of marriage. Individually, *ọmọ-ilé* occupied the position of *ọkọ* in relation to the in-coming
aya. As I noted earlier, the translation of *aya* as "wife" and *ọkọ* as "husband" imposes gender and sexual constructions that are not part of the
Yorùbá conception and therefore distort these roles. The rationale for
the translation of the terms lies in the distinction between *ọkọ* and *aya* as
owner/insider and nonowner/outsider in relation to the *ilé* as a physical
space and the symbol of lineage.[37] This insider-outsider relationship was
ranked, with the insider being the privileged senior. A married anafemale
is an *abiléko* — one who lives in the house of the conjugal partner. This
term shows the centrality of the family compound in defining the status
of residents. The mode of recruitment into the lineage, not gender, was
the crucial difference — birth for the *ọkọ* and marriage for the *aya*. Since

there were no equivalents in the Western cultural logic, I have chosen to use the Yorùbá terms in most places. Henceforth, the specific sexual *ọkọ* of an *aya* will be called her sexual conjugal partner.

In theory, it was only the sexual conjugal partner of the *aya* who had sexual access. The rest of the *ọkọ*, his siblings and cousins, regardless of anatomic sex, were also her *ọkọ* but did not sexually engage her. Some might claim that there was a possible gender distinction among *ọkọ* since in this heterosexual world only the anamales could copulate with an *aya*. Such a reading would be incorrect because in the universe of *ọkọ*, it would have been sacrilegious for anatomic males older than an *aya*'s particular conjugal partner to be sexually involved with her — again, the predominant principle at work was seniority, not gender. According to the system of levirate, younger members of the family upon the death of an *aya*'s conjugal partner could inherit rights in and access to the widow if she so consented. An older person could not inherit from the younger. Anafemale *ọkọ* were not left out even in this form of inheritance; they too could inherit rights to the widow, while the sexual privileges were then transferred to their own anamale offspring if need be. Therefore, it is clear that there was no real social distinction between the anafemale *ọkọ* and the anamale *ọkọ*. Furthermore, because of the collective nature of the marriage contract, it was possible to imagine a marital relationship that precluded sex — other rights and responsibilities being paramount.

The hierarchy within the lineage was structured on the concept of seniority. In this context, seniority is best understood as an organization operating on a first-come-first-served basis. A "priority of claim"[38] was established for each newcomer, whether s/he entered the lineage through birth or through marriage. Seniority was based on birth-order for *ọmọ-ilé* and on marriage-order for *aya-ilé*. Children born before a particular *aya* joined the lineage were ranked higher than she was. Children born after an *aya* joined the lineage were ranked lower; to this group, she was not an *aya* but an *ìyá* (mother). It is significant to note that the rank of an *aya* within the lineage was independent of the rank of her conjugal partner. For example, if an old member married an *aya* after his own offspring had married, she (the father's *aya*) ranked lower than all the offspring's *aya*, because they preceded her in the lineage. This occurred regardless of the fact that he, as an elderly member of the lineage, might rank higher than everyone else. This fact again shows that each person's rank was independently established and underscores my point that the timing of entry into the clan, not gender, determines ranking.

The hierarchy within the lineage did not break down along anasex lines. Although anafemales who joined the lineage as *aya* were at a dis-

anafemales only when moving into lineage → does the same apply for men? Deemed deference when [illegible]

advantage, other anafemales who were members of the lineage by birth suffered no such disadvantage. It would be incorrect to say, then, that anatomic females within the lineage were subordinate because they were anatomic females. Only the in-marrying *aya* were seen as outsiders, and they were subordinate to ọkọ as insiders. Ọkọ comprised all ọmọ-ilé, both anamales and anafemales, including children who were born before the entrance of a particular *aya* into the lineage. In a sense, *aya* lost their chronological age and entered the lineage as "newborns," but their ranking improved with time vis-à-vis other members of the lineage who were born after the *aya* entered the lineage. This fact dovetails very nicely with the idea in Yorùbá cosmology that even actual newborns were already in existence before they decided to be born into a specified lineage. So the determinant for all individuals in the lineage was when their presence was recorded. The organization was dynamic, not frozen in place as gendered organizations are wont to be.

Against this background, the following statement by anthropologist Michelle Rosaldo is misleading and a distortion of Yorùbá reality: "In certain African societies like the Yorùbá, women may control a good part of food supply, accumulate cash, and trade in distant and important markets; yet when approaching their husbands, wives must feign ignorance and obedience, kneeling to serve the men as they sit."[39] It is clear in this statement that the word "wives" is automatically universalized to refer to all anafemales, while the term "men" is used as a synonym for husbands, as in Western societies. As explained earlier, these are not the meanings of these categories in Yorùbá language and social structure. What this statement fails to point out is that in the Yorùbá context, the term ọkọ (translated here as "husband") encompasses both anamale and anafemale. Therefore, the situation described in the quote cannot be understood in terms of gender hierarchy, as Rosaldo has done. Indeed, the same courtesies, such as kneeling, referred to in the above passage were accorded by *aya* to the anafemale ọkọ, members of their marital lineages, as a matter of course. Another interesting caveat is that mothers used ọkọ 'mì (literally, "my ọkọ") as a term of endearment for their own children, signifying that these children, unlike themselves, were insiders and belonged in their marital lineage.

In a study based in Lagos, anthropologist Sandra T. Barnes, using a feminist framework, assumes that Yorùbá anafemales are subordinate to anamales. Thus she interprets the observed deferral of *obìnrin* as a deferral to male authority figures. She then postulates a contradiction between her observation and the cultural ethos that "women are as capable as men."[40] Barnes misinterprets whatever it was that she observed.

The paradox that she articulates here is of her own making since hierarchy and authority, as I have consistently shown, to this day do not depend on body-type (more commonly known as gender). Furthermore, Barnes's interpretation of the proverb *Ọ̀kùnrin réjò tóbìnrin paà, kéjò ṣáá ti kú* (If a man sees a snake and a woman kills the snake, what is important is that the snake should be dead), which she cites as proof of the cultural ethos of gender equality,[41] is simplistic because she assumes the proverb is timeless. A more attentive reading of the proverb suggests the presence of gender categorization and hints at a contestation, if you will, of ongoing claims regarding the capabilities of *ọkùnrin* and *obìnrin*. A more contextualized reading would place the proverb in the historical context of the recent colonial transformations in which in certain circles group interests are being put forward in the idiom of gender.

Inside the lineage, the category of members called *ọkọ* were anamales and anafemales, but the category *aya* appeared to be limited to just anafemales. Beyond the lineage, however, this was not the case. Devotees of the *òrìsà* (gods/goddesses) were referred to as the *aya* of the particular *òrìsà* to whom they were devoted. The devotees were *aya* to particular *òrìsà* because the latter enjoyed the right of ownership / membership, just like members of a lineage enjoyed the right of membership vis-à-vis in-marrying *aya*. The devotees were outsiders to the shrine, which was home to the *òrìsà*. Indeed, S. O. Babayemi, a Yorùbá social historian, observing devotees of the deity Ṣàngó, notes that male worshipers, "like the female members..., are referred to as wives of Ṣàngó."[42]

The foregoing elucidation of the occurrence of the social category of anamale *aya* in the religious realm should not be discounted by relegating it solely to this realm. Yorùbá society was not and is not secular; religion was and is part of the cultural fabric and therefore cannot be confined to one social realm. As Jacob K. Olupona, the historian of religion, notes: "African religion, like other primal religions, expresses itself through all available cultural idioms, such as music, arts, ecology. As such, it cannot be studied in isolation from its sociocultural context."[43]

Within the lineage, authority devolved from senior to junior, the oldest member of the lineage being at the helm. Because, in general, most of the adult anafemale *ọmọ-ilé* were assumed to be married and resident in their marital compounds, there is a tendency in the literature to assume that the oldest and most authoritative member was invariably an *ọkùnrin*. This is not correct for a number of reasons. The cultural institution of *ilémosú* referred to the presence of adult anafemale *ọmọ-ilé* in their natal lineages. *Ilémosú* was associated with the return to natal lineages of anafemale ọmọ-ilé after many years of marriage and sojourn in their marital compounds. The adult obìnrin members of the lineage were known collectively as the ọmọ-oṣú.

If the anafemale member was the oldest person present in the lineage, then she was at the apex of authority. The presence of anafemale ọmọ-ilé and their children in their natal lineages was not uncommon given the fact that patrilocality was neither universal nor a permanent state in many marriages. In many status-privileged lineages, female ọmọ-ilé did not necessarily move to their marital lineages even after marriage. Samuel Johnson noted that "some girls of noble birth will marry below their rank, but would have their children brought up in their own home, and among their father's children, and adopt his totem."[44] Similarly, N. A. Fadipe recognized that

> if the mother's family is influential, a child may lean towards the maternal uncle more than he leans towards his own father. Whether the mother's family is influential or not, if at any time a man felt himself being crowded out either physically or psychologically from his own extended-family, he would find a welcome in the compound occupied by his mother's family.[45]

Although Fadipe went on to argue that a person's rights in his/her mother's family are somewhat more limited than in his/her father's family, the fact that certain lineages trace their ancestry through a founding mother suggest that there is reason to challenge this claim. Additionally, there are historical figures like Efúnṣetán Aníwúrà, the Ìyálóde of Ìbàdàn, who in the nineteenth century was one of the most powerful chiefs in the polity. She had risen to this position of preeminence by having claimed the leadership of the Olúyọ̀lé lineage, which was actually the lineage of her mother's birth.[46] In the contemporary period, my own personal experience and research corroborate the findings of Niara Sudarkasa, who conducted her study in Aáwẹ́, an Ọ̀yọ́ town, in the early 1960s. Sudarkasa writes:

> When a man has been brought up in his mother's compound, and resides there with his wives and children, he would usually be regarded as part of the male core of the house even though he belongs in his father's lineage.... There is the case of a man in his sixties whose father's compound is Ile Alaran in the Odofin quarters but has lived in his mother's compound (Ile Alagbẹdẹ) since he was a very young boy. This man is a member of his father's lineage, he has property rights which accrue from membership in the idile, and his adult sons may build houses on the land in Ile Alaran.

Nevertheless, this man built a two-story house at Ile Alagbẹdẹ and is the most influential man in that compound. He is referred to by the members as the Bale. . . . Whenever a member of Ile Alagbede is involved in a dispute with a person of another compound, it is to this man that the Bale of the other compound would look for settlement of the matter.[47]

Notwithstanding the fact that in the literature the head of the family is usually described as the *baálẹ̀* (the eldest anamale), there are lineages even today that are led by anafemales. In Ògbómọ̀sọ́ in 1996 there were two female village heads — Baálẹ̀ Máyà and Baálẹ̀ Àrójẹ — representing their lineages and holding the hereditary titles. These females were first citizens of both their lineages and the village. It is, then, a gross misrepresentation to assume that anatomy necessarily defined the line of authority inside the lineage. The oldest residents of the lineage were usually the *ìyá* — the mothers of the lineage. These were the old mothers who were usually in a position of authority over their children, including any *baálẹ̀* who was one of their offspring. They were collectively known as *àwọn ìyá* (the mothers), and no major collective decisions could be made without their participation individually and as a group. Because they were usually the longest-living residents of the lineage, they controlled information and carried the lineage memory. Considering that this was an oral-based society, one can begin to appreciate the importance of their positions.

The privileged position occupied by *àwọn ìyá* can be shown by considering the dominant role of the *ayaba* (palace mothers) in the politics of Old Ọ̀yọ́. The power associated with longevity was institutionalized in the role of the *ayaba* in the political hierarchy of Ọ̀yọ́. I will discuss this in the next chapter, but it is important to note here that their power derived from experience and memory, "as many of them [had] lived through the reign of two or more Aláfin."[48] The *ayaba* were next in line of authority to the *aláàfin,* and they wielded the power of the rulership in both the capital and the provinces. The household head in the Ọ̀yọ́ setting should not be interpreted as some de facto or de jure leader who was in control of all decisions. Since the lineage was segmented and was a multilayered and multigenerational group in which a variety of collective, sometimes conflicting and individual, interests were represented, the notion of an individual head of household is more misleading than elucidating. In the *agbo ilé* (compound), power was located in a multiplicity of sites, and it was tied to social role-identities that were multiple and shifting for each individual depending on the situation.

Descent: Agnatic or Cognatic?

There has been considerable discussion about the nature of Yorùbá descent. A number of anthropologists have described the pattern of descent as patrilineal. However, both Johnson and Fadipe elaborate its cognatic aspects; their work is supported by my own research. Eades also challenges the idea that the system of descent is agnatic, postulating that scholars' misconceptions stem from the fact that they see the patrilineage as the "natural" unit of analysis without looking at intrahousehold dynamics.[49] Eades is correct in asserting that within the household there is a great deal of segmentation — the primary grouping being the omo-iyá.[50] This is similar to what Felicia Ekejiuba terms a "hearthhold"[51] in Igbó society; it is composed of a mother and her children. In Yorùbáland, siblings of the same mother have the strongest bonds, and often half-siblings (who share a common father) do not associate as much with each other if their mothers do not have a close relationship.

To return to Old Ọ̀yọ́ society, we can say that the inheritance system provided strong evidence for the cognatic nature of the kinship system. Since only consanguinal relations inherited from each other, neither oko nor aya inherited from the other's property. Siblings and children of both anamales and anafemales were the primary beneficiaries. Therefore, it was necessary for children to know their relations on both sides. The strong incest taboo also necessitated awareness of kinship ties on both the mother's and the father's sides of the family.

The focus on the patrilineage by anthropologists is of particular significance in deconstructing the imposition of gender in Yorùbá society. The concentration on the patrilineage focuses only on the role of anafemales as aya (which, in reality, was but one role among many that they fulfilled in Old Ọ̀yọ́ society), ignoring their roles as omo-ile (members of the lineage). Since marriage did not lead to membership, we must pay close attention to the natal lineage, which remained the primary lifelong source of social identity, access, and support, material and otherwise. Indeed, an anafemale offspring retained her full rights in and obligations to her natal compound, whether she was married or not, to the extent that her children were able to lay claim to property in the compound or get access to land by invoking their mother's rights. Though a female was an aya (in-marrying resident) and usually also an ìyá (mother) in her marital lineage, she was first and foremost an omo (offspring/member of the lineage) and an oko (owner/member) in her natal home, which gave her access to its means of production. Failure to look at the different roles and location of anafemales within relationships produces an inaccurate picture.

Marriage: A Family Affair

In Ọ̀yọ́-Yorùbá society, marriage was essentially a relationship between lineages. Contractually, it formalized the conferral of paternity rights of the lineage of the groom to the children born in the course of the marriage. In exchange for this right, goods and services were transferred from the groom's lineage to that of the bride. The goods were given as the bride-wealth, while the services were rendered lifelong. The payment of the bride-wealth by the groom's family conferred sexual access and paternity. It did not confer rights over her person or labor. The establishment of paternity rights in no way displaced the right of the mother and her lineage to the children. The apparent need to publicly establish paternity rights reflected not paternal dominance but the taken-for-grantedness of the rights of mothers over their children.

The contractual arrangement called marriage involved a long process, since it often incorporated a period of betrothal. It was marked by an exchange of gifts and a number of ceremonies acknowledging the relationship between the two lineages. The journey of the bride to the compound of the groom was described as ìṣèyàwó (the making of the bride) from the perspective of the bride's lineage. From the perspective of the groom's lineage, the journey was referred to as the igbéyàwó (the carrying of the bride). The bride was carried over the threshold into the lineage by relatively newly arrived aya, who were thus juniors in the hierarchy.[52] This singular act underscored the collective nature of the marriage and the shared responsibility it entailed for different lineage members and residents. Ìyàwó means "bride," although in the contemporary period it has become synonymous with aya, referring to an anafemale spouse.

The bride on her wedding day exhibited her distress, which underscored the import of the impending change in her living arrangement. Her trepidation was symbolized in the performance of ẹkún ìyàwó, literally, the lamentations of a bride. Here is an example:

> How does one prevent being disgraced, child of Lalonpe?
> How does one guard against making mistakes,
> When one gets to the husband's house?
> How does one guard against making mistakes,
> So that one behaves like an adult?
> That when one is asked to do something
> That demands maturity of mind,
> One does not behave like a child?[53]

Cnhusm ?

As a collective, the lineage of the bride ranked higher than that of the groom in social intercourse because according to the cultural conception, the former had done the latter the favor of providing access to children through its offspring. This was the reason all members of the *aya*'s family could and did command obeisance from the conjugal ọkọ and members of his lineage.

The single purpose of the bride-wealth was to confer sexual and paternity rights, not the rights to the bride's person, her property, or her labor. It is important to note that there was no anamale access to fatherhood without taking on marriage obligations. But fatherhood was possible without sexual conjugal involvement — even impotent conjugal partners could be fathers as long as they had gone through the marital process culminating in the payment of the bride-wealth. In the case of impotence of the sexual conjugal partner, the *aya* could have sexual relations with a member of the family or an outsider. The child would be regarded as that of her partner since fatherhood did not depend on being the biological father. Marriage, then, was of overwhelming importance for the ọkùnrin, since without it their paternity rights could not be established. Its primacy can be discerned in the following verses from the Ifá corpus in which the theme of "wifelessness" is predominant:

> Ifá divination was performed for Eji Odi,
> Who was going to the market of Ejigbomekun,
> Weeping because he had no wife.
> Eji Odi was told to perform sacrifice.[54]

Another verse goes:

> Ifá divination was performed for Orunmila
> When he was practicing divination without a wife.
> Could he possibly have a wife?
> That was why he performed divination.[55]

Apart from the *ìdáàna* (payment of bride-wealth), bride-service was also a feature of Ọ̀yọ́ marriages. It denoted the lifelong goods and services the groom was expected to provide to his in-laws, most notably the bride's parents. N. A. Fadipe, writing over fifty five years ago, describes the scope of bride-service obligations:

Among the many obligations of a man to the family of his fiancee which were assumed directly upon the formal betrothal of the couple to each other were services of various kinds which may be classified as follows: (1) those which recur annually; (2) those whose nature and extent were known but whose time of occurrence cannot be easily predicted; (3) those whose nature and extent were known but which were of a contingent character depending on circumstances outside the control of either party; (4) those whose nature and extent could not be forecast but which were the consequences of a course of action on the part of either the fiancee's parents or other members of her family; and (5) fixed obligations timed according to the discretion of the male partner or his parents during his minority.[56]

Although monogamous marriages were the norm, polygamy represented the dominant idiom through which marriage was conceptualized. In fact, marriages in which there were multiple conjugal partners represented only a fraction of the population. But the fact that all *aya* of a lineage were ranked in a single hierarchy and in relationship to one another as co-*aya* gave the impression that they were all married to the one conjugal partner. Having said that, the collective nature of marriage was underscored by the real interest held in a marriage by *omo-ilé* who were junior to the sexual partner of any particular *aya*. Members of the family had an interest in making a good match because marriage into the wrong family could introduce hereditary diseases into the family, and this would affect their own or their children's marriage chances. A good match was important because of the system of levirate — the transfer of rights in the widow to another member of the family after the death of her conjugal partner (a transfer that occurred only if the widow consented to it). Anafemale *omo-ilé* had a similar interest because they too could inherit rights in the widow, the sexual aspects of which they could transfer to their own anamale child, if the widow accepted such an arrangement. Beyond the symbolic, we begin to understand the extent of collective, individual, and very real interest held by all lineage members in the *aya-ilé*.[57]

The interest in polygamy was directly related to the need and importance of bearing children and safeguarding their health. The main reason for marriage was procreation. If marriage fulfilled other needs in Old Ọyọ́ society, they were secondary. Children were considered *ire* (blessings, the good). They were the ultimate raison d'être of human existence.[58] Therefore, the stability of the marriage rested on whether children were produced and their survival maintained. For the bride, the right to become a mother superseded all other considerations in marriage. If a marriage did not become fruitful within the first few years, a female could become restless and move on. Important as it was to give birth, once children were born, their survival became paramount and subsumed any other interests that were perceived to be in conflict with it. Consequently, the new mother practiced postpartum abstinence — abstaining from sexual intercourse from as early as pregnancy until the time the child was weaned off the breast (two to three years), as it was believed that sexual activity and early pregnancy would endanger the life of the infant. The new father could have sexual intercourse if he had other conjugal partners.

There is no question that postpartum abstinence was adhered to. There are enough empirical studies — even in the more recent period, when the practice is not as common — to show that everybody took it as imperative to the child's survival.[59] Beyond this concern, there were structural reasons for abstinence. The structure of the compound and the allocation of space in this densely populated arena meant that there was really no privacy, especially since, in the main, personal interests could not really be separated from collective interests.

As an illustration of the possible dilemmas of living so close to one's relations, let us assume that a conjugal partner was finding it difficult to abstain from sex with the new mother. At the very least, he would need her cooperation to break the taboo. The notion that the conjugal partner could forcefully impose himself on his *aya* is at best very tenuous. We must remember that couples did not share rooms; the *aya*'s room was usually shared with her children and others in her care. Furthermore, rooms were very small; many members of the household slept in the verandah. Thus there was relatively little privacy, and privacy would have been a necessary condition for breaking taboos or spousal abuse. Consequently, the prevalent idea in some feminist literature that marriage was set up universally with the interest of males as paramount[60] is not borne out in this cultural context. Instead, Yorùbá marriages were set up to ensure the survival of children, and the culture conceived of early sexual activity for a new mother as dangerous to the child.

The general attitude of *obìnrin* toward polygamy ranged from seeing it as desirable to tolerating it, a tolerance based on an appreciation of its benefits. It was in the interest of the anafemale *ọmọ-ilé* to have a large retinue of *aya-ilé* to call upon when help was needed. In this regard in particular, polygamy was an ungendered privilege determined by the reciprocity established between each individual *aya* and individual *ọkọ*. It was also in the interest of a senior *aya* to be in a polygamous marriage because the responsibility of cooking devolved to the junior *aya* in the multiple marriage; therefore, it was usual for *aya* to initiate the process of polygamy for her conjugal partner. She did not see it as contrary to her overall interest. Some of these views are clear in the response I got from an "elderly mother," Àlàrí at Òkè Màpó, whom I interviewed in Ìbàdàn. When I mentioned to her the idea that some people feel that polygamy is detrimental to the interest of the *aya*, she had this to say:

*Èyin alákòwé, ẹ tún dé nùu. Bẹ́ẹ̀ náà l'ẹ wípé aya gbọ́dọ̀ bá ọkọ da
owó pọ̀. Wọ́n a bí wọn pọ̀ ni? Ṣ'ẹẹ ríi, ohun tẹ́'yin ńrò un, ò jẹ́ bẹ́ẹ̀.
Bọ́rọ̀ ọmọ bíbí bá ti kúrò ńbẹ̀, ti ọkọ si ńṣe ojúṣe rẹ̀, kín ló tún kù?
Ọkùnrin a ńṣe iyọ̀ tá ní láti máa fi sọ́bẹ̀ lójoojúmọ́ ndan? kín laá
wá fi gbé wọn tira gbá-gbá?*

[You learned people (alluding to my Western credentials), there
you go again! The other day you were all advocating the merits
of having joint finances with one's *ọkọ*. Were you born together?
(I.e., Are conjugal partners consanguinal relations?) So long as an
obìnrin fulfills her need for children and he fulfills his obligations,
what else? *Ọkọ* is not salt that you have to have in your food on
a daily basis. What is this desire to lock oneself in a suffocating
embrace?]

Her response underscores a number of important points: (1) children
as the supreme purpose in marriage, and children being the first obli-
gation of the couple to each other; (2) the norm of separate finances of
a couple, showing that there is no notion of a conjugal estate; (3) the
privileging of consanguinal ties over those of conjugality; (4) a view
of monogamy as not inherently desirable or positive; (5) the generation gaps in the society deriving primarily from the introduction of
Christianity and other Western ideas and institutions.

Aya and Some Aspects of Social Structure

Any discussion of social roles would not be complete without examining some of the linkages in family roles and social structure from
the standpoint of the *aya*. Inside the marriage, couples had obligations
to and certain expectations of each other. To that extent, they had
reciprocal claims on each other's labor and time. They both had differing responsibilities to both lineages. Town endogamy was predominant,
which meant that it was usual for an *aya* who had moved to her partner's lineage to see members of her own family on a daily basis. Based
on the seniority hierarchy, the conjugal partner ranked higher than his
aya inside the lineage, but his authority, like the authority of any senior person, was limited. He did not have control over the *aya*'s labor
or her property. All adults had their own obligations that they had to
fulfill. Within marital lineages, these responsibilities included monetary
and labor contributions made as an *aya-ilé* (member by marriage). As

an ọmọ-ilé, inside natal lineages, there were obligations to members of one's own lineage. For example, one could be asked to contribute to the wedding ceremonies of one's sibling. Beyond the lineage, many persons belonged to an egbẹ́ (town association), which was a way of establishing status. For many obìnrin, the greatest form of accumulation was to acquire a large aṣọ (wardrobe of cloth) for their own personal use and later for their anafemale offspring. There were particular styles of expensive woven cloth that a properly situated iyá had to have in her ìtẹ́lẹ̀ àpótí (bottom box).[61] Many mothers engaged in a lifelong process of accumulating cloth for their anafemale child and accumulating bride-wealth payments for their anamale child. Against this background, we can begin to appreciate the delicate balancing of a multiplicity of interests for any one person.

Aya had her property, and the conjugal partner had his. The absence of the notion of a conjugal estate and the fact that in the inheritance system couples could not inherit each other's property underscore the necessity for the aya to be gainfully employed. The inheritance system was predicated on the idea that only consanguinal relations could inherit from one another. Siblings and children of the deceased were the primary beneficiaries.

The general household division of labor was based on age relativity, with younger people and children usually having the responsibility for cleaning up after meals. Within the lineage, the aya cooked, not the obìnrin in general. Further, the seniority system in the lineage meant that an anafemale member who was not an aya did not have to cook. Therefore, it was possible that an ọmọ-ilé (birth member of the lineage) would never have to cook if she did not want to. Similarly, aya with appropriate seniority did not have to cook. In a polygamous[62] marriage, the responsibility for providing food for the conjugal partner passed to the younger aya. This was one of the major attractions of polygamy for many aya — it passed on certain responsibilities. Given the disassociation of seniority from menial jobs, it is not surprising that cooking devolved to juniors.

A major responsibility of an aya was to wá ńjẹ (find food) for her conjugal partner. The use of the verb wá (to look for, to find) as opposed to sè (to cook) is instructive in understanding the business of meal procurement. It is possible that it speaks to the fact that a great deal of food consumed was bought in the streets and markets of the town. It is not clear exactly when professional cooking developed in Yorùbáland, but it is likely that it is linked to urbanization. Clearly, however, the practice of cooking food for sale in the streets has a long history in the area. Hugh Clapperton and Richard Landers, who visited Ọ̀yọ́ in the 1830s, discussed the various kinds of cooked dishes they were able to buy in the markets.[63]

Because *aya* were very busy and were engaged in pursuing their own livelihoods, much of the food that was consumed daily did not originate in the family; it was bought. The idea that an *aya* had to *cook* for her conjugal partner thus needs qualification. As Sudarkasa observed:

> When men are working in the fields surrounding the hamlets, for breakfast, they eat ẹko or akara which they buy for cash or on credit from the women who hawk about the farmlands. For their midday meals, some farmers boil and eat one or two slices of yam in the fields. Occasionally women cook for their husbands during the day, however, since they are often working in different places; the husbands do not usually expect their wives to prepare any meals except that which they eat in the late afternoon after returning from the fields.[64]

In general, some dishes and meals were more likely to be bought than others. For example, ọkà (a dish based on yam flour) and ẹ̀ko (a dish based on corn flour) were more often tied to the verb *dá* (to cut from a large quantity) than *se* (to cook). Breakfast was usually bought food (not homemade), as young and old *lọ dá ẹ̀ko mu* (procured *ẹ̀ko*). Certain time-consuming dishes seem to have passed from home-based production into the commercial domain early in the social organization of towns. Ẹ̀ko tútú, ègbo, ọ̀lẹ̀lẹ̀, èkuru, and àkàrà readily come to mind. No dish, however, was absent from the menu of *iyá olóónjẹ* (professional food sellers). The example of Àdùkẹ́, the food seller in this verse from the Ifá corpus, is not unusual:

> Ifá divination was performed for Àdùkẹ́,
> Offspring of kind-hearted people of ancient times,
> Who cooked maize and beans together in order to make a better life.
> She woke up early in the morning,
> Weeping because she lacked all the good things.
> Àdùkẹ́ was told to perform sacrifice,
> And she did so.
> After she had performed sacrifice,
> She became an important person.
> She had money.
> All the good things that she sought after
> Were attained by her.
>
> "When we cook beans and maize together,
> All the good things of life fill up our home."[65]

The need for each and every adult to provide for themselves and to fulfill family and other social obligations was taken for granted. Therefore, the need for *aya* to pursue their own livelihoods was recognized, protected, and promoted. This was no doubt one of the factors that shaped not only the family division of labor and recipes but also the economy. The professionalization of cooking not only provided an occupation for some but also freed many mothers from cooking so that they could go to the local markets or engage in farming and long-distance trade.

Aya did not cook at home every day, a fact that speaks to the issue of time allocation. An *aya* usually did not cook one meal at a time. The mainstay of the cuisine was *ọbẹ̀* — a stew that consists basically of meat and/or vegetables, pepper, oil, and spices. The Yorùbá preference for stewing over other forms of cooking probably developed because stews keep their flavor and even tend to taste better days after the initial cooking. *Ọbẹ̀* is an all-purpose dish eaten with a variety of carbohydrate staples, such as *iyán, àmàlà, ẹ̀bà, láfún,* and *ẹ̀kọ. Ọbẹ̀* is cooked to last at least three to four days so that daily cooking is a matter of reheating the *ọbẹ̀* and buying the carbohydrate. All this suggests that cooking for the family was not and is still not central to definitions of family life. Night markets were (and are) a feature of Ọ̀yọ́ social structure. They were first and foremost food markets. The establishment of night markets may have been a response to the need to procure dinner for the family, since many an *aya* had been absent from home all day and sometimes for weeks on end when they pursued long-distance trade. Economic geographer B. W. Hodder, in his diachronic study of Yorùbá markets, correctly concluded that

> night markets in which women connect their local communities with the town's main sources of foodstuff can only be understood in the context of the local Yorùbá habits of feeding. The bulk of the working class population eats food that has not been prepared in their own homes.... The explanation for this phenomenon of outside cooking and eating, however, is also bound up with the fact that women put trading first in their interests.[66]

Gender-Framed Debates: Bride-Wealth, Polygamy, Sexual Access, and Control

Bride-wealth has been presented in a negative light by Western interpreters of many African societies. In some quarters, its meaning has been distorted, reduced to a transactional exchange akin to buying a wife.

In his study of kinship, anthropologist Claude Lévi-Strauss described bride-wealth as an exchange of brides for goods.[67] Much subsequent scholarship has simply built on Lévi-Strauss's claims. A classic piece of feminist scholarship in this regard is Gayle Rubin's elucidation of Lévi-Strauss's concepts.[68] Rubin's essay — which sees women as victims, not beneficiaries, of the institution of marriage — is often used as the sole and unquestioned evidence in the feminist search for (i.e., creation of) patriarchy in African societies. For example, in a book on the Shona of Zimbabwe, Elizabeth Schmidt brings together Lévi-Strauss and Rubin to support her assertion that in precolonial Shona society, "while men have certain rights in their female kin, including the right to dispose of them in marriage, women do not have reciprocal rights in their male kin. They do not even possess full rights to themselves."[69]

Although Yorùbáland was not Shona society, the fact that Schmidt does not provide independent evidence (other than Lévi-Strauss) of "bride-wealth as female-kin disposal" leads me to believe that she is making the common mistake of homogenizing all African if not all so-called tribal societies. This often leads to a failure to look to each society for the meaning of its institutions. Furthermore, Shona society, like that of the Yorùbá, incorporates female members, just like their male counterparts, as having an ownership interest in their natal lineages.

Schmidt's book, then, is an example of a long trend of Western misreadings of African cultures, misreadings caused by a failure to view those cultures as they are, on their own terms. For instance, there is an overemphasis on bride-wealth as goods transferred from the lineage of the groom to that of the bride; little or no attention has been paid to bride-service — a tradition that set out the lifelong obligations of the groom to the lineage of the bride. The reciprocal nature of the marriage contract has become lost in the discussion.[70] Similarly, the gendered and singular focus on patrilineality has resulted in the erasure of the fact that daughters, just like sons, had a lifelong interest in and participated in the lineage of their birth, be they married or not.

Like bride-wealth, the practice of postpartum abstinence has been described by various scholars as sexual control of the female and an example of the limitations imposed on anafemale members in African societies. The debate should be placed in comparative context — that is, attention should also focus on societies where such a practice did not exist. Western societies are one good example of this. The Yorùbá practice of postpartum abstinence contrasted sharply with practices in European marriages of the same historical time period, marriages in which husbands had unlimited sexual access to their wives. This meant that European wives had no control over their bodies, since men's "conjugal rights" included unlimited sexual access regardless of the welfare of the child, the age of the child, or the health of the mother. In his book *A History of Women's Bodies,* social historian Edward Shorter documents the pain, the anguish, and the danger that the male sexual privilege and lack of consideration caused for European women:

> Put yourself in the shoes of the typical housewife who lived in a town or village then. Neither she nor anyone else had any idea when the "safe" period for a woman was; and for her, any sexual act could mean pregnancy. *She was obliged to sleep with her husband whenever he wanted.* And in the luck of the draw, she could become pregnant seven or eight times, bearing an average of six live children. Most of these children were unwelcome for her, for if one single theme may be said to hold my story together, it is the danger to every aspect of her health that ceaseless childbearing meant.[71]

Shorter's thesis is that the medical advances between 1900 and 1930 that enabled European women to gain some measure of control over their fertility also contributed to their being able to shift priority to questions of politics. For Shorter, "ending the physical victimization of women was a precondition for feminism."[72] His analyses and other feminist postulations of marriage as slavery provide a good background to the question of why feminism developed in the West.

Whatever the debates about the origins of the Western feminist movement, women's control over their bodies remains the cornerstone of agitation for women's rights. This is not surprising, given the history sketched above. Yorùbá conjugal history, however, was different, particularly given the fact that male sexual expression was not privileged over female sexual expression, female well-being, and children's survival. The primacy of having children, which held for all adult members of the society, meant that the mother's health was of paramount importance; it was safeguarded to ensure that she would be able to bear and give birth to children. Postpartum abstinence, which resulted in child-spacing, also limited the number of babies any one woman could produce — which safeguarded the health of anafemales. Then and now, having a large number of babies is detrimental to a woman's health. The Yorùbá also placed the responsibility for contraception where it belonged: with the couple and the family, not just the *aya* as an individual.

To be sure, polygamy and postpartum abstinence have been interpreted as signs of male dominance and articulated as detrimental to the interests of women. Polygamy is often interpreted as a sign of male privilege and female subordination.[73] This view, however, is not only simplistic but incorrect, particularly when the contemporary situation is read back into history. For one thing, in Yorùbáland, because *obìnrin* did not constitute a social category, they had no collective interest as a group. An anafemale was interested in her natal lineage in part because it was a source of a large retinue of *aya-ilé*, who could be of help to her. That phenomenon was complemented by the interest of the *aya* to have all her *oko* take a personal interest in the children and material responsibility for them. Commentators have often claimed that polygamy was detrimental because it violated the exclusive sexual rights of an *aya* to her conjugal partner. However, one should not assume that every *aya* necessarily valued having an exclusive sexual right to her conjugal partner. Even at the individual level, if the ramifications of the variety of interests anafemales may have are examined, it is possible to see that polygamy is not inherently incompatible with the interest of the *aya*. Polygamy in Ọ̀yọ́ society is best apprehended as an ungendered privilege depending on the situation and particular interests being focused upon at any moment. Consequently, imposing a gendered interpretation on it amounts to misrepresentation.

Like all marriage forms, polygamy as a social institution is not inherently good or bad. There are good marriages and bad marriages, polygamous or monogamous. The history of monogamous marriage in the West and feminist articulations of how oppressive to women and children this institution has been do not reveal monogamy as a system that inherently promotes a wife's interest. With respect to "women's interest," its value as an alternative to polygamy is thus hardly clear. In an article on the thorny issue of polygamy in the Christian church, Bernard Adeney, having argued that polygamy should have no place in the church, still makes a thoughtful remark that is relevant to my argument. He advocates that for church membership,

> not just a person's marital status but also how well its responsibilities are fulfilled [should be] considered. If a man with only one wife neglects her, has affairs, or is abusive and does not show the fruits of repentance, he may be excluded from membership. On the other hand, an old man who has lived for many years with two wives and currently treats them well may be welcomed into the Church.[74]

Responsibility is the key word.

It will be helpful to examine more closely the notion of women's interest, a notion around which the antipolygamists like to present their views. Assuming there is indeed a category "women," what are the interests attributed to them? If it is in the wife's interest to abstain from sex for a period after delivering a baby, then monogamy is not necessarily a positive influence; evidence from Western societies is clear on this issue. Furthermore, in any given situation certain interests conflict with one another. Choosing one means losing the other. The important thing is the freedom to determine which of the interests is the most important. So when a young Ọyọ́ woman, after five years of marriage, asks her conjugal partner to sọ mí di méjì (marry another ìyàwó), it does not mean that she is naive about the possible problems that could arise. She probably has made a comprehensive appraisal of her own interests and has determined which were worth pursuing. Traditionally, the *aya* frequently initiated the process of polygamy for her conjugal partner; when she did not, her consent had to be sought. The point is that the *aya* had agency.

Still, the issue of polygamy calls for further analyses, given the misconception about the benefits to the social group labeled "men." Perhaps the most interesting issue concerning the existence of polygamy in Old Ọyọ́ is not so much about women's oppression as about men's status. We might ask: If some *ọkùnrin* had multiple conjugal partners, doesn't that mean (ruling out overt demographic imbalance) that there were many *ọkùnrin* who did not have legitimate access to even one anafemale? Polygamy can, therefore, be interpreted as an institution of male deprivation/discipline rather than male privilege or sexual license. Abiola Irele, for example, recommended highly what he called the "discipline of monogamy" in opposition to the African traditional polygamy.[75] The reason for Irele's enthusiasm for monogamy is not clear, considering the physical and sexual exploitation that many Western women continue to be subjected to in their monogamous suburbs. Male discipline is not inherent in monogamy. With regard to a polygamous society, the question of discipline is very pertinent. Where lies the discipline? Discipline for whom and to what effect? This line of reasoning calls into question the idea of anamales representing a social grouping — polygamy, after all, essentially gives some males more legitimate access at the expense of other males. The idea of a uniformity of interests of anamales in opposition to an assumed anafemale collective interest needs to be interrogated.

In Old Ọyọ́, it was usually younger anamales who found themselves in the position of not having legitimate sexual access. As noted earlier, marriage involved the paying of bride-wealth by the lineage of the groom to that of the bride. In a situation where there was no overt demographic imbalance, polygamy could be sustained only by having *ọkùnrin* and *obìnrin* marry at different ages; thus, on average, anafemales got married at around sixteen to eighteen years of age — eight to ten years earlier than males. It is possible that the late age at which anamales married, relative to anafemales, correlated with the amount of time needed to accumulate the bride-wealth. All this combined to mean that many Ọyọ́ males did not have legitimate sexual access for many years of their adult lives. Even males with two *aya* could be forced into abstinence if both of them become pregnant at the same time, which was not unusual. At another level, it is pertinent to pose the question: What did males who had no wives do to get sexual satisfaction? This question is posed deliberately against the backdrop of sociobiological notions of unbridled male sexual needs caused by overflowing testosterone. Although a number of scholars make the claim that in Old Ọyọ́, the ideal was for brides to remain virgins, it is apparent that there were some other institutions that predisposed toward premarital sex. What was important was that such a relationship be recognized by both families and be well on its way to conclusion as marriage with the payment of the bride-wealth. Even so, this could not have been a total solution to the problem of many bachelors — to engage in this type of premarital relation still necessitated that the anamale's family had some wealth accumulated. In short, the system overall curtailed sexual activity for the unmarried. This undercuts the image of African male's unbridled sexual activity (the "testosterone brigade")[76] that has been projected in various racist and masculinist discourses. Male preoccupation with sexual intercourse seems to be exaggerated by both researchers and some males in the contemporary period. Many ọkùnrin, just like obìnrin, did abstain from sexual intercourse. Homosexuality does not seem to have been an option.

Given that, there does exist in Yorùbáland an institution called *àlè*, which is best described as a sexual relationship between married or unmarried ọkùnrin and married obìnrin. This institution may be a means for getting rid of some of the steam, so to speak. For many Yorùbá, the *àlè* relationship is a difficult thing to talk about, especially given that the Christian and Western oversexualization of African peoples has made some Yorùbá moralistic about sexual matters. I describe it as an institution because it is present in the society; it is talked about; and it has its own "rules of the game." During my research, many persons were willing to talk about it only as something other people do. Based on that research, I would say that it is tolerated, if not accepted, for married persons to engage in sexual friendships. The *àlè* relationship is often emotionally and sexually charged, in contrast to the marriage relation, which has procreation as its primary focus for both ọkùnrin and obìnrin. The *àlè* institution raises questions about how Yorùbá see sexuality, an issue that cannot be treated here. Suffice it to say that in the past, and still in many quarters, issues of sexuality were not really issues of morality; the advent of Christianity and Islam have changed this. The prevalence of *àlè* relationships cannot be precisely determined historically, but one can date it back to at least the 1850s. Its existence is documented more recently in studies of a large number of situations in which would-be divorcées are already pregnant by their prospective partners. The latter must come forward to pay reparations to their present conjugal partners and to claim paternity of the unborn child.[77]

One could argue that the existence of such a practice in recent history does not mean that it is an ancient institution. This line of argument is plausible, but in the oral traditions, particularly those relating to the *òrìsà* (gods), it is not unusual to hear how one male *òrìsà* or the other *gbà* (takes away) the *aya* of another. The innocence of the *aya* suggested by the verb *gbà* is interesting enough, but my point is that the idiom is used here in exactly the same way in which the act is framed among humans. Yorùbá gods behave like humans; indeed some of them are deified human beings. The trend since the imposition of Christianity and Victorian values is to curtail sexual freedom for *obìnrin*. Consequently, it is more logical to postulate that the *àlè* institution has deep indigenous roots — it could not have originated with Christian moralizing about sex or Victorian restrictions on women.

Gendered Visions: Spaces, Faces, and Places in the Division of Labor

In its hey-day, Ọyọ́-ile was a centre of trade, goods reaching its markets from the Atlantic and from towns in the West Sudan beyond the Niger, and being sold alongside the produce of Yorùbáland itself. —ROBERT SMITH, *The Alaafin in Exile*

In studies of society as such, the concept of the gender division of labor is invoked like a mantra, its universal and timeless existence being taken for granted. Niara Sudarkasa describes a "division of labor by sex" in Old Ọyọ́ society in which males are classified as farmers and females as traders.[78] Some scholars have gone to the extent of elevating this concept from the terrestrial world of humans to the celestial world of the gods. For example, B. Belasco, in his discussion of Yorùbá society, posits a sexual division of labor among Yorùbá deities on the assumption that there is a consensus about which gods are male and which ones are not.[79] The debate about the division of labor in Old Ọyọ́ society is therefore actually framed by questions about when women became dominant in trade. Although this was regarded as a curiosity if not an anomaly, this gen-

der division of labor was rarely questioned. Anthropologist Jane Guyer
writes:

> The sexual division of labour among the Yorùbá seems *less clearly
> embedded in an elaborate cultural logic of male/female differences
> and oppositions*. Discussions of the division of labour by sex are
> phrased in terms of pragmatism rather than metaphysics, and I
> have not found in the literature any detailed analysis of the link
> between the concept of femininity in religious thought and the
> feminine tasks of everyday life.[80]

Guyer is correct about the absence of a gendered cultural logic, but she
is mistaken in assuming that the Yorùbá division of labor did not in-
volve metaphysics: it did; it was just not a gender metaphysics; it was
a lineage-based one. Subsequent discussion will bear this out. Further,
Guyer could not find notions of "feminine tasks" simply because such
a notion of gendering work did not exist in the indigenous Yorùbá
conception.

In many other cultures, tasks like cooking were limited to women.
In Yorùbáland, as I have shown in a previous section, it was *aya,* not
obìnrin, who cooked. Furthermore, cooking could not be stereotyped
as the work of the *obìnrin* because *okùnrin* regularly cooked on their
extended trips to the farm — their *aya* were rarely with them because
they were seeking their own livelihood. Recall Sudarkasa's observation
that "for their midday meals, some [male] farmers *boil and eat one or
two slices of yam* in the fields."[81] Similarly, warfare, which in many
cultures is constructed as a masculine enterprise, was not projected as
such in Yorùbáland. Because effectiveness in war involved control of
mystical and supernatural forces, much of which was controlled by *iyá
mi òsòròngà* (metaphysical mothers — sometimes inappropriately called
witches), it was not possible to reduce participation in war to gender
questions.[82] Historically, there were many *obìnrin* who engaged in com-
bat and emerged as war heroes. One of the most picturesque accounts
of the Ọ̀yọ́ in battle — a scene described by Johnson and elaborated by
Robert Smith, who collected oral traditions in Ọ̀yọ́ and the provinces —
concerns the battle of Ilayi with Borgu; the Ọ̀yọ́ were led by Aláàfin
Ọ̀rọ̀mpọ̀tọ̀, who was a "woman king":[83]

> The Ọ̀yọ́ losses were great and their army would have been routed
> except for an unusual incident. Among the Ọ̀yọ́ dead was one of
> the foremost of the Esho [Noble Guard], the general bearing the ti-
> tle of Gbonka. Orompoto created a new Gbonka on the field, and
> when this man fell, [s]he made a third who, again, was slain. The

third Gbonka had been transfixed in death by the Borgu arrows in a kneeling posture with his mouth open and his teeth bared as though grinning. To the Borgu, it seemed that this was a living warrior impervious to their arrows who laughed at their efforts. In their alarm, they ceased to press their attack, and the Ọ̀yọ́, who had been on the point of retreat, rallied and finally gained victory.[84]

In addition, one should not gloss over the fact that in the nineteenth century, war was a communal affair. We have excellent documentation of this in studies by J. F. Ade Ajayi and Robert Smith.[85] All this taken together indicates that the assumption of a gender division of labor — like the assumption of other gender constructs in Old Ọ̀yọ́ society — represents a mistaken imposition of an alien frame of reference.

In order to comprehend the Ọ̀yọ́ division of labor, we must consider it at two levels — one concerning space and the other personnel. At the spatial level, the primary arenas in which work took place were the oko (farmlands), which were miles away from town. It was an agrarian society, most of whose members were àgbẹ̀ (farmers). The farm stood in contrast to the ìlú (town), the urban center in which people had their ilé (compounds). The farmland was primarily seen as a place of work, although oftentimes farmers had an aba (hut) in which they spent weeks if required. The ìlú was seen as a place of rest and as the place to enjoy the good life. As it is said, Ilé là'bọ̀ 'simi oko (Home is the place of rest after any journey, even the one to the farm). Within the towns, people engaged in a number of occupations. Trading in various goods was predominant. Traded goods included crops like iṣu (yams), processed food like èlùbọ́ (yam flour), and luxury goods like aṣọ (cloth). The more specific arena in which trade took place was the ọjà (market), the major one usually in the center of town next to the ọba's palace. There were various smaller markets in the neighborhoods; often they were associated with specific products. Beyond the boundaries of Ọ̀yọ́, there were other polities with which people traded that had their own market systems, organizations, and specialties.[86] Due to the fact that the economy had some degree of specialization, certain professions and crafts like weaving, smithing, surgery, divining, hunting, dyeing, and calabash-carving were associated with certain lineages.

As to personnel, farming and trading were open to the whole population. Distinction among the traders was made, however, based on the (1) type of goods sold (e.g., aláṣọ was the cloth dealer; elélùbọ́ was the seller of yam flour; olónje was the food seller); (2) the distance traveled (the long-distance trader was aláròbọ̀ — one who comes and goes);

and (3) the scale of operation (e.g., *aláte* was a retailer who sold at the smallest unit). None of these roles was conceived as being limited by anatomic sex. For this reason, one of the most unfortunate terms used in the study of traders in West Africa and now continent-wide is "market women." As was noted in chapter 1, this term gives the impression that the X chromosome or the female anatomy is the primary qualification for becoming a trader, when, in fact, in many African societies, the category of traders and their various distinctions are not based on the anatomy. Usually the prefixes *iyá* and *bàbá,* in the case of Yorùbá, are added to the designation as a sign of respect and indication of age, not gender. Thus we have *iyá* (mother) *aláso* and *bàbá* (father) *aláso,* both cloth traders. Though there may or may not have been many *okùnrin* food sellers, in the Òyó conception, what that food seller was doing was not different from what the *bàbá aláso* was doing. *Wón nsòwò ni* (They are both basically trading).

The genderizing of the *ojà* (market) in the literature also calls for an examination. Toyin Falola has argued unconvincingly that the Yorùbá market was supremely women's space.[87] The reduction of the most public and the most inclusive space in the society to a gender-specific, exclusive "women's space" constitutes a gross misrepresentation. The *ojà* was in close relationship with the *àáfin* (palace), both sharing the center of the town. In G. J. Afolabi Ojo's words, "The Oba could watch from a reasonable distance the regular assembly of his people. In addition, since it was the hub of economic activities of the people, the market was situated in the center of town."[88] The very public and nonexclusive nature of the *ojà* was apparent in common sayings like *ayé lojà, òrun nílé* (The earth is a market, and the otherworld is home). It was also said that *wèrè tó bá ti w'ojà, kòsee wò* (A mentally unstable person who enters the market can never be cured). The claim being articulated in this saying is that once crazy people went to this very public space and were acknowledged as mad by all who saw them, they would be labeled as crazy. Due to the sheer number of persons in the market, it would be impossible ever to shake the label of "incurably mad," and therefore the possibility of healing was removed. In addition, the *ojà* was literally and metaphorically a crossroads where a multitude of peoples from different walks of life, different towns, different nationalities, and even different "beings" met. Because people approached the market from different places and from various directions, it was said that *ònà kán ò w'ojà* (There is not one route to the market). Moreover, it was also believed that spirits dwelled in the marketplace and that *òrìsà* (gods), like Èsù and other supernatural and invisible beings, were present in this arena.[89] Could Falola tell us the "gender identity" of these invisible beings? Obviously, in the Yorùbá conception, the *ojà* was the most open realm in the whole town, identified with no single group. Though night markets — running from 6:30 to 10:30 — occurred, it was understood that by midnight, the marketplace had to be vacated by humans and turned over to the spirits. Why, then, would Falola privilege those who occupied the market during the day over those who were present from midnight on? Doing so discounts the Yorùbá conception in favor of the Western viewpoint. Falola privileges the physical over the metaphysical, which is not the Yorùbá norm. Besides, the markets were not just for trading; they were also meeting points for people from all walks of life. Markets were also places for reenactment of important historical rituals of state. The mythology about *ọbá m'ọrọ̀* and the *ènìyàn òrìsà* was "performed on the first occasion in the royal market."[90] Sudarkasa's description of the night market in Aáwẹ́ and Ọ̀yọ́ is also telling:

> The night markets are more important social centers than are the daytime markets. The night markets are places where people celebrating important occasions bring their entourage and drummers. At Akesan market in Ọ̀yọ́, hardly a night goes by without the appearance of a group of dancers in the marketplace. People celebrating weddings, funerals, and other occasions dance to the market on one of the nights during which the celebrations take place.[91]

From the foregoing, it is impossible to understand why Falola would single out a group called women and hand them this prime space, even as he is telling us that they are a socially marginalized group. Of course, he does not explain how he arrived at this conjecture. Like other scholars, he assumes what he sets out to prove — the existence of "women" as a social category and their universal subordination. Such a claim is, as I have argued, a spurious one and cannot be supported by the evidence. The specialized professions and crafts were the prerogative of specific lineages in the polity. The division of labor here was lineage-based in that lineage membership, not the anatomy, was the prerequisite to practicing such professions. This division of labor was perceived at a metaphysical level. Members of the specialist lineages were seen to have an exclusive mandate from the *òrìsà* that made it possible to properly carry out their professions. Other members of the society were deemed incapable and indeed unacceptable for this reason. In his discussion of occupational guilds in precolonial African societies, Cheikh Anta Diop explains the discriminatory basis of occupational access: "A subject from outside a trade, even if he acquired all the skill and science of a calling which was not that of his family, would not be able to practice it efficiently, in the mystical sense, because it was not his ancestors who concluded the initial contract with the spirit who had originally taught it to humanity."[92]

Hunting is a good example of this. Though hunters are usually presented as anamales, it was more likely for an anafemale from a hunting compound to become a hunter than for an anamale from a nonhunting compound to become one. This is due to the fact that although hunting required material weapons like bows, arrows, and guns, the most important weapons in the arsenal were family mandates from the gods, medicines, potions, incantations, and talismans, all of which were closely guarded family secrets. My research in Ògbómòsó bears out that hunting is still regarded more as a family vocation than as a gender-specific profession. I interviewed a female hunter (iyá ọdẹ), Dorcas Àmàó, who was then about seventy-six years old and was still active as an ọdẹ (hunter). She dressed like her male counterparts and worked as a security guard like other hunters. During the igbẹ festival, she joined with them to fire her gun and perform other rituals. Born into a hunting lineage, she told me the story of how she became an active hunter.[93] In 1981, she had a dream in which her deceased father, who had been a seasoned hunter, appeared in a group of other departed forebears, all dancing the akitinpa (dance of hunters). As they danced toward her, she joined in the dance and her father handed her a gun and commanded that she must start to "shoot her gun." She went on: Nigbati eniyan o gbo do déjàá (One must not disobey). She had no choice but to do her father's bidding. When I asked her whether she expressed any concern to her father in the dream that she was female, she said she had had no concern about that. In fact, the particular concern that she expressed was that she was a Christian — she perceived a conflict between her family vocation and her chosen religion, but her father replied Èsìn ò ní kí a má ṣ'orò ilé (Religion does not prevent us from practicing our family vocation and rituals).[94] At the time of this event, she lived with her husband's family, but she immediately left for her natal compound to announce the occurrence. There was no opposition on the part of any member of her hunting family; if anything, they were all jubilant that their dead father chose to f'ara hàn (appear to her). One of her younger brothers who hunted actively himself taught her how to fire a gun, and she soon acquired one herself. Her case thus demonstrates that anatomic difference was not elaborated into a reason for exclusion. In societies where there is a sexual division of labor, it is usually accompanied by an ideology that seeks to restrict each gender to its own specific arena. There are no such ideologies in the Yorùbá world-sense.

The experience of Karin Barber, a scholar of Yorùbá oral traditions, can serve as a further indication of the disjuncture between Western assumptions about gender and the Yorùbá understanding. In her book *I Could Speak until Tomorrow,* Barber makes the observation that "there are few situations in which women are told they cannot pursue a certain course because they are women."[95] She then goes on to discuss the case of a female diviner-priest who from the Western perspective is an exception in a male-dominant occupation: "When I tried to discover how people accounted for this extraordinary behavior, no one ever suggested that there was anything odd about it. Men and women alike asserted that no code was transgressed by her actions and that no disapproval was directed at her."[96] Barber concludes, however, that this avowed cultural principle of openness and women's freedom of choice is limited in practice. This may well be, but if it is, it is because she has recorded twentieth-century Yorùbá society, a society in which ideas about gender are increasingly becoming entrenched. However, there is a more fundamental disjuncture between the categories being invoked by Barber and those being invoked by her Yorùbá informants. Despite Barber's observation that the Yorùbá world is not dichotomized into male and female, her own conceptual categories are, and she in fact calls the Ifá (god of divination) world, "the man's world." It is from her viewpoint, therefore, that the position of the anafemale *aláwo* (diviner-priest) seems extraordinary. Barber considers maleness as a qualification for becoming a diviner-priest. In contrast, for her Yorùbá informants, the anasex of this *aláwo* was not an issue. What was most important for them was her education (an achieved attribute) and, more importantly, her family connections (an ascription). This is what one informant had to say about the female *aláwo:*

> She learnt Ifá. If a woman goes to school she becomes an educated person; if she learns Ifá, she becomes a babalawo. Her father was a babalawo, so was her husband, so she picked up little by little from them. There was never a time when the association of babalawo said she had no right to participate in their activities. ... The verses she learnt were the same as those of other babalawo. Once she learnt she was a babalawo ...[97] Both men and women come to consult her.[98]

From the Yorùbá frame of reference, it would have been more remarkable if this woman had become an *aláwo* without her father or any other ancestors having been one. Because occupations were lineage-based, it was not remarkable that she was carrying on her family profession as other *babaláwo* and other children must have done in Yorùbáland. This *aláwo* was not an exception in the universe of diviner-priests because, like most of the others (male or female), she inherited the profession. As would be said in Yorùbá, Ó bá olá nílé ni (It is all in the family).[99] The same applied to blacksmiths, weavers, or any of the other occupations that existed in Old Ọ̀yọ́. Both ọkùnrin and obìnrin were represented in all occupations.

Interrogating the Gender Framework

In spite of the evidence to the contrary, scholars have used gender to account for the division of labor in Old Ọ̀yọ́. Samples of such discourse are presented in this section to demonstrate the invention of a gendered society and to highlight other related questions. In taking the gender division of labor for granted, scholars have focused on accounting for what they saw as female predominance in trade. A number of researchers have made the claim that trading was a female profession that took place mostly in town. Farming, in contrast, was associated with males and was assumed to take place in the farmlands, which were on the outskirts of towns, often miles away. This spatial aspect of the division of labor, therefore, has been used by researchers as the basis of explicating the Yorùbá division of labor. Like F. J. Pedler,[100] B. W. Hodder posits that female predominance in rural marketing may date back to conditions of internal insecurity that made it unsafe for men to move away from the farms, while women enjoyed relative immunity from attacks.[101] It is not clear why Hodder believed that females were immune from attack. In fact, historical sources do not support this hypothesis — consider, for instance, the numbers of Yorùbá obìnrin and children who were sold during the Atlantic slave trade.[102]

Anthropologist Niara Sudarkasa, analyzing the historical records that document female trading, concludes that females mostly traded locally, within the towns; very few of them engaged in interurban trade. In addition, she suggests that the reason males, not females, were the farmers in the nineteenth century was that "farming could not be left to other than those who also had the responsibility of defending the society against attack by hostile groups."[103] Thus, she concludes, farming and soldiering went hand in hand because both took place outside the safe haven of the town gates. Plausible as this line of thinking might seem, the dichotomous presentation of farming and trading has the effect of belying the relationship between the two and undermining the role of obìnrin in farming and indeed in production in general.

The primary goods of trade in Yorùbá society were foodstuff that traders procured from farms and carried on their heads into the towns.

Yams and other basic foodstuff were processed and then sold in the markets. This does not, however, prove that there was always a great spatial separation of farms and towns. Johnson's records cast a shadow over the farm/town, gender-framed divide when he describes how "towns in the plain that are greatly exposed to sudden attacks, or those that have had to stand long sieges, have a second or outer wall enclosing a large area which is used for farming during a siege."[104] Furthermore, a number of documented accounts by European explorers and missionaries describe female participation in interurban trade. For example, Hugh Clapperton noted in his journal the following observation of Yorùbáland: "We passed several people, principally women, heavily laden with cloth, plantains and a paste from pounded Indian corn."[105]

Another aspect of Sudarkasa's viewpoint foreshadows some feminist theories that have been used to explain the sexual division of labor in the West and elsewhere. I refer specifically to the idea that because females are mothers, they cannot be engaged in activities that take them too far away from the "domestic sphere."[106] Thus, Sudarkasa postulates that motherhood is the primary reason for the domestication of females in general. Following the conventional wisdom in African studies that long-distance trade was the province of males, Sudarkasa argues that even in Yorùbá society, despite the dominance of females in trade, long-distance trade was the province of males. She reaches this conclusion because long-distance trade necessitated being away from home for weeks at a time, and this she posits as incompatible with child-care responsibilities. "In traditional Yorùbáland (as in the present day society) it was *mainly* women past the age of child-bearing who engaged in long-distance traffic, which necessitated their being away from their homes for weeks or even months at a time. Those women who had responsibility for their children traded in the local markets."[107] Based on the assumption that motherhood domesticated females, it is logical to conclude that it was mainly menopausal women, who did not have child-care responsibilities, who were engaged in long-distance trade. In that case, female long-distance trade would be an exception and not the rule. But such a projection is based on Western cultural norms.

The Yorùbá construction of motherhood was far different from that which is projected in these Western-based fantasies. To begin, the obligations of motherhood, like those of fatherhood, were the primary reason for gainful employment for all adults and the primary incentive to accumulate was the need to provide a dowry and bride-wealth for one's children. The notion that it was only old mothers who engaged in long-distance trade is thus problematic—when the women became old, these primary economic needs had already been met. Furthermore, with individual aging came changes in the family cycle — children were expected to provide for parents, and grandmothers in particular were expected to help take care of their grandchildren. Parents expected their children to take care of them in their old age; the social status of both parents and children depended on it. Therefore, the image of an old mother past the "bloom of life"[108] (however it is defined) engaged in long-distance trade is not supported by the evidence.

Indeed, the socioeconomic realities of Yorùbáland challenge the theory of motherhood as a domesticating role — part of the Yorùbá definition of motherhood was that mothers must provide for their children materially. Sudarkasa herself is quite clear about this; as she notes, motherhood was an *impetus* rather than an *obstacle* to economic activities. Since the period of actively giving birth extended over a long period of time, dividing mothers into two groups (i.e., young ones and those past the bloom of life) is too narrow and reductionist. There were other kinds of mothers — ones who neither had infants nor were menopausal. It is understandable to postulate that having a newborn had an effect on all of a woman's engagements. But for how long? In addition, many mothers of newborns would have had other children, and it is hardly conceivable they would not have taken their responsibilities to their other children into account in the structuring of their lives.

Furthermore, the living arrangements in large compounds, offering a multiplicity of mothers and fathers, meant that child-rearing was not an individualized experience that devolved only to mothers. Many mothers were able to share child-care responsibilities among themselves, freeing large numbers of mothers of childbearing age to engage in whatever activities they pleased. Children were often supervised by older children; old people (of all stripes) participated in care-giving; and babies were transported on their mothers' backs and other backs to the market. Once it is recognized that the division of labor also encompassed seniority and generational factors, it is not difficult to see how motherhood was compatible even with long-distance trade. As I already noted, even the so-called local trade had a long-distance aspect because foodstuff for trade had to be brought in from farms that were often miles away.

Decomposing the Concept of a Gender Division of Labor

The proclivity to impose a gender division of labor on Old Ọ̀yọ́ society stems from a number of assumptions. One is that such a division is universal and timeless. It is necessary to unpack the concept of a gender division of labor. Felicity Edholm, Olivia Harris, and Kate Young distinguish between (1) analyzing the sexual division of labor as "the differential assignation of tasks"; this is "merely stating in another way that gender differentiation is realized in specific social activities"; and (2) analyzing "on what basis tasks other than those of procreation and lactation are assigned to one sex or the other, i.e. the content of the sexual division of labor, and of the nature of appropriation of, and exchange between, sex-specific products."[109] However, as I have demonstrated above, there were no gender-specific products or assignment of tasks in Old Ọ̀yọ́. Both okùnrin and obìnrin were represented in all professions, the basis of assignment, if any, being lineage membership.

Edholm, Harris, and Young go on to suggest that because heterosexual coupling is the foundation of the division of labor, scholarly analyses of gender difference in roles/occupations should be based on conjugal roles — husband/wife or mother/father. This approach is problematic with regard to Old Ọ̀yọ́ because there was no conjugal couple as such, and married persons did not form a productive unit. Indeed, the existence of polygamy rendered the complementary conjugal-role model inapplicable. With regard to the mother/father model, both mothers and fathers had "bread-winning" obligations to their children. Mothers seem to have been more prominent and critical to their children's existence and survival on a daily basis; but fathers also had very prominent parts to play in the lives of their children, particularly during rites of passage, such as marriage, that were of great importance in Yorùbá society. Indeed, the parental model in Old Ọ̀yọ́ society encompassed much more than the roles of mother and father. It was more a division of labor between the idí-ìyá (maternal kin — the mother's house) and the idí-bàbá (paternal kin — the father's house). An anafemale belonging to the paternal kin, for example, would play the role of the father as she enacted the obligations of the father's side.

Thus, we cannot apply a simple notion of complementarity between the role of fathers and the role of mothers on a daily basis. First, a more complex notion of complementarity would transcend the individuality of mothers and fathers and should be placed in the context of the lifetime of the ọmọ (child). Second, the presence in the agbo-ile (compound) of multiple generations and children of different ages opens up the issue of the division of child-care among residents. Third, casting the division of labor in Yorùbá society in conjugal-role terms ignores the fact that siblings had concrete responsibilities toward each other and toward the various aya and offspring. Fourth, the primary responsibility of adult anamales and anafemales was not necessarily to each other as conjugal partners; siblings and parents of both had a claim on resources, sometimes, in fact, a first claim.

Edholm, Harris, and Young further argue that in some situations, the critical question is not whether certain tasks were "sex-specific" (the question that has dominated the literature) but who controlled labor and the products of the labor[110] and which tasks were most highly valued by the culture. Motherhood was the most valued institution in Yorùbáland, and anything that made an *obìnrin* a more effective mother was promoted, even if it impinged on other people and other engagements. Recall the Yorùbá attitude toward postpartum abstinence. *Aya* and *ọkọ* controlled the products of their own labor as there was no notion of a conjugal estate. This property relation was demonstrated in the inheritance system in that couples did not inherit each other's property. With regard to trading versus cultivating, there is no evidence to suggest that one was more valued than the other at the time. However, it is well documented that Yorùbá people then and now valued town living; they associated it with the good life and with social intercourse. This may suggest that in spatial terms, the location of traders in town could be perceived as more advantageous. To say that traders were thus seen as more important is to overstretch the limits of the evidence. On a related issue, Sudarkasa proposes that in the nineteenth century, soldiering was more valued than farming in Ìbàdàn, one of the Yorùbá polities.[111] Ìbàdàn had gained military ascendancy, and military adventurism had become an avenue for males to gain wealth. As a result of this development, farming during this time period was regarded as drudgery.

The problem of categoricalism maybe another factor in accounting for the inclination to erect a gender division of labor. R. W. Connell identified one of the major features of the categorical approach in social theory as the focus on "the category as a unit, rather than the processes by which the category is constituted, or the elements of its constituents.... The social order as a whole is pictured in terms of a few major categories — usually two — related to each other by power and conflict of interest."[112] Categoricalism is clear in the analysis of the Ọ̀yọ́ social order, where in spite of a variety of possible economic engagements and the complexity of the division of labor, anamales are reduced to farmers and anafemales to traders. Connell goes on to discuss how the gender division of labor is mapped in categorical analysis. "Analyses of the sexual division of labor, for instance, have usually set up the gender categories as a simple line of demarcation in economic life, adding a complexity by mapping the twists and turns of this line in different societies." He further argues that only a few scholars concern themselves with " 'the making of a woman's occupation,' . . . a question which, by making the process of constructing categories a central issue, leads away from the abstract logic of categoricalism."[113] Jane Guyer's observation about the categorical way in which occupations are defined is also instructive. With regard to farming, she writes: "One has to put aside the essentially European designation of farming as a single occupational category in order to understand the logic of the division of tasks in these [Yorùbá and Beti] systems."[114] Likewise, one has to remember that people had multiple occupations; for example many diviner-priests were also farmers. Many people farmed to trade. Hence, the separation of trading and farming in the literature is unwarranted.

This section has highlighted the gender categoricalism of interpreters of Ọ̀yọ́ society. I have argued that the making of the categories "men" and "women" and the mapping of such onto occupations like farmers and traders, respectively, in a society in which ọkùnrin and obìnrin were represented in both occupations, are without foundation and so are nothing but an imposition of an alien model that distorts reality and leads to false simplification of social roles and relationships.

Statistics have been the most crucial basis for establishing categories. Therefore, foundational to many analyses is what can be called a "statistical categoricalism." Based on this, the argument is made that men and women were disproportionately represented in the different categories. Thus if traders were mostly women, then trading is categorized as a woman's job. This process discounts the numbers in the oppositional category (which scholars themselves have set up), and those numbers are usually ignored and contribute nothing to the discussion. The major problem with statistical categoricalism is that it sets up the categories "men" and "women" a priori and then uses statistics to validate unproven assumptions. Statistics are not innocent — they are collected in terms of a research focus that is underpinned by presuppositions about the nature of human life and societies. Statistics only do what the researcher wants them to do. Hence, in reference to Old Ọ̀yọ́ society, statistics presented to support the claim that there was gendering are actually the work of scholars themselves performing a statistical gendering.

From the standpoint of this book, the existence of men and women as social categories must be proven before a statistical analysis to show their prevalence is performed. Furthermore, we must go back to the most fundamental argument of this book — unlike in Western societies, human anatomical differences were not the basis of social categories in Yorùbáland. Statistics are nothing but a "body count"; they are just another way of validating the Western notion that physical bodies are of necessity social bodies.

Anthropologist Jane Atkinson has shown that in the Wana society of southeast Asia all social roles are equally open to men and women. She puzzles, however, over why statistically women are less represented in the prestigious profession of the shaman. She concludes that "a Wana woman who becomes a powerful shaman has not broken the rules but beaten the odds."[115] Odds are the supreme language of statistics and speak to the Western obsession with measurement and the preoccupation with "evidence that we can see."[116] The odds here are not made by the Wana; they are actually Atkinson's very own inventions. Atkinson does acknowledge that Wana world-sense is different from the Western worldview. What is missing in many Western-derived analyses is the realization that more important categories may be at work, categories informed by and constituted from the indigenous frame of reference. It is possible, for instance, that most of the Wana shamans or Yorùbá diviner-priests could turn out to be firstborns. The researcher cannot know this if birth-order is not a conceptual category of research. Other crucial categories could be those who were born under the full moon or the second child of the second wife. One could go on, but the point is that Western categories like gender are globalized and deployed as universally valid even as other more important local categories may have been rendered irrelevant and therefore inconceivable. The argument being made here is not irrelevant to Western societies either, because there could be other fundamental categories that are equally important in interpreting these societies. Racial categories come readily to mind. In Western societies too, seniority and birth-order are important factors in determining access, opportunities, and personal identities of people; yet these variables have not been given as much attention as they should. In a study of radicalism in Western societies, Frank Sulloway contends that birth-order is the most important factor determining who will become a rebel in the family.[117] Accounting for why certain variables are privileged by researchers over others is important for understanding societies and for social theory. In the written discourse on the Yorùbá, gender is privileged over seniority only because of Western dominance in the conceptualization of research problems and in social theory.

Gender as a Theoretical and Ideological Construct

As I have demonstrated repeatedly above, in Western discourses, gender is conceived as first and foremost a dichotomous biological category that is then used as the base for the construction of social hierarchies. The body is used as a key to situating persons in the Western social system in that the possession or absence of certain body parts inscribes different social privileges and disadvantages. The male gender is the privileged gender. But these observations are not true of the Yorùbá frame of reference. Thus gender constructs are not in themselves biological — they are culturally derived, and their maintenance is a function of cultural systems. Consequently, using Western gender theories to interpret other societies without recourse to their own world-sense imposes a Western model.

Edholm, Harris, and Young conclude that "the concepts we employ to think about *women* are part of a whole ideological apparatus that in the past has discouraged us from analyzing *women's* work and *women's* spheres as an integrated part of social production."[118] I could not agree more with the idea that concepts are part of the ideological apparatus. However, these scholars fall into the very ideological trap they elucidate — they deploy the concept "women" as a given rather than as a part of the "whole ideological apparatus." Woman/women is a social construct, although it is invoked asocially and ahistorically. There were no women in Yorùbá society until recently. There were, of course, obìnrin. Obìnrin are anafemales. Their anatomy, just like that of okùnrin (anamales), did not privilege them to any social positions and similarly did not jeopardize their access.

The worldwide exportation of feminist theory, for example, is part of the process of promoting Western norms and values. Taken at its face value, the feminist charge to make women visible is carried out by submerging many local and regional categories, which in effect imposes Western cultural values. Global gender-formation is then an imperialistic process enabled by Western material and intellectual dominance. In effect, one of the most important recommendations that emerges from my analysis of Yorùbá society is that in any consideration of gender construction, researchers should be concerned about not only the "whatness"[119] of gender but also the "whoness" — because one determines the other. That is, when scholars say that gender is socially constructed, we have to not only locate what it is that is being constructed but also identify who (singular and plural) is doing the constructing. To return to the building metaphor used earlier, how many of the bricks for erecting the edifice come from the society in question? How many from scholars? And, finally, how many from the audience?

The problem of gender in African studies has generally been posed as the woman question, that is, in terms of the issue of how much women are oppressed by patriarchy in any given society. Women and patriarchy are taken for granted and are therefore left unanalyzed and unaccounted for. However, in mapping the Yorùbá frame of reference, it became clear that the social category "woman" — anatomically identified and assumed to be a victim and socially disadvantaged — did not exist. Assuming the woman question a priori constitutes an unfounded application of the Western model, privileging the Western way of seeing and thereby erasing the Yorùbá model of being.

In conclusion, what the Yorùbá case tells us about gender as a category is that it is not a given. Thus, as an analytic tool, it cannot be invoked in the same manner and to the same degree in different situations across time and space. Gender is both a social and historical construct. No doubt gender has its place and time in scholarly analyses, but its place and its time were not precolonial Yorùbá society. The time of "gender" was to come during the colonial period, which will be discussed in subsequent chapters. Even in reference to those periods, gender cannot be theorized in and of itself; it has to be located within cultural systems — local and global — and its history and articulations must be critically charted along with other aspects of social systems.

Colonization
↓
gender.

Chapter 3

Making History, Creating Gender

THE INVENTION OF MEN AND KINGS
IN THE WRITING OF ÒYÓ ORAL TRADITIONS

•••

When we speak of African traditions or history we mean oral tradition; and no attempt at penetrating the history and spirit of the
African peoples is valid unless it relies on the heritage of knowledge of every kind patiently transmitted from mouth to ear, from
master to disciple, down through the ages.
— AMADOU HAMPATE BA, "Approaching Africa"

OF ALL THE THINGS that were produced in Africa during the
colonial period — cash crops, states, and tribes, to name a
few — history and tradition are the least acknowledged. This
does not mean that Africans did not have history before the white man
came. Rather, I am making distinctions among the following: first, history as lived experience; second, history as a record of lived experience
that is coded in the oral traditions;[1] and, third, written history. The
last category is very much tied up with European engagements with
Africa and the introduction of "history-writing" as a discipline and a
profession. Indeed, it is important to acknowledge that African history,
including oral traditions, was recorded as a result of the European assault. This underscores the fact that ideological interests were at work
in the making of African history as is true of all history. Tradition
is constantly being reinvented to reflect these interests. A. I. Asiwaju,
for example, in an essay examining the political motivations and ma-
nipulations of oral tradition in the constitution of ọbaship in different
parts of Yorùbáland during the colonial period, writes: "In the era of
European rule, particularly British rule, when government often based
most of its decisions over local claims upon the evidence of traditional

80

history, a good proportion of the data tended to be manipulated deliberately."[2] This process of manipulation produced examples of what Asiwaju wittily refers to as "nouveau rois of Yorùbáland."[3]

The concept of "invented traditions"[4] is useful for probing the reconstitution of African oral traditions in the contemporary period. I deploy it to acknowledge the implication of the present in the past, rather than making a "presentist"[5] claim that the past is solely fabricated to reflect present interests. J. D. Y. Peel's elaboration of the idea of "stereotypic reproduction," or the mutual conditioning of the past and present, is a more useful approach in this instance. Peel states: "Where possible, present practice is governed by the model of past practice and, where change does occur, there is a tendency to rework the past so as to make it appear that past practice has governed present practice."[6]

The notion of invented traditions does not necessarily imply dishonesty; the process is usually much more unconscious. In fact, it is a testament to the immediate nature of evidence and the positionality of any particular recorder of the past. As Arjun Appadurai reminds us: "Though the past is inherently debatable, it is not an infinite and plastic symbolic resource, wholly susceptible to contemporary purposes.... Rather, the past is a rule-governed and therefore finite cultural resource. As with other kinds of cultural rules, anything is possible, but only some things are permissible."[7] What is permissible is culture-bound. The idea expressed in the notion of permissibility is that the extent to which the past is malleable for present purposes is limited. Although many things can change, some things must remain the same. The task for historical sociology is to see which institutions have changed and which ones have remained the same in content and in form and what historical processes and cultural forces made such changes and continuities "permissible," to use Appadurai's term. It is also important to note that there is a positive reading of the notion of invented traditions that recognizes that traditions as a body of knowledge are in and of themselves not static but dynamic and part of a process in people's lived experiences. Consequently, the idea of "invention" does not suggest that there are no real traditions; furthermore, it does not mean that change in and of itself nullifies the existence of tradition as a whole.[8] The Yorùbá conception of tradition (àsà) speaks to the issue of the interplay between the past and the present and the agency of the person who "recounts" history at any point in time. Olabiyi Yai explicates àsà as follows:

> Something cannot qualify as àsà which has not been the result of deliberate choice (sà) based on *discernment and awareness of historical practices and processes* (ìtàn) by individual or collective orí

[the personal destiny that is chosen prior to coming into the world of humankind]. And since choice presides over the birth of àsà (tradition), the latter is permanently liable to metamorphosis.[9]

Since the colonial period, Yorùbá history has been reconstituted through a process of inventing gendered traditions. Men and women have been invented as social categories, and history is presented as being dominated by male actors. Female actors are virtually absent, and where they are recognized, they are reduced to exceptions. Historian Bolanle Awe makes a similar observation when she writes that piecing together "women's history" has been difficult because of "the dearth of information [about women's achievements], particularly documentary evidence; . . . some outstanding women in history have been mistaken for men, and their achievements [have been] attributed to male rulers!"[10] In an earlier essay, Awe alluded to a distinction between African historiography, with its male bias, and African oral traditions, which are inclusive of all segments of the population. It becomes clear, then, that the notion of "women's history" as articulated by the "Western feminist international"[11] is problematic with regard to Africa. Underlying the idea of women's history are the assumptions (1) that whatever accounts of the past we have now are actually men's history; and (2) that accepting such a conceptualization would be legitimizing claims that we already know to be false in the case of many African societies. If we must "recover women's history," we as scholars cannot be ahistorical in our approach. The question is, When did this history get lost? And how was it possible in our societies for the histories of "men" and "women" to be thus separated? In short, the concept of gender bias in history itself calls for a close examination in that it privileges the Euro-American tradition of male-dominant history over the African oral traditions, which were often inclusive. Such a privileging makes sense in the contemporary period, but with regard to the long duration of Yorùbá history, for example, it really has no place. In the effort to correct the male bias of recent African historical documentation, scholars might begin with a fundamental reexamination of such historiographies as UNESCO's *General History of Africa* and *Ground Work of Nigerian History,* both of which Awe notes are male-biased.[12] The work of African historians like Awe to place women back in history should be applauded, particularly against the background of the male-dominant historical reconstructions of the last century and a half. In accounting for "pasts," however, conjunctural factors[13] are no less important than historical events and sociocultural facts. One must ask, What are the origins of this male-biased African historiography? And more importantly, Why does written history by and large continue to be androcentric?

Consequently, my own concern is not with "women's history" per se. Rather, my focus, more fundamentally, is to question the historicity of the gendered interpretation of Ọ̀yọ́ oral traditions in the work of many contemporary historians. My goal is to draw attention to the fact that writing Yorùbá history has been a process of gender attribution in which kings and men have been created from oral traditions that were originally free of gender categories. In order to trace and account for these processes, I interrogate the work of Samuel Johnson,[14] the pioneering historian of the Yorùbá, and other writers who have touched upon the question of gender in Ọ̀yọ́ historiography. Issues of language, the transmission of knowledge, the social identity of historians, and the collection and cultural translation of oral traditions will also be addressed. Furthermore, images of the past as presented in Ọ̀yọ́ art will be examined, taking into account the "gendered gaze" that has been introduced in the interpretation of the past by art historians.

Finding the King in Every Man

Much of Ọ̀yọ́-Yorùbá history has been written in the traditional event-centered mode of historical documentation, replete with its overrepresentation of wars, kings, and great men. This focus, which assumes an undefined interest, has led to the idea that male actors dominated to the detriment of (and in the virtual absence of) "women." In the previous chapter, I showed that gender categories did not exist as such in Old Ọ̀yọ́ society — gender was not an organizing principle. Seniority defined by relative age was the dominant principle. Thus, social categories deriving from an elaboration of anatomic distinctions — categories like "men" and "women" or kings — did not exist. Ọ̀yọ́ social categories were gender-free in that the anatomy did not constitute the basis for their construction and elaboration. Access to power, exercise of authority, and membership in occupations all derived from the lineage, which was regulated from within by age, not sex.

With regard to Old Ọ̀yọ́ historiography, then, the categories "men" and "women" had to be invented. This invention, however, was not systematic. Its original impetus was rooted in the assumption that gender is a natural way of categorizing in any society and that male privilege is the ultimate manifestation of such categorizing. This assumption was carried forward from European history as the model of global history, and because of colonization and the educational training of historians of African origin, many such historians have not made a departure from the Western model, which they have in the main accepted as given. Invaluable as their work has been, it is salient to question in its entirety the assumption in the historiography that gender was a category in the societies of Old Ọ̀yọ́ and indeed Yorùbáland. In the same way, the attendant notion of male dominance based on the privilege of penis possession has to be thoroughly interrogated. Such articles of faith have to be proven first, not taken for granted or used as bedrock for subsequent discussion. What and who constitutes the category "men" and what constitutes male interests should be explained.

Conversely, the premise promoted more recently about the so-called position of women also has to be deconstructed. It too is fundamentally flawed when it takes gender categories and interests as timeless givens. Furthermore, it is prejudicial against females: since it assumes male dominance, it transforms females in positions of power into "males" or exceptions. If the focus is shifted from the status of women to the status of men, it may be possible to situate some theoretical perspectives in a historical and cultural context. I seek to bring together sociocultural and conjunctural factors in the interpretation of Ọ̀yọ́ oral traditions. I posit, therefore, that the emergence of men and women as social categories in Ọ̀yọ́-Yorùbá discourse was a historical process and that any interpretation of history that assumes these categories to be timeless is inherently flawed.

It is important to understand that this is not a polemical objection to a male-dominated society. My focus, rather, is to systematically scrutinize the building blocks of historical knowledge. What is being questioned is the claim in Yorùbá historiography that Old Ọ̀yọ́ society was male-dominant, when no evidence has ever been adduced for this position. Ọ̀yọ́ history and tradition were reconstituted during the colonial period, and the indigenous world-sense and frame of reference have been subverted in the process of constituting the new social categories — men, women, and kings in particular.

In the first part of this chapter, I interrogate specifically the dynastic lists of aláàfin (rulers) that have been presented by various local and foreign recorders of the past. These lists purport to show that male rulers were the norm and that if there were any females, they were exceptions. The question that then arises is: Given the non-gender-specificity of Ọ̀yọ́ names, pronouns, and social categories, how did historians decipher the gender of all the aláàfin on the lists? Put another way: Considering the difficulty of identifying anatomical sex at a spatial and temporal distance and in the context of the Yorùbá language, how were the "recorders" of the lists able to identify as male particular rulers, especially those who ruled before the nineteenth century, a period in which there were no written eyewitness accounts?

N. A. Fadipe notes one important aspect of the problem of deciphering gender in Yorùbá at a spatial and temporal distance from the subject: "[The] introduction of the third person singular personal pronoun ó into a passage of written Yorùbá, in which persons and things of various genders have previously been mentioned, is apt to prove irritating...because ó may mean he, she, or it."[15] The source of Fadipe's irritation lies not in the Yorùbá language but in the more recent imposition on the society of the European predilection for gender-categorizing. One cannot blame the Yorùbá for not creating gender constructs. The real problem is the mistranslation and distortion that have resulted from the process of imposing Western models in the reconstruction of the Yorùbá past.

Ultimately, the argument being made in this chapter is not about whether females have been constructed as absent among the Ọ̀yọ́-Yorùbá rulers, but about the presentation of the aláàfin as men; also, the chapter challenges the projection of the power of the rulers as being founded on the existence of male privilege and male interest. The idea that privilege inhered in the male body-type was introduced into the scholarship about the Yorùbá without careful examination of the Yorùbá cultural ethos and parameters of information-coding and, therefore, without justification. In Old Ọ̀yọ́, there were no legal, linguistic, or cultural gendered specifications for access to given offices and positions. Before creating the category "kings" it was necessary to first create the category "men." That done, men were handed the rulership of the empire, while the residual part of the society was designated the domain of another category — labeled "women." This process derived from the uncritical assumption that Western categories were universal. Thus as Yorùbá oral traditions became part of global history, they acquired the coloring of the dominant cultural institutions of their time — both Western secular and Christian. In these traditions, power and authority are believed to be the prerogative of the male sex, and therefore gender interests are at the base of political institutions.

Thus historians and other scholars of Old Ọ̀yọ́ society who have made these assumptions should be pressed to provide proof (1) that a gendered reading of Yorùbá traditions is valid; (2) that a system of rulership existed that was based on male interest and male-only succession; (3) that the political hierarchy was dominated by males; (4) that maleness constituted a particular social interest that promoted males as a group over females; and (5) that such a gendered system is timeless. A survey of the documentation of Ọ̀yọ́ history shows that all the categories that were gender-free have now become gendered and male-specific. Offspring have been turned into sons, siblings into brothers, rulers into men, and *aláàfin* into kings — at least at the level of language. Anafemales who occupied thrones have been routinely demoted to regents. This is part of the process of the patriarchalization of Ọ̀yọ́ history, a process in which the masculinization of the *aláàfin* and the aristocratic class in general has played a significant part. This process has also stimulated another one, namely, the feminization of certain positions, whereby the society-wide influence of females in power has been narrowed to an undefined interest, distinct from the rest of the community. The genderization of Ọ̀yọ́ history also surfaces in the field of art history, where discussion of the visual world takes on sexual dimensions.

Talking History: Listening for Men

The story of the publication of the Reverend Samuel Johnson's *The History of the Yorùbás* is fascinating in itself, though there is no space to tell it here. Suffice it to say that even though the original manuscript had been completed in 1897, it was not published until 1921. Johnson was a Yorùbá, a Sàró,[16] whose legacy to his people was a documentation of their history. There is no question that his motivation for writing was nationalist, and his role in the documentation of Yorùbá history cannot be overstated. Robin Law, a historian of the Ọ̀yọ́ Empire, asserts:

> The historical traditions of Ọ̀yọ́ did not constitute a history of Ọ̀yọ́, until put together for this purpose by a literate historian such as Johnson. In an oral society, there is not so much *a* traditional history as a range of historical traditions, each tradition (or at least each group of traditions) with its own function and institutional context.[17]

Though one could agree with Law's pronouncement on Johnson's seminal role in constituting Ọ̀yọ́ historiography, from the perspective of the Yorùbá the various *ìtàn* (narratives) and information encoded in *oríkì* (praise poetry) constitute their account of the past, with or without Johnson's intervention. It must be emphasized that the realization in postmodern Western historical traditions that points of view are implicated in historical documentation, and that historical facts at any given point in time are a result of contestation, is not new — such a realization has always been taken into account in the presentation of Yorùbá historical traditions. *Ìtàn* and *oríkì* are critically deployed in Yorùbáland with their perspectival role in mind; therefore, there are no mystifying notions of objectivity.

Reverend Johnson's influence on Yorùbá historiography cannot be overestimated at the level of either written history or oral traditions. In fact, his work is being reabsorbed into Yorùbá oral traditions in a process of feedback.[18] Like any pioneer, Johnson and his work have been critiqued by a number of subsequent scholars and commentators. His bias in favor of the state of Ọ̀yọ́ has been noted,[19] and his Christian partisanship has been acknowledged. From the perspective of this study, however, what is of interest is Johnson's dynastic list purportedly showing all the aláàfin who had ruled Ọ̀yọ́ since its inception. B. A. Agiri has done a comprehensive critique of many aspects of Johnson's account.[20] Robin Law and Robert Smith have raised questions about the factuality of this list vis-à-vis the number of aláàfin, the chronology of the events, the regnal lengths, and even the order in which these rulers reigned.[21] What has attracted little attention is the unquestioned assumption that the aláàfin were males and that any females among them were exceptions.

Based on his interviews with the arókin, official historians of Ọ̀yọ́, Johnson compiled a dynastic list reproduced here from the appendix of his book (see fig. 1). Johnson differentiates Òdùduwà and Òrànyàn from the others, explaining that these first two "kings" did not reign in Ọ̀yọ́. The third aláàfin — Àjàká — was said to have been called to the throne a second time (as the fifth "king"). Iyayun, a female, is mentioned as having ruled only as a regent. The rest of the names listed are presented as male aláàfin.

However, Johnson's own elaboration of the history of succession and the evidence presented by other historians show that there is reason to believe that some of the aláàfin that ruled Ọ̀yọ́ before the nineteenth century were female. For example, A. L. Hethersett, another Yorùbá local historian, who served as the chief clerk and interpreter to the British in Lagos in the 1880s and 1890s, put together from oral tradition an Ọ̀yọ́ dynastic list in which Gbagida was identified as a female aláàfin.[22] Gbagida appeared on Johnson's list but under a different name — Johnson interpreted it as a nickname for Onisile, the twenty-fourth ruler on his list.[23] This fact demonstrates that looking at "proper" names is not sufficient for determining the maleness or femaleness of any aláàfin. Indeed, Johnson himself had asserted that in Yorùbá, "proper names rarely show any distinction of sex; the great majority of them apply equally well to males and females."[24] More recent scholarship has also shown that the twelfth ruler on Johnson's list, Ọ̀rọ̀mpọ̀tọ̀, was a female and that there were two other previously

Figure 1
Dynastic List (from Johnson)

1. *Oduduwa*	20. *Ayibi*
2. *Oranyan*	21. *Osinyago*
3. *Ajaka*	22. *Gberu*
4. *Sango*	23. *Amuniwaiye*
5. *Ajaka*	24. *Onisile*
6. *Aganju*	25. *Labisi*
Regent Iyayun	26. *Awonbioju*
7. *Kori*	27. *Agboluaje*
8. *Oluaso*	28. *Majeogbe*
9. *Onogbogi*	29. *Abiodun*
10. *Ofinran*	30. *Aole*
11. *Eguoju*	31. *Adebo*
12. *Orompoto*	32. *Maku*
13. *Ajiboyede*	33. *Majotu*
14. *Abipa*	34. *Amodo*
15. *Obalokun*	35. *Oluewu*
16. *Ajagbo*	36. *Atiba*
17. *Odarawu*	37. *Adelu*
18. *Kanran*	38. *Adeyemi*
19. *Jayin*	

unmentioned anafemale ọba (rulers): Adasobo (Òfinràn's mother) and Bayani (Ṣàngó's sister). Robert Smith, who collected oral traditions from various categories of officials in Ìgbòho and New Ọ̀yọ́ in the 1960s, writes about yet another anafemale ọba: "This account of the military success of Òròmpòtò's reign...confirmed that the warlike Òròmpòtò was a woman....One informant at New Ọ̀yọ́ added that Òròmpòtò reigned for twenty years...as a woman king (ọba obìnrin)."[25]

The presence of female rulers certainly raises questions about the assumption of an all-male succession system. For one thing, the female aláàfin, irrespective of their numbers, cannot be dismissed as exceptions, unless there was a clearly stated rule from which they were being excepted. Thus far, no such rule has been shown to exist. The more fundamental question raised by the presence of female aláàfin is not why their numbers are few, because that is not yet known for a fact, but how gender, female or male, was assigned in the first place. In other words, the issue is not why only four aláàfin are identified as females but how the rest of them were identified as males. The larger question concerns the nature of the institution of *aláàfin* in Old Ọ̀yọ́ and historians' representation of it.

Johnson was aware of the gender-free nature of Yorùbá categories in relation to English and expressed reservations about the influence on Yorùbá of English gender categories. Nevertheless, his Western and Christian training had already shaped his perceptions about the linkages among gender, leadership, and cultural-custodial knowledge. The presence of a male-biased gender ideology is indicated in the introduction to his book, when he urges his other "brethren" to follow in his footsteps and inquire about the histories of other parts of Yorùbáland "because it may be that oral records are preserved in them which are handed down from *father to son*."[26] In line with Western ideology, Johnson's phrasing locks out anafemales from the process of historical transmission and knowledge-production. It could be argued that the apparent gender bias in the preceding quote is superficial, being merely a translation matter. However, this does not appear to be the case. For one thing, language is important in and of itself; second, Johnson's gender bias becomes clearer and his worldview is better apprehended as we examine the totality of his writings on historical events and Ọ̀yọ́ cultural institutions.

In any interview process, the formulation of inquiry can be a clue to the nature of information sought and shapes how such knowledge is to be organized. Law notes that

> oral information is normally offered only in response to a question, and both its content and its form are greatly influenced by the questions asked.... The problem about literate historians' use of oral traditions is not so much that they falsified what they heard (though this undoubtedly sometimes occurred) as that by the very process of seeking out oral information, they changed its character.[27]

Johnson relied exclusively on the *arókin* (royal bards)[28] for information about the earlier period of Yorùbá history. However, his account could not have been identical to what he heard from the *arókin*, for the following reasons: first, the difference in the nature of oral history and written history;[29] second, the relationship between language and translation; third, the mediating and interpretive role of Johnson the recorder, which he himself commented on. For instance, he observed that the *arókin* often presented him with different versions of some events; one can only surmise that he as the literate historian selected one, which he then reconciled with the grand narrative of Ọ̀yọ́ history he was in the process of producing.

Johnson's biases were likely to have affected his role as a recorder of oral tradition, particularly at the points of collection, translation, and transmission. From the perspective of this work, the most problematic aspect of his interpretation is the notion that succession to the throne was open only to male members of the family. Though there are no records of the questions he asked the arókin to elicit the information he collected from them, it is possible to speculate on what form of interrogation he used. Law has suggested that Johnson might have asked: "How many Kings of Ọ̀yọ́ had there been, and in what order did they reign?"[30] What is interesting is the implication of these questions in Yorùbá translation, since it is likely that Johnson rendered them in Yorùbá rather than in English. My interest is in the first part of the question, which I translate as follows: Ọba/aláàfin méèló ló ti gun orí ìtẹ́ ní ìṣẹ̀dálẹ̀ ìlú Ọ̀yọ́? In the two languages, the question differs in one crucial sense, namely, that in English, king is a male category, while in Yorùbá, both ọba and aláàfin are gender-free, making the translation of one into the other at best obfuscatory. Clearly, the importance of language cannot be overemphasized as a code for transmitting or interpreting perceptions and values enframing otherwise factual information; words are not gender-free in and of themselves — it is the meaning that attaches to them in the larger societal frame of reference that determines what they represent. Johnson no doubt listened to what the information-keepers had to say, but because there was such a vast gap between his frame of reference and that of the interviewees — a gap revealed in the divergence in the language structures — the arókin may have given a response to a question that he *did not ask,* namely: How many rulers (male and female) have there been? Thus when the royal bards gave him the names of rulers, they would not have excluded females, while he, having asked for ọba, which he interpreted as kings (a male Western category), would have assumed they were all male. Yet neither aláàfin nor ọba translates as "king."

Still, beyond Law's wording of the question, it is possible to initiate narratives of the past by posing the question differently. For example, Taló tẹ ìlú yǐ dó? Tani o tẹ̀lé e? (Who founded this town? Who followed?), is a common way of starting history lessons in Yorùbáland.[31] Because the question in Yorùbá is gender-free, the names presented in the arókin's response cannot be identified as specifying male or female gender. Òrányán or Ṣàngó was the founder of Ọ̀yọ́; neither the names nor the deed of founding a polity suggests any gender-specificity; in the oral traditions, both anamales and anafemales have been known to found lineages and towns. For example, there are multiple oral traditions about the person of Òdúdúwà, the Yorùbá progenitor, and the first

"mythical" ruler on Johnson's list. According to some *ìtàn*, Òdúdúwà
was male; according to others, the progenitor was female. The burning
questions remain: How does a contemporary historian like Johnson select the appropriate gender for a ruler, particularly that of those who
reigned before the nineteenth century and for which there were no eyewitness accounts?[32] How did Johnson know the sex of each *aláàfin?*
How did he know, for instance, that Onisile, the twenty-fourth *aláàfin*
on his list, was male? The simple answer is that he did not know. Johnson simply took for granted that *aláàfin* were "kings," and therefore
male, since this was perceived to be the natural order of things given
what obtains in a Western milieu, where his educational training and
sensibility had been formed.

Robin Law has asked the question of how truly traditional is traditional history. Using Yorùbá oral tradition as a case study, he concluded
that "Johnson's King list was not a traditional one, but a creation of
his own. Or, rather, perhaps, a creation of the *arókin* under Johnson's
influence.... There is no need to believe that any of Johnson's aláàfin
are inventions."[33] Law is perhaps correct to assume that Johnson did
not invent any particular *aláàfin;* however, the attribution of male gender to almost all of them is nothing but an invention. The invention
lies in the reinterpretation of the institution of *aláàfin* as parallel to European kingship. The list itself may not have been invented, but the
gender of particular rulers was invented. Law's wording ("How many
Kings of Òyó have there been, and in what order did they reign?") of
Johnson's hypothetical question to the *arókin* reflects the dilemmas of
"translating cultures" — the problem is clear in many writers' references
to these gender-free rulers' lists as "kings' lists" (gendered male). In the
next section, beyond language, a more detailed examination of the process of creating androcentric institutions in Òyó history and culture is
undertaken.

Passing on History: The Men's Relay

Defining the exact rule of succession in Old Òyó is essential. Historians
such as J. A. Atanda rely on Johnson for an understanding of succession
in Old Òyó.[34] Others, like Law, observe that "the mechanics of succession at Òyó are imperfectly known,"[35] but in spite of that observation
they still go on to cite what I call Johnson's hypothesis of "*àrèmo* succession." B. A. Agiri concludes that "nothing specific could be remembered
about early succession patterns, and ... Johnson remedied this deficiency
in the way he thought most appropriate."[36] What is at issue is precisely

what Johnson thought was most appropriate, why he thought that this
was the most likely mode of succession, and what its implications are
for the writing of Ọ̀yọ́ history.

According to Johnson, Old Ọ̀yọ́ succession was male-exclusive — access being based on primogeniture. He claims that in the earlier days,
"the eldest son naturally succeeded the father."[37] But as Agiri reminds
us, "There was at least one occasion, even during the earliest period,
when a son, Egunoju, was succeeded by his *sister,* Orompoto."[38] And
Smith reports that "informants at New Ọ̀yọ́ have said that Òfinràn
began his reign under the regency of his mother Adasobo."[39] Johnson
elaborates the early system of succession:

> The very first official act of the new King after his coronation is
> to create an Aremo.... The title is conferred on the eldest son of
> the sovereign in a formal manner, the ceremony being termed the
> "christening" as of a newly born child, hence he is often termed
> "Ọmọ" by way of distinction.... When the King is too young to
> have a son, or his son is a minor, the title is temporarily conferred
> upon a younger brother, or next of kin that stands in place of a
> son, but as soon as the son is of age, he must assume his title.[40]

An interesting part of Johnson's elucidation of the position of the *àrẹ̀mọ*
is the notion that it changed over time, in that there was a period during
which, because of the suspicion of patricide by some previous *àrẹ̀mọ,*
it became part of the law and constitution that the *àrẹ̀mọ* had to reign
with his father and also die with him.[41] Even with the alleged changes,
Johnson maintains that succession remained male-exclusive. A male successor, he postulates, was chosen from among the "members of the royal
family; he was one considered most worthy, age and nearness to the
throne [also] being taken into consideration."[42]

However, a reappraisal of Johnson's narrative brings to light certain information that is not accounted for by the framework of a
male-exclusive succession. For instance, the term *àrẹ̀mọ* actually means
firstborn. We see this common usage of the term in the *oríkì* (cognomen)
of Aláàfin Ládùgbòlù (1920–44), as recorded by J. A. Atanda:

> *Àrẹ̀mọ Awero, b'e ba nlo 'le mole*
> *Teru t'omo ni o yo*
> *B'e ba ri baba.*[43]

> [The first born of Awero, when he visits Mole's lineage compound,
> Both slave and free-born would rejoice
> At seeing the father.]

Awero is the personal *oríkì* of a female; presumably, therefore, this is Aláàfin Ládùgbòlù's mother's name, and Ládùgbòlù is addressed here, as his mother's firstborn. This does not mean, however, that he was also his father's firstborn, considering that the royal family was usually polygamous. Hence, when Johnson wrote, for example, that the crown fell to Àjàká's son, Aganju,[44] or that Onigbogi was one of the sons of Oluaso, he was probably translating the Yorùbá word *ọmọ* into the English "son." It could well have been translated as "daughter of" or "brother or sister of" (when siblings were of different generations, the younger was referred to as the *ọmọ* of the older one). In fact, the best translation of *ọmọ* in this context is "descendant of or relation of." It should also be noted that there was no indication as to the anasex of the person being descended from: there was often no reference to mother or father, and since a subject could equally inherit from both father and mother, one cannot assume one anasex. Recall that Òfinràn, the tenth *aláàfin* on Johnson's list, was said to have inherited the throne from his mother Ọba Adasobo. A number of *aláàfin* were more explicitly identified with their mothers' heritage — most notably, Ṣàngó, whose mother was said to be a Nupe royal offspring. Hence Ṣàngó's appellation, Ọmọ Elempe, the descendant of Elempe, ruler of the Nupe.[45]

Having translated the gender-free *àrẹmọ* into the gender-specific "Crown Prince," Johnson was faced with the task of accounting for what happened if the firstborn was female. He did this by ascribing to the female *àrẹmọ* the title "Princess Royal," which was supposed to be conferred formally in the same way as the title "Crown Prince."[46] However, after her investiture, the female *àrẹmọ*'s formal role, according to Johnson, seems to have ended. This perspective could have derived from the general practice whereby, in the larger society, on marriage, female offspring took up residence in the household of their conjugal family — marriage residence being patrilocal. However, patrilocality was not universal. It was also commonplace for female offspring of royalty to stay in their natal compounds even after marriage and raise their children in their natal lineages. This practice is encapsulated in the saying, *Ọmọ ọba ò kí ngbé lé ọkọ* (Female royal offspring do not dwell in their marital house).[47] Johnson himself observed that "some girls of noble birth will marry below their rank, but would have their children brought up in their own home, and among their father's children and adopt his totem."[48] Given that the children of such female royal offspring were raised in the royal household, this introduced the possibility of succession passing through females, as acknowledged by Johnson: "The right to the throne is hereditary, but exclusively in the male line or the male issue of the King's daughters."[49]

However, Johnson's historical accounts of succession for some *aláàfin* contradict the hypothesis of male-exclusive succession. Two are discussed below. One concerns Osinyago, the twenty-first *aláàfin* on his list. According to Johnson, "*Osinyago* who succeeded to the throne was equally worthless.... His firstborn son, like his father, was of a grasping propensity, which led to his early death. The second child [Omosun], though a female, was masculine in character, and *she considered the rank and privileges of the Àrèmọ (Crown Prince) her own.*"[50] On the one hand, if one assumes a male-only succession, then Omosun's attitude would seem not only eccentric but virtually insurrectionary. Thus Johnson felt the need to masculinize her, another pointer to his Western, gendered consciousness in which female leadership could be accounted for only by the infusion of a certain dose of masculinity. On the other hand, if the perception of ungendered succession is adopted, it becomes obvious why she would have regarded the throne as her entitlement: there simply were no restrictions on an anafemale ọmọ taking the throne. The origin of the dispute between Omosun and her male cousin, revealed in the above quotation, shows that she had been involved in governance since the dispute between the two arose over "the right of appointing a new Aséyìn at the death of the then king of Ìṣéyìn [a tributary state of Ọ̀yọ́]."[51]

Another example concerns Johnson's presentation of Iyayun as an *ayaba* (royal consort) who allegedly became a regent: "During *Kori's* minority, *Iyayun* was declared regent; she wore the crown, and put on the royal robes, and was invested with the *ejigba*, the *ọ̀pá ilẹ̀kẹ̀* and other royal insignia and ruled the kingdom as a man until her son was of age."[52] In the traditional Ọ̀yọ́-Yorùbá inheritance system, inheritance devolved through consanguinal, not conjugal, lines. The question then arises as to the whereabouts of all the other members of the royal family, the large pool of siblings, parents, and cousins from which it would have been more likely to select a successor. The practice of regency in Europe, in which the throne passes to a wife through her minor son, is in principle alien to Yorùbá culture. Thus it is not likely that an *ayaba* (royal consort), who is not a member of the lineage, would have been allowed to take over the throne under any circumstance. In fact, it would have been most unacceptable to the royals and the *ọ̀yọ́ mèsì* (council of chiefs), who would have regarded it as the ultimate usurpation. Johnson may have introduced this alien concept to explain what he considered to be an exception (a female occupying the throne); having been glaringly convinced that this ruler's female sex could not be glossed over.

However, given Yorùbá cultural values and practices, it is more likely that Iyayun was on the throne simply because she was a descendant of the previous *aláàfin*, who might have been her father, mother, brother, sister, uncle, or aunt. In other words, she was more likely to have been an *omo oba* (descendant of a previous ruler) than an *ayaba*. There may indeed have been some confusion over the identity of Iyayun, in that Johnson also presents her as an *omo oba* from one of the provincial towns, which raises the question of what her natal identity really was.[53] It is also probable that there is confusion about the order of succession, in that Iyayun may have reigned before her son, and he may actually have inherited the throne from her. In any case, it is difficult to believe that she was an *ayaba* who ascended the throne. The *ayaba* had their roles, next to the *aláàfin*, in the political hierarchy; they occupied many different positions, which Johnson himself went to great lengths to explain.[54] Given all this, it would seem that the proposal of a female regency is largely a fabrication, being the easiest way to reconcile the historical fact of an *obìnrin* occupying the throne with Johnson's working assumption of male-only succession. In this process, Johnson distorted anafemale rulership.

Against this background, Robert Smith's account of Aláàfin Oròmpòtò can be evaluated. Smith collected oral traditions from the *arókin* in the 1960s, gaining information that had not been recorded by Johnson. Here is Smith's account:

> This account of the military success of Orompoto's reign [surprisingly] makes...the assertion,...confirmed reluctantly by the authorities at New Òyó, that the warlike Orompoto was a woman, [a] sister and not [a] brother of Egunoju. The most specific account is that she took over the government because of the youth of Ajiboyede, Egunojo's son. One informant at New Òyó added that Orompoto reigned for twenty years, not merely as a regent (*adele*) but as a woman king (*oba obinrin*)....*The persistent reference to Orompoto as a woman becomes more feasible when it is recalled that there has already been at least one, possibly three, female regencies in earlier Òyó history.*[55]

In this case, Oròmpòtò was an *omo oba* (royal offspring) in her own right. The fact that she reigned instead of her brother's son does not mean she was a regent (a temporary representative of a true ruler). This is not the first instance of collateral succession, even in Johnson's account. Plausibly, she reigned because she was the appropriate person to be on the throne at that time, given that in Yorùbá culture, one's children's inheritance rights were not automatically superior to those of one's siblings. Her reign of twenty years also suggests that she was recognized to be a genuine *aláàfin* in her own right. What is pertinent with regard to the interpretive role of the scholar is that even when Smith quotes an informant as specifying that Ọ̀rọ̀mpọ̀tọ̀ was a "woman ruler," he still has to strive to grapple with the concept of a female ruler, which he can only justify by framing it with the regency concept, just as Johnson did before him. Since ọba (ruler) is not gender-specific in Yorùbá, the new phrase ọba obìnrin (woman ruler) is awkward. It would be interesting to know whether it was introduced by the informant or by Smith.

During research in Ògbómọ̀ṣọ́ I found a present-day female ruler of Máyà, a village that used to be under Ọ̀yọ́ jurisdiction. The present baálẹ̀ (village head),[56] Olóyè Mary Ìgbàyílọlá Àlàrí is female, and I was able to conduct a series of interviews with her in Ògbómọ̀ṣọ́ in March 1996.[57] She was made the baálẹ̀ on December 20, 1967, by the late Ṣọ́un of Ògbómọ̀ṣọ́ Ọlájídé Ọláyọdé, which meant that she had already spent twenty-nine years in office. She was the unanimous choice presented by her family for the office. During our conversation, I asked why she was chosen by the family and whether anyone had raised objections to her claiming the title because she is female. She replied that there had been no objections and that she had in fact been drafted by her family members after they had come to the conclusion that she was the best person in the family to do the job. She proudly enumerated her accomplishments as baálẹ̀. In Àróje, another village in the Ògbómọ̀ṣọ́ environs, there was another female ruler. I made several attempts to interview her but was unsuccessful. She died in May 1996. The present Ṣọ̀un (monarch) of Ògbómọ̀ṣọ́ (Ọba Ọládùnní Oyěwùmí), who made her the baálẹ̀, told me that she was the rightful person for the throne. The Ṣọ̀ún pointed out that in certain Yorùbá polities and lineages male gender is not a prerequisite to occupying the throne. Baálẹ̀ Máyà was married at the time she took office, and she said that she enjoyed the support of her husband and his family.

Like Johnson, other historians evidence the same unresolved dilemmas about gender in Yorùbá history. Law questions the claim in Hethersett's list that Gbagida (= Onisile), the twenty-fourth aláàfin on Johnson's list, is female: "The claim that this ruler was a woman is difficult to account for."[58] Law does not explain why such a claim is difficult to accept, but given the sociocultural ethos and historical evidence, his own dismissal of female rulers needs to be scrutinized. Further, the idea that the female royal offspring were disenfranchised is equally difficult to sustain, given the existence of present-day female rulers, the lack of evidence that most of the listed aláàfin were male, and Yorùbá inheritance laws. Many contemporary historians seem to be creating Ọ̀yọ́ history in a cultural vacuum; if they paid attention to other institutions, cultural values, and practices, then it would be clear that some of their basic assumptions needed to be accounted for.

Smith has noted that the Ọ̀yọ́ dynastic list may have been considerably shortened because many earlier aláàfin have been forgotten "because they descended from the female line and were later replaced by descendants in the male line."[59] J. D. Y. Peel confronted the same problem of gender and the rulers' list in the state of Ilesha, another Yorùbá domain. According to him, despite the oral narratives regarding at least six female rulers, none of the contemporary ruling houses would want to claim descent from the females, as they believe it would weaken their claim to the throne. This echoes the reported reluctance by the authorities in New Ọ̀yọ́ to confirm to Smith that Aláàfin Ọ̀rọ̀mpọ̀tọ̀ was a woman and again underscores the need to determine the precise time in Yorùbá history at which the presence of women in positions of rulership, power, and authority became perplexing to certain sections of the population. Thus for Peel, "it is impossible to know what has happened to produce the tradition of so many 'female' Ọwá (rulers), though a sociologist's strong inclination is to believe that the problem lies in the [retelling of] tradition rather than the event."[60] Although the political systems of the different Yorùbá states should not be homogenized, Peel's observation is relevant to this discussion, although his observation needs to be restated to remove the gender bias. Thus the concern should be not what happened to produce the tradition of so many females but what happened to produce the tradition of so many males and male-only succession in the retelling of history. When and why did the tradition of anafemale succession become invalid in many of these polities?

Having questioned the social identity of scholars and its effect on their interpretations of Ọ̀yọ́ history, there seems to be a need to examine the conceptual gap regarding gender in the cultural translation of Yorùbá sensibilities into English and vice versa. This raises the question of the relationship between Yorùbá categories, which are truly gender-free and therefore generic, and English categories, which privilege the male even when they appear to be generic. Given that the study and reconstruction of Yorùbá history are undertaken by both Yorùbá and Euro-American historians, there is a possibility that when the historians of Yorùbá origin use the word "king," for example, they may mean a gender-inclusive category like the Yorùbá ọba. A number of historians (e.g., Babayemi, Agiri, Asiwaju), even as they write about kings' lists and kings, do not seem to be questioning the historicity of female aláàfin, which leads the issue to whether they assume the category "king" to be gender-neutral like ọba or aláàfin. The reverse seems to be the case for many of the Europeans. (I examine the question of language, literature, cultural translation, and audience in chapter 5.) The argument here is not that contemporary African historians are less androcentric than their Euro-American counterparts. Rather, the point is that the way in which English is being used may reflect different language and cultural realities. My experience of English-language usage in Nigeria suggests such a possibility.

A good example of a scholar assuming that the institution of the ọba is gender-free is demonstrated in A. I. Asiwaju's account of the state of Ketu, in southern Yorùbáland. He recounts a most interesting event, which incidentally is consigned to a footnote in his book. In his discussion of the proliferation of alákétu (rulers of a Western Yorùbá precolonial state that now straddles Nigeria and the Republic of Benin), he counts three claimants to the title in the 1970s. One was a female from Brazil: "One other Alaketu, a woman, based in Bahia, South America, even visited Nigeria in 1974 with such pomp that she tended to eclipse the existence of the West-Africa based ones!"[61] That Asiwaju does not subject the anasex of the self-styled alákétu from the Yorùbá diaspora to analysis nor see it as a cultural aberration may be due to his recognition that succession in many pan-Yorùbá states was not gender-based and that therefore the appearance of a female ruler needed no explanation. The position of Ketu in Yorùbá historiography lends credence to the idea that female rulership in Ketu has historical grounding. Ketu was one of the Yorùbá polities that is accepted as having been founded by one of Òdúdúwà's daughters, not a son.[62]

In the contemporary period, the general aristocracy seems to have been masculinized along with the aláàfin. Thus, without being based on any evidence, an assumption has been introduced that members of the ọ̀yọ́ mèsì (council of chiefs), the ọmọ ọba chiefs (royal offspring title-holders), and the arọ́kin (royal bards and historians) were all male in the past. The ayaba (royal consorts — mothers of the palace who held various key authority positions in the political hierarchy) appear to be the exception to the rule of male dominance in the political hierarchy of Old Ọ̀yọ́ as presented by historians beginning with Johnson.

In the interpretations of oral traditions, many writers, local and foreign, assume that the phrase "descendant of" in genealogies denotes a succession of father to son, even when it is clear that numerous successions pass from sibling to sibling. Peel noted the widespread father-to-son preference in the elaboration of historical succession of rulers in many West African states and concluded:

This was no doubt a translation of an order of succession into its closest genealogical analog. . . . It is very common in West African dynasties with a widely rotating succession that an early period is alleged to have had a father-to-son succession, which is so easily and economically explained as an artifact of the later genealogical system itself, that we would be very chary of assuming a real change of succession without clear additional evidence.[63]

Peel is certainly correct about this rendering of succession in English as father-to-son, but one cannot always assume that the oral traditions in the African languages and cultures are equally male-exclusive in letter and in spirit. Consider this example. In a different essay on the making of history, Peel postulates a Yorùbá model of historical reconstruction based on the saying *Bàbá ni jíngí* (Your father is a mirror), which he interprets as expressing the idea that "the physical appearance, aptitudes, spiritual affinities, [and] social position of a father [are] best echoed in his sons."[64] Even if one accepts his interpretation that the saying is about lineal inheritance, he is simply wrong to suggest that inheritance of any kind — including physical appearance — devolves only from father to son. Such an interpretation is not suggested by the Yorùbá rendering. Furthermore, in Yorùbáland, anamale and anafemale offspring equally inherit from the father; more importantly, inherited attributes are not necessarily seen to derive from biology precisely because fatherhood is socially constructed. As I pointed out in the previous chapter, the claim to fatherhood is based on marriage to the mother of the child; being the genitor is neither a necessary nor a sufficient condition for the claim to fatherhood. Of course the genitor and the father in most cases are one and the same; but in cases where they diverge, the claim of the conjugal partner of the mother of the newborn supersedes that of the genitor. Thus as regards Yorùbá social practice and cosmology, Peel's biologized and hence gendered model is untenable since inheritance of all types of attributes passes through the mother also. In fact, the saying *Bàbá ni jíngí* is part of a larger unit; it is part of a poem that articulates Yorùbá ideas about parental bonds and inheritance in which both mother and father are represented:

> *Ìyá ni wúrà.*
> *Bàbá ni jíngí.*
> *Níjọ́ ìyá bá kú ni wúrà bàjẹ́.*
> *Níjọ́ bàbá bá kú ni jíngí wọmi.*
>
> [Mother is gold.
> Father is a mirror.
> When mother dies, the gold is ruined.
> When father dies, the mirror drowns. (my translation)]

Finally, it should be noted that from the Yorùbá perspective, fathers can be reincarnated in their anafemale child, given that anatomical attributes are not privileged and do not determine social practices. Recall Johnson's explication of the office of the *iyámọdẹ* (one of the anafemale high officials in the palace) as embodying the spirit of the *aláàfin*'s "fathers."[65] In the religious realm, spirit possession does not discriminate based on anatomic sex: Ṣàngó (the thunder god) manifests itself in both male and female devotees. The primary problem of rendering Yorùbá history and indeed other aspects of the culture, then, is the imposition of the Western, overly physicalized and gendered model of apprehending the world. Perhaps the *Bàbá ni jíngí* conceptualization is appropriate if we all agree that the *bàbá* (father) in question is the West. Yorùbá historiography mirrors Western history; that much many African scholars have argued about African history in general.[66]

Interpreting History: Creating Men

The problems of interpretation of Yorùbá history and culture, particularly with regard to the issue of gender, can also be attributed to the linguistic and cultural translation of Yorùbá into English. This can be demonstrated by using the two major sources of oral tradition, *ìtàn* (historical narrative) and *oríkì* (praise poetry). In 1988, a group of historians visited Ọ̀yọ́ to record the views of the *arókin* on their "own professional activities and history."[67] In response, one of the *arókin*, Ọ̀nà-Alaro, told the following *ìtàn* to highlight their role as consolers of the *aláàfin* in time of crisis. One of the researchers, P. F. de Moraes Farias, reports the response in both Yorùbá and English:

Tí nǹkan bá ti ṣe Ọba, ọba óò pé wón ọ́ lọ pè wá wá. Tí àwọn ìjòyè bá ti sọ báyìí pé nǹkan báyìí ó ti ṣe Ọba báyìí, Ọba báyìí nǹkan ṣe é rí. Ọba báyìí nǹkan ṣe é rí, yóọ̀ báá póùn náàà gbà, Ọlóun ló wí pé ó wá bẹ̀. Ó lè jẹ́ pé ọmọ ọba kán lè wà, kó jẹ́ pé ọmọ rẹ̀ dóódù ẹni-à-bí-àṣọlé dóódù rẹ̀, kó fò sánlẹ̀ kó kú, gbogbo àwọn tí wón wà lódọ̀ rẹ̀ ò ní lè wí. Wọn ó lọọ gbé e pamọ́. Ni wọn ó wàá pé, "Ẹ lọ pArókin wá." Láá wà sọ pé, "Báyìí, báyìí, báyìí, a gbọ́ pómọ rẹ báyìí ò sí;... ọmọ ti Lámọín báyìí náà sì wá bẹ̀ẹ̀, ọmọ ti Làkésègbè náàá si wa bẹ̀ẹ̀," yóọ́ báá póùn gbà. Àwa làá lọọ sọ.[68]

[If something happens to the Ọba, the Ọba [the Aláàfin] will send for us. As soon as *his* chiefs tell us that such and such a thing has happened to the Ọba, [we will tell him about] another Ọba to whom something similar also happened. So *he* will say that *he* accepts [gbà] it because it is Ọlọ́run's making. Suppose a prince, the firstborn of the Ọba [Aláàfin], dies. The courtiers will not dare give the news to the Ọba. They will go and hide the corpse. Then they will say, "Go and call the Arọ́kin." Then we will tell *him*: "We hear that this son of yours has died.... The son of so-and-so [an Ọba] once died in the same way. And so did the son of somebody else [another Ọba]." And then the Aláàfin will say he accepts [gbà] it. We are the ones who will go and tell him.][69]

In a number of ways, the translator of this piece has been careful. Most notable is the rendering of the ungendered Yorùbá words *Lámọín* and *Làkẹṣẹ̀gbè* into the apparently non-gender-specific English "so-and-so" and "somebody else." Because the Hausa/Arabic derived loanword *dóódù*, which has become part of Ọ̀yọ́ vocabulary, is sex-specific, being a male designation, the translation of the first *ọmọ ọba* (child of ruler) as "prince" is acceptable. However, the subsequent uses of *ọmọ*, which are gender-free in the Yorùbá original, also end up being translated into "son." Similarly, there is nothing to indicate the anasex of the hypo-thetical *aláàfin* (ruler), but s/he is transformed into a man in the English translation by the use of the pronouns "he," "his," and "him." Thus do all the characters in the story acquire the male gender, even though with the exception of a reference to *dóódù* in the case of one character, there is nothing in the *arọ́kin's* speech to warrant such an assumption for the rest of them, who number at least three.

The same distortion and inaccuracy are replayed in the next *ìtàn* (narrative) that the *arọ́kin* narrate. The protagonist is another *ọmọ ọba* named Akuluwe, who this time is a female. This is indicated in the fact that the *aláàfin* told the *oníkòyí* (ruler of Ikoyi) to make her his bride.[70] Farias suggests that a female was necessary in this story because the ac-tion depended on the protagonist being taken away — embarking on a journey; and since the logic of Ọ̀yọ́ marriage demands that the female be taken away, it follows that a female protagonist was indispensable in the story. There is an element of overinterpretation in making such an assumption. Two facts show this: (1) it was commonplace for royal fe-males upon marriage not to move to their marital lineages; and (2) male royal offspring often lived in the provinces, so they too made journeys in and out of the Ọ̀yọ́ metropolis all the time. The *ìtàn* is as follows:

Ọba tó jẹ tẹ̀lé Òrànányán, Ọba Àjàká Dàda Àjùòn tí àdàpè ẹ̀ ń jẹ Ọba Àjàká lÓyọ̀ọ́ ile, ọmọ kanṣoṣo tó bí.... Gbogbo Ọ̀yọ́ Mèsì lóun ó fẹ́ ẹ, kò fẹ́ wọn. Wọ́n wọ́nríbáa Baálẹ̀ ìlú, kò fẹ́ wọn. Gbogbàwon tó lóun ò fẹ́.... Òkòyi ló lóun ó fẹ́ẹ. Ọba ní kó lọ fi ṣ'aya. Ńgbà Óńkòyí ń lọ, tóó ń mú un lọọlé, ibi tí ilẹ̀ ṣú wọn si, wọ́n pebẹ̀ ni Gbọ́ngbọ̀n. Ọ̀ wá sunbẹ̀. Oorun ti wọn wáá sùn ńbẹ̀, ní gbà tílẹ̀ ée mọ ilé jo . . . Ọmọ Ọba jóná, ó jóná sí ìlú yen. Ńgbà Óńkòyí wáá délé, ó wí pé "Òun dáràn o! Ọmọ t'Ọ́ba fóun, òun ló kú. . . . Wọ́n ni ó pe àwọn ọmọọ̀ rẹ, pẹ̀lú sẹ̀kẹ̀rẹ̀ ii. Oníkòyí ni babánláa bàbá tiwa.

[The Ọba [the Aláàfin of Ọ̀yọ́] who ruled after Òrànmíyàn, Ọba Àjàká Àjùòn, this is his name. Ọba Ajàká at Ọ̀yọ́ Ilé. *He had one daughter.* All the Ọ̀yọ́ Mèsì [members of the royal council] said they wanted to marry her, but she refused. She also refused the Baálẹ̀ [chiefs] of many towns. All the ones she said she would not marry . . . Then she said she would marry the Ọba of Ìkòyí, and the Aláàfin gave her hand in marriage. When the Oníkòyí was taking her home, nightfall caught them at Gbọ́ngbọ̀n. During the night, the house in which they slept caught fire. . . . The princess was burned to death. . . . He was told to call upon his own children with this Ṣẹ̀kẹ̀rẹ̀. The Oníkòyí is our grandfather.][71]

In the Yorùbá original, this female offspring is said to be Aláàfin Àjàká's *ọmọ kanṣoṣo tó bí*[72] (ruler's *one and only child*) (my translation). In the Farias translation, it is rendered as "He had one daughter." This is inaccurate because it gives the impression that Àjaká had other children — sons — thereby minimizing the gravity of his daughter's death. This in turn compromises the point of the story being told by the *ònà-aláró*, which is to establish the origins of the institution of *arókin* in Ọ̀yọ́ history. The *ònà-aláró* (an *arókin* — royal bard) recounted that the institution developed to console a particular *aláàfin* in the moment of the greatest crisis of his life as a parent and a ruler — the death of her/his only child. The oral account as rendered in Yorùbá is clearly different from the English version in letter and in spirit. It would be interesting to know how the *arókin* would have reacted to the English version, since it clearly undermines the import of their institution in that the task of consoling a ruler who has lost an only child is more weighty than that of consoling one who has lost one of many children.

Next, it will be helpful to explore the relationship between gender and *oríkì* (praise poetry), the other important source of information about the Yorùbá past. *Ìtàn* (narrative), we have seen, did not for the most part reveal anasex categories. According to Awe, there are three forms of *oríkì* dealing with human achievements:

1. *Oríkì ìlú* (towns), deals with the foundation of a town, its vicissitudes, and its general reputation among its neighbors.

2. *Oríkì orílè* (lineages), gives the characteristics of a patrilineage by focusing attention on a few illustrious members of the lineage whose attributes are supposed to typify the main features of the lineage.

3. *Oríkì ìnagijẹ* (individual personalities), deals mainly with individuals. The poem could outline those qualities that mark him (or her) out for distinction or it could be a combination of these and his/ her pedigree, in which case some of the oríkì orílè is included.[73]

As Awe articulated, the *oríkì* of individual personalities (also called *oríkì bòròkìní* — i.e., praising of important persons) are the most informative for historical reconstruction. She further asserts that

> Oríkì ìnagijẹ...could be a very fruitful source for historical reconstruction.... Because its scope is more limited in the sense that it concentrates on one individual and therefore covers a relatively shorter period of history, the *oríkì* can give detailed and direct information which can be more easily fitted into available historical evidence on the period.[74]

Since the *oríkì ìnagijẹ* are portraits of important personalities, it would seem that information about the sex of the person in question would be readily available. But even then, as Awe immediately points out, "this type of *oríkì* is not always easily available for the more remote period of Yorùbá history."[75] Because the focus of this chapter is the pre-nineteenth-century period, that remark is directly relevant here. Thus, there are serious limitations on relying on *oríkì ìnagijẹ* to decipher the anasex of Ọ̀yọ́ rulers. Karin Barber, in a paper on *oríkì*, suggests that the events of the nineteenth century provided ample opportunity for self-aggrandizement, to the extent that the number of notable personalities increased exponentially and that the genre of *oríkì* of notable personalities itself witnessed not only amplification but also stylistic changes in performance.[76]

To go back to the question of delineating the gender of historical figures, it may be possible to discern the anasex of historical personalities based on the use of personal *oríkì* (cognomens) that appear to be gender-specific. Proper names do not indicate gender, but these cognomens, which also function as names, seem to suggest anatomic-specificity. Adeboye Babalola asserts that personal *oríkì*, unlike given names, are an indication of what the parents hoped for a particular child.[77] Names usually denote the circumstances of birth. Àlàké, Àdùnní, and Àlàrí are cognomens associated with females, and Àlàmú, Àkànní, and Àlàdé are a few associated with males. It is possible, therefore, that if in the *oríkì* or *ítán* the cognomen of the personality is given, then one may be able to ascertain anasex. For example, the *oríkì* of the lineage of Òkò contains the following lines:

Ààrẹ Àlàké jíbọ́la Àlàké Ajíbọ́rò lóko...
Ààrẹ Àlàké ọmọ agédé gudù Ọba Ìgbàjá.[78]

[The leader Àlàké Ajíbọ́rọ̀ loko...
The leader *Àlàké*, one that fought fiercely, killing without mercy, the ruler of Ìgbàjá.]

Since Àlàké is the personal *oríkì* (cognomen) of a female, these lines show that the Òkò lineage has a revered founding female ancestor. One major drawback to relying on cognomens is that they are not always used instead of proper names. In Johnson's dynastic list, for example, only one or possibly two names appear to be cognomens — namely, Àjàgbó and Atìbà, which are male cognomens. The thirty-six other names listed are given names and are therefore not gender-specific. Similarly, the one hundred and forty-two lines of the *oríkì* of Balogun Ìbíkúnlé, a notable nineteenth-century figure presented by Awe in her study, contain no mention of his cognomen, although we learn that he was the father of 'Kuejo, and we also learn the names of myriad other notable personalities with whom he fought in war.[79]

Another problem that arises even when the cognomens are mentioned in a particular *oríkì* genre is to determine who is specifically being addressed, since there is a proliferation of names. Karin Barber collected the oríkì of Wínyọmí, a founding father of Òkukù. The following lines provide a good illustration of this problem:

Winyomi Enipeede[,] Head of the Hunters[,]
Aremu, blocks the road and doesn't budge, Enipeede, one who fills the coward with apprehension...
Àlàmú said[,] "If you get into trouble to the tune of two thousand cowries..."
He said, "Your own father will take his cut of the settlement[.]"
European cloth does not wear well[.]
Winyomi said[,] "what it is good for is showing off."[80]

In the foregoing piece, there are a number of appellations, and presumably all refer to Winyomi; however, the presence of the two cognomens — Àrẹ̀mú and Àlàmú — suggests that reference is to more than one person, since an individual can have many given names but usually only one cognomen. Indeed, this issue raises the question of the conflation of identities in *oríkì* that makes it difficult to untangle the genealogical detail and individual identities presented. Barber correctly asserts that "a social history that attempted to use *oríkì* to recover patterns of personal relations would meet with...difficulties. *Oríkì* do not record the genealogical relationships of the subjects commemorated in the *oríkì*. Genealogical relationships...seem actually to be obscured, rather than clarified and preserved, by the *oríkì*."[81] It is also true that a history that purports to assign the sex of personalities on the basis of *oríkì* allusions alone is fraught with problems. Furthermore, as Barber shows, even the "I" of an *oríkì* chant moves continually between male and female, adult and child, insider and outsider, specific and generalized persona.[82]

The *oríkì* genre, with its multiplicity of references, carries within it an indeterminacy with regard to questions of individual social identity. Another source of complication in regard to the issue of shifting identities lies in the fact that the different units of the *oríkì* have different sources and variable dates of composition, even though they are recited as if they derive from one source and one lineage. Individual identity in Old Ọ̀yọ́ derived from communal identity, and a subject's *oríkì* would include lines from both the maternal and the paternal lines. In performance, however, all the events and attributes appear to pertain to only one descent line.

Finally, because particular physical and moral attributes have their own stock epithets, they introduce another lack of specificity even into the individualized *oríkì inagijẹ*. A number of attributes that have their own poems are tallness, shortness, generosity, and dancing ability. These are introduced to enhance any personality with the said attribute during an *oríkì* performance.[83] If an anamale or anafemale subject is being addressed, and if s/he is identified as tall or short, the appropriate epithet would be incorporated. It is no wonder, then, that Barber, who sought to make a distinction between male and female *oríkì*, concluded that such a distinction is not possible. Writing about the *oríkì* of prominent women, she observed that "these oriki are very close in tone and in imagery to the personal oriki of big men. There are no recognizably 'women's oriki.'"[84] But there are no men's *oríkì* either. Steeped in the male-as-norm framework of the West, Barber is using men as the frame of reference. Consequently, she continues to project erroneously the idea that there are men's *oríkì* though there are no women's *oríkì*. There are neither men's *oríkì* nor women's *oríkì*. *Oríkì* in Yorùbáland are gender-free in all regards. My own experience and research demonstrate that lineage *oríkì* are not gender-specified. In my interview with Baálẹ̀ Máyà, I asked her if she had a different *oríkì* from the family *oríkì*. She was puzzled by my question and pointed out to me that her lineage *oríkì* is the same as any member of the family. In the autobiographical pamphlet she gave to me, she had a section on *oríkì* of the different village heads that have ruled Máyà, including herself.[85]

Barber's own work shows clearly that *oríkì* is neither male-exclusive in subject matter nor female-exclusive in performance or composition. The limitation of her research is actually a limitation imposed by her insistence on using Western gender categories even as she correctly asserts that the Yorùbá world is not dichotomized into male and female. More specifically, she insufficiently appreciates the fact that the *oríkì* of the lineage are as much the product of female as of male members of the lineage. The character and identity of a lineage derive from the personality and remarkable deeds of any member of the lineage, which are then generalized to all the other members. The following passage is a good illustration of the nature of lineage *oríkì*. Barber presents us with the *oríkì* of Babalọlá, a prominent male member of the Ẹlẹ́mọ̀sọ́ lineage:

> Babalọlá, the child opens its arms, the child delights its father,
> The way my father walks delights the Iyalode.
> Enigboori, child of the father named Banlebu ["meet me at the dye-pits"],
> *If people don't find me in the place where they boil ijokun dye,*
> *They'll meet me where we go early to pound indigo,*
> Enigboori, that's how they salute the father called "Banlebu."[86]

In the interpretation of this *oríkì* provided to Barber by the elderly sister of Babalọlá, it becomes clear that the italicized lines are actually a reference to a daughter of the compound who is noted for her sexual liaisons. The lines mean: "If you don't find her in one place, you'll surely find her in another" — in other words, in the house of *some* man or other![87] Yet these are the lines from a lineage *oríkì* that is being used to salute a prominent male member of the family. What this shows is that the character and identity of the lineage as projected in *oríkì orílẹ̀* (lineage *oríkì*) are an emblematization of characteristics derived from past observations coupled with present behavior of any person in the lineage regardless of anasex. The more fundamental implication of this fact has to do with the nature of Ọ̀yọ́ lineages. The *ìdílé* (lineage) have been called patrilineages in the scholarly literature, but as I showed in chapter 2, the concept distorts both what actually goes on inside these lineages and the local conception of them. Mothers and female offspring are as central in the determination of the identity and characteristics of these institutions as are fathers and male offspring. The patrilineage is not so much the father's house as the father's house as inflected by the mother's identity. Thus, children of the same father but different mothers are not inserted into the lineage in the same way; neither would their personal *oríkì* be identical, as these also draw from the mother's background.

In a Western-dominated world in which gender is invoked as a fundamental and universal category, there is a preoccupation with establishing gender. It must be understood, however, that in the Yorùbá past, gender categories were not part of the frame of reference; gender, therefore, cannot be used as the fault line in the reconstruction of the past. In the contemporary period, invocations of gender have to take into account the history of genderization, scholars themselves being a part of that process, which is ongoing.

The Residualization of "Women" and the Feminization of the *Ìyálóde*

Thus far, this discussion of the process of grafting gender onto Yorùbá history and culture has addressed the creation of "men," as exemplified by the masculinization of universal authority categories such as the aristocracy in general and the *aláàfin* in particular. Running *pari passu* was a complementary and equally important process, the creation of "women" by scholars in general. This process rests on acceptance by these scholars of three questionable assumptions: first, the genderization of Yorùbá society, a process in which the universal world-sense is split into male and female; second, the notion that male dominance and privilege are the natural manifestations of these differentiations; and, third, that by implication the residual societal attribute of deprivation is ascribed to females. When those who assume that men are the measure of all things are confronted with incontrovertible evidence about anafemales who were in positions of power and authority, they tend to explain the latter away as exceptions, as temporary representatives of men or male interests, or as stooges of the oppressive patriarchy; or they try to reduce their significance by positing that they held sway over anafemales only.

Against a background in which social identity is gendered and an idea of the "status of women" is introduced, projecting anafemales as forever unempowered, the work of pioneering Yorùbá social historian Bolanle Awe — well known for going beyond the event-centeredness that characterizes the field of history — has been invaluable in presenting an alternative tableau. In an essay entitled "The Iyalode in the Traditional Political System of the Yorùbá,"[88] she endeavored to place the office of the *iyálóde* squarely among the pantheon of Yorùbá political positions in which it belonged. There is no mention of an *iyálóde* in Johnson's account of the powerful mother-officials who dominated the political hierarchy in the Ọ̀yọ́ metropolis. The person he identified as being in charge of the market is the ẹni-ọjà: "She is in charge of the King's [aláàfin's] markets, and enjoys all the perquisites accruing therefrom.... She has under her (1) the Olosi who has joint responsibility with her for the market, and (2) the Aroja, or market keeper, an officer whose duty it is to keep order, and arrange the management of the market, and who actually resides there."[89] Johnson's omission suggests that there was no iyálóde in Old Ọ̀yọ́ and lends credence to the idea that the title is more associated with the provinces and was elaborated at a later time period, probably with the development of new states like Ìbàdàn following the fall of Old Ọ̀yọ́ in 1836. In my conversations with the Ṣọ̀ún of Ògbómọ̀ṣọ́, Ọba Oyěwùmí,[90] he mentioned that there are a number of chieftaincy titles in present-day Ògbómọ̀ṣọ́, such as ọ̀tún and òsì, that were constituted only in recent history owing to the influence of Ìbàdàn.[91] He went on to say that Ìbàdàn is a republic, whereas Ògbómọ̀ṣọ́ and Ọ̀yọ́ are monarchies; thus these newly imported chieftaincy titles were at odds with the monarchical organization. I asked whether the title iyálóde, which is now present in Ògbómọ̀ṣọ́, is one of the Ìbàdàn imports. Ọba Oyèwùmí pointed out that the title was not traditional to the Ògbómọ̀ṣọ́ polity. In my interview with the iyálóde of Ògbómọ̀ṣọ́, Olóyè Ọládọjà Àdùkẹ́ Sánní,[92] she said that the first iyálóde was installed in Ògbómọ̀ṣọ́ only during the time of the Yorùbá wars. In fact, she noted that the pioneer iyálóde had been conferred with the title in recognition of her bravery during those troubled times. This would make the title a relatively recent addition in Ògbómọ̀ṣọ́.

Johnson mentions an iyálóde in some of the provincial towns, but his account does not tie her to the market, suggesting a wider arena of power. Nevertheless, an interrogation of the office of iyálóde is necessary to this study, given the way in which the office has been elaborated as a prototype of female leadership and its deployment without regard for historical time and differences in pan-Yorùbá political organizations.

The particular appellation iyálóde is associated with Ìbàdàn in particular, a state that emerged within the Ọ̀yọ́ political system in the nineteenth century. It was also known in Abẹ́òkúta, another new state. In other polities, such as Àkúrẹ́ and Òndó, there were two chieftaincy titles, arísẹ and lóbùn, respectively, which were also known to be held by women. However, it should not be assumed that all these titles had the same meaning and function throughout Yorùbáland, since to do so would be to level and homogenize political posts that were in operation in different politicocultural centers at different historical time periods. Indeed, a number of scholars have documented the differences in the organization of Yorùbá states, showing why chieftaincy titles and the bases and functions of particular title-holders cannot be assumed to be the same. Awe acknowledges this when she observes, "It is clear that it is impossible to make sweeping generalizations about the position of the Iyalode or of women generally within the Yorùbá political system."[93]

Given the interrogatory mission and ongoing scrutiny of the building blocks of knowledge and the reappraisal of Yorùbá historiography, it is perhaps cogent to reexamine some of the basic assumptions in the historiography of the *iyálóde*. The title *iyálóde* means "mother of public affairs," and according to Awe, the holder of that office was the voice or spokesperson of women in government:

> Her most important qualifications were her proven ability as a leader to articulate the feelings of women, . . . and . . . , in contrast to the male chiefs, who would be involved in the organization of war, the reception of foreign visitors, and so on, it is not unlikely that the women chiefs would be involved in the settlement of disputes between women, the cleanliness of the markets, and other female concerns.[94]

It is apparent that these observations are based on several erroneous assumptions: that women and men constituted separate social categories with differing interests; that the office of *iyálóde* represented a women's chieftaincy system separate from and parallel to that of men; that the female anatomy was a primary qualification for the office of *iyálóde*; and that the alleged predominance of females in trading occupations implies that markets were female concerns. The prefix *iyá* (mother) suggests anafemale. But it also means "older woman"; therefore, it is an indication of adulthood, seniority, and consequently responsibility and status. Thus *iyálóde* can also be translated as "older anafemale in charge of public affairs." *Ìyá* and *bàbá* are normally used as prefixes in describing the engagements of a particular adult female or male, respectively. Thus a male chief is called *bàbá ìsàlè* (older male, leader); a female food seller is *iyá olónje* (older female seller of food); and a male cloth-weaver is *bàbá aláso* (adult male maker of cloth).

However, the other part of the title — *òde* (public affairs) — goes beyond the person, indicating that the responsibilities of the office encompass a much wider domain than is commonly attributed to it. Someone in charge of the markets would have had authority over the community's economy, regulating supply and demand, product pricing, allocation of stalls, tolls, fees, and fines. Furthermore, if the background of Yorùbá polities, which were heavily engaged in warfare, and the emergence of Ìbàdàn or Abéòkúta as military states are considered, the connection between war and the economy becomes clearer. Hence it was perhaps no coincidence that in the nineteenth century, Ìyáọlá, the first *iyálóde* of Ìbàdàn, was given the title because of her contributions to Ìbàdàn's war efforts. According to Awe, "Like the male chiefs, she contributed her quota of soldiers to Ìbàdàn's ad hoc army where a corps of domestic slaves were trained to fight."[95]

Similarly, Madam Tinubu, after an illustrious career, received the title of *iyálóde* of Abéòkúta in "appreciation of her bold deeds." These included the supply of guns and ammunition to Abéòkúta soldiers during the wars between the states of Abéòkúta and Dahomey.[96] As for Efunsetan, another *iyálóde* of Ìbàdàn, her interest in public affairs extended to foreign affairs. Well known for her extensive wealth, she constituted a formidable opposition to the ruler of Ìbàdàn, À[à]rè Látósà. Awe records that "she challenged his [Latosa's] foreign policy that alienated Ìbàdàn from her neighbors, and resisted his domestic policy that tended toward the establishment of sole rule, contrary to Ìbàdàn's tradition of oligarchic government."[97] Thus from Awe's accounts, the careers of the individual *iyálóde* — Iyaola, Madam Tinubu, and Efúnsetán — suggest that they were not circumscribed by any considerations of anasex. The general national interests, such as the economy, domestic policy, defense, and foreign affairs, did not fall outside their purview.

There is also the question of which women the *iyálóde* were supposed to be concerned with. The general assumption is that a major constituency were anafemale traders. Because of the predominance of anafemales in the occupation of trading, in the literature, the term "trader" has become virtually synonymous with "market woman," which in turn is used interchangeably with the word "woman." However, an *egbé* (guild) of traders is misrepresented as a women's group, for traders were not categorized on the basis of anatomy. Rather the type of goods, trade distance, and so on, determined the composition of individual *egbé*. Hence, for instance, even if all food sellers were anafemales and belonged to a food sellers' guild, this did not make it a women's group, because the qualification for membership derived not from the anatomy but from the commonality of economic activity. My discussion of statistical categoricalism in the previous chapter dealt with the issue of whether a legitimate argument can be made about the statistical prevalence of anafemales in a particular trade. Suffice it to say here that the question of gender and numbers does not arise from the Òyó frame of reference; it, of course, fits in very well with the Western bio-logic framework. The question itself already presupposes gender cat-

gender as a nature

egories as a natural way of organizing society, a claim that is challenged by Ọ̀yọ́ cosmology and social organization.

Thus if the *iyálóde* had jurisdiction over disputes within the market-place or regulatory responsibility for environmental sanitation, or if they served as a channel for communication between people in the market-ing profession and governmental authorities, describing them as being concerned with women's interests would seem to be the result of a con-ceptual straitjacket. It constitutes a failure to view the *iyálóde*'s functions comprehensively.

This brings the discussion to the task of determining what in Old Ọ̀yọ́ society could have constituted a distinctly women's political inter-est, which the *iyálóde* or any feminized female official was supposed to represent. From what is known about Old Ọ̀yọ́'s political and social or-ganization, anatomical females were, alongside males, arrayed around diverse interests deriving from status, occupation, lineage, and so on. Some of these interests, such as those of the *aya* (anafemales married into a lineage) and *ọkọ* (anafemales born into a lineage), sometimes conflicted. Within the Old Ọ̀yọ́ political system, the most significant conflicting tendencies were between the *aláàfin*, on the one hand, and the *ọ̀yọ́ mèsì* (the council of chiefs), on the other.[98] In the elabo-rate palace administrative machinery that protected the interests of the *aláàfin* against the *ọ̀yọ́ mèsì* were the *ayaba* (royal consorts), "old moth-ers" who occupied positions including the royal priesthood of Ṣàngó, the national religious denomination of *òrìṣà* worship. In the adminis-tration there were also *ìlàrís* (anafemale and anamale), some of whom served as bodyguards. As Awe observes of the powerful mothers in the palace: "They were . . . in a position of great influence because they had direct access to the king. Even the *Iwarefa,* his highest officials, had to go through them to arrange rituals, festivals and communal la-bor. Tributaries of the Ọ̀yọ́ Kingdom could only approach the Aláàfin through them."[99] Awe further suggests that their positions were said to "undermine the effectiveness of the *iyálóde*" (that is if, in fact, there was such a chieftaincy). The disjuncture between the powerful mother-officials and the alleged *iyálóde* suggests a dissonance that preempts the homogenization of anafemales as a sociopolitical category.

The foregoing again illustrates that a gendered framework of analysis is an alien imposition that seriously distorts the rendering of pre-colonial Yorùbá history. Considering that anatomical maleness was not a qualification for other chieftaincy posts and political representation of corporate interest by ward chiefs, presenting the office of the *iyálóde* as one for which the primary qualification was anatomical femaleness re-sults in the exceptionalization of the *iyálóde*. Similarly, presenting them

pre-colonial Yorùbá history

Woman motherhood exception

as being concerned solely with women's interests, which in precolonial Yorùbáland were not separate from general lineage and societal interests, has the consequence of feminizing the post and thereby whittling down its significance.

Images of History: Ọ̀yọ́ Art and the Gendered Eye

In light of the prevailing thesis of this book that Yorùbá society was not organized along gender lines, the focus of this section is to analyze the images of Èṣìẹ́. These are a collection of over one thousand stone sculptures located in Èṣìẹ́, a Yorùbá town of Ìgbómìnà composition in present-day Kwara State. Most Ìgbómìnà claim Ọ̀yọ́ origins. The images — soapstone figures representing men, women, children, and animals — have been dated to the twelfth to fourteenth centuries; they range in height from five and one-half inches to over forty inches. Scholars have long been concerned about the relationship between art and the social order and whether art reflects society or responds to the same structural principle as the social organization. In an essay on Yorùbá verbal and visual arts, M. T. Drewal and H. J. Drewal correctly assert that "the structure of the arts and the structure of society are homologous and reflect Yorùbá aesthetic preference, but, more importantly, these structures are a concrete manifestations of the Yorùbá conception of the nature of existence and being. They articulate ontological thought."[100]

The origins of the stone images of Èṣìẹ́, as they came to be known, remain a great mystery, especially as they apparently did not originate in the present site but seem to have been transported there. This is interesting because many of the pieces weigh over fifty pounds (some weigh over one hundred pounds). They were brought to the attention of the Western world in 1933 by H. G. Ramshaw, school superintendent for the Church Missionary Society (CMS). Subsequently, a number of European scholars visited the site and wrote about the Èṣìẹ́ sculptures. The most comprehensive work to date, *Stone Images of Èṣìẹ́, Nigeria,* is by Philip Stevens; it was published in 1978. The book fulfills the twofold mission of evaluating the ethnographic and archaeological data and presenting an extensive photographic catalogue.[101] The aim of this section is to interrogate Stevens's gender-specific interpretation of the sculptures and to evaluate the assumption of historians of Yorùbá art about the naturalness of gender categories. Ethnographic data should provide clues to comprehending the images and allow for a reverse dialectic — an interpretation of the images as clues to ethnography.

Stevens describes the variety of the sculptures in the Èṣìẹ́ collection:

Most are seated on stools; a few are standing. Some apparently reveling, laughing, playing musical instruments; most of them are armed as if for war. Their features suggest a great diversity of influences.... The figures have been propitiated since the latter part of the 18th century when the present inhabitants claim to have arrived on the site and found them.[102]

The Èsìé images are a concrete manifestation of the Ọ̀yọ́-Yorùbá conception of the nature of being and existence as determined by lineage membership and social roles, which are not defined by gender. At the heart of one of the gendered renderings of the Èsìé images is the fact that many of the figures are carrying arms, including daggers, bows, and quivers. The sculptures appear to depict social roles. Stevens writes, "Fully one-third (about 325) of the pieces are female, and of these about a quarter (85) are armed, as if for war."[103]

Using the framework of a lineage-determined division of labor, rather than a gender-based one, it is possible that the figures, both female and male, represent the ọmọ-ilé (offspring) of one the lineages associated with warfare and hunting, such as Èṣọ́, Òjè, or Ilé Ọlọ́dẹ. Thus the arms-bearing females are more likely to be ọmọ (offspring) than aya (anafemales married into the lineage), and, as has been demonstrated in the previous chapter, the position of a female offspring in a lineage did not differ from that of the male, both deriving role authority from lineage membership. Stevens, however, perceives these "militaristic females" as aberrant and then proceeds to genderize their weapons: "Of the total number of such militaristic figures, an interesting correlation does appear: men are archers and wielders of daggers; the women carry cutlasses. In fact, no figure that is positively female (T35 is questionable) wears a quiver; only a few of the males hold cutlasses."[104] In this manner, gender is fostered as a given, and realities that cannot be accounted for by this fabrication are thus exceptionalized. Interestingly, once the notion that all the figures holding cutlasses are female is accepted, it becomes virtually impossible to look at a cutlass-carrying figure without seeing a female. In other words, once the sex of the figures is assumed and the sex-appropriateness of the weapons is assumed, then the weapons become a way of identifying sex and vice versa.[105] The process is at best circular. It should be reiterated that there was nothing in Ọ̀yọ́ culture that dissociated anafemales from carrying cutlasses or machetes. Art historian C. O. Adepegba in his analysis of the metal staff of Òrìṣà Oko, the god of agriculture, had this to say: "The Yorùbá word for staff seems inappropriate, as the square-ended, flat-edged object resembles [more] a sword or cutlass than a staff....The staff is meant for female devotees: male devotees carry strung cowries."[106] Even if one were to subscribe to the idea of gender-specificity in Yorùbá life, the preceding assessment of Òrìṣà oko by Adepegba shows that "women" are the cutlass-carriers, which is diametrically opposed to Stevens's working assumption that male figures are the more likely to carry weapons.

This leads to a fundamental question: How are viewers able to determine the sex of each of the figures? Stevens seems to acknowledge that apprehending sex in Yorùbá discourse can be an ambiguous adventure, and he proffers some guidelines:

> In West African sculpture, determining the intended sex of the fig-ure is difficult. Where they are exposed, the genitals are certain indicators, but the breasts are sometimes equally pronounced in both sexes. Hairstyles, jewelry and dress do not appear to cor-relate sexually in the Èsìẹ collection.... I have relied on breast accentuation.... Where the breasts are more than mere nubs, I have designated the figure as female.[107]

But using the breasts as an index of gender still has certain limitations. In real life, many women do not have breast accentuation, which is prob-ably a better indication of female youthfulness — prime motherhood — than just femaleness. Also, several figures are wearing bow straps cov-ering their breasts or nipples, which makes it impossible to determine breast accentuation. Consequently, Stevens's statistical analysis of how many figures are female and his correlation of sex to weapon type re-veal more about the workings of a gendered gaze than it does about the sculptures themselves.

The art historian John Pemberton has written about the Èsìẹ images as part of his interpretation of the Ọ̀yọ́ visual world and religious ico-nography. However, it appears that his representations are not only gendered but illustrate what a number of feminist and other scholars have postulated about Western visual arts: that is, the gaze is always a male gaze — the beholder is always male. In a beautifully illus-trated book entitled Yorùbá: Nine Centuries of Art and Thought, Henry Drewal, John Pemberton, and Rowland Abiodun display samples of Yorùbá art forms with commentary, situating them in their different lo-cations. Pemberton, in the section on Ọ̀yọ́ art, comments on one of the Èsìẹ pieces that is identified as a male:

> Seated male figure, Esie... The artist conveys the authority of his subject in the composure of the face and the directness of the gaze, as well as the seated position and gesture.... The expressive power

of this carving is that the artist not only depicts a social role but makes one aware of a person who held the role.... There is a fleshy quality in the once-powerful shoulders and arms. One feels the weight of the man in the abdomen as it protrudes above the sash and in the spread of the hips as he sits on the stool.[108]

He also comments on a comparable (in posture and composure) figure that he identified as female:

> Seated female figure... The Esie female figure holds a cutlass, which rests on her right shoulder as a symbol of office.... Note the delicate scarification marks on her forehead. The height of her elaborate coiffure is equal to that of her face, emphasizing the importance of the head.... The head and face of the woman are exquisitely modeled. She has an elaborate hairstyle, powerful forehead above deeply recessed eyes, and a fullness of the lips. The strings of beads around her neck, her youthful breasts, and the fullness of her abdomen are evidence of her beauty and power as a woman.[109]

Above we established that among the Èsìé figures there is no gender-specificity, a principle that would cover coiffure, scarification, and adornment. Given that, the marked difference in how these two images are presented becomes very apparent. The male image is discussed in terms of social roles, the female in terms of adornment. The authority of the man is vested within him — composure, gaze, gesture; the woman's authority derives from a symbol. The spread of the male's abdomen spells weightiness, the fullness of the female, beauty. Even where the word "power" is used to describe her, it is in the context of her womanhood — the "power of a woman." Power to do what? In popular Nigerian parlance today, this allusion would be taken to mean "bottom power." In other words, her power is not about authority but derives from her ability to exercise influence based on the commodification of sexuality. Such a delivery mimics the presentation of female beauty to a male voyeur in European art.

Yet, using the ungendered model postulated by this work, it is possible to comprehend that the Èsìé figures are not depicting power and authority in a sex-specific manner. For example, the youthfulness of some of the identifiable females and their depiction as figures with authority could suggest that they are in their natal lineage (probably a hunting one), which then explains the naturalness of their carrying arms. From the perspective of using the images as evidence for certain social claims, this interpretation suggests that the figures are best analyzed as

Nothing sex specific

a collection — a reflection of the prevalent communal ethos — not as individual characters without a context. As I showed in the previous chapter, until recently war in Yorùbáland was not conceptualized as a masculine activity.

The gendered gaze is also apparent in Pemberton's representations of religious iconography, exemplified by that of Ṣàngó, the thunder god. For example, all his selections of religious worship show female devotees and priests. Most of them are in what he interprets to be subservient positions, whereas most of the males are in authority positions. Yet it is clear from other sources that even the *aláàfin* "prostrates before the god Ṣàngó, and before those possessed of the deity calling them 'father.'"[110] According to Pemberton, "The unpredictable, capricious, self-serving *òrìṣà* is also the one who imparts his beauty to the woman with whom he sleeps. He is the giver of children."[111] Such language is imbued with implicit sexual references that suggest that the female priests worship the god as a male sexual figure. Pemberton claims that Ṣàngó is praised by women in a song:

> Where shall I find *Jebooda*, my husband?
> He dances as he sings with us.
> He-who-destroys-the-wicked-with-his-truth . . . ,
> He-who-spends-a-long-time-in-Oya's-grove;
> For when we wake up,
> You who serve the whole world, father of *Adeoti*,
> I will pay homage to you my father.[112]

Contrary to Pemberton's assumption, it is not only "women" who worship Ṣàngó. The term "husband" is a mistranslation of the Yorùbá word ọkọ in the text and in no way constitutes evidence that only females use such a chant. Ṣàngó is the ọkọ of his worshipers because he is the house-owner and they are the outsiders. It is accepted terminology for devotees and priests of òrìṣà (deities or gods) to be called ìyàwó (consorts). Recall S. O. Babayemi's assertion that "male worshippers, . . . like the female members, . . . are referred to as wives of Ṣàngó."[113] Indeed, Pemberton does include a photograph of a "wife" of another god, Òrìṣà Oko, in the collection.

The relationship between Ṣàngó and his congregation is neither gendered nor sexualized. Ṣàngó is not the only òrìṣà who gives children. There are at least two female deities, Oya and Ọ̀ṣun, who are specifically worshiped for their ability to give children. Therefore, it is erroneous to attribute Ṣàngó's children-giving powers to his male anatomy.

While the sexualization of Ṣàngó worship may have made it difficult for Pemberton to acknowledge the òrìṣà's male devotees, the same cannot be said for anthropologist James Matory, who reveals another facet of the sexualized view. He interprets the categorization of the male adherents as *ìyàwó* — which he glosses as "wife" — as a sign of symbolic if not actual homosexuality. In the Geertzian mode of "thick descriptions [inventions]," his interpretations are so thick they curdle. Thus in Matory's writing, Ṣàngó priests appear as drag queens and transvestites. His dissertation, "Sex and the Empire That Is No More: A Ritual History of Women's Power among the Oyo-Yorùbá," explores the symbolism of the Yorùbá verb *gùn,* which he glosses as "to mount." He explicates: "Indigenous lay testimony illustrates Oyo's rise and fall in dramatic images of gender relations. This imagery I, along with other scholars, have glossed as 'mounting,' which in Ọ̀yọ́ religion and politics structures the delegation of authority from god to king, king to subject, husband to wife, and ancestor to descendant."[114]

Obviously, the very premise on which Matory rests his study is alien to the Yorùbá conception. Categories like "king" do not exist; the so-called lines of authority he presents are fabrications in that authority does not flow in the directions he has articulated; and of course the gender categories he depicts are his own inventions. No flow of authority between *ọkọ* and *ìyàwó,* for instance, can be characterized as a gender flow since both categories encompass anamales and anafemales. Likewise, his introduction of homosexuality into Yorùbá discourse is nothing but an imposition of yet another foreign model. Wande Abimbola, a scholar of Yorùbá history and oral traditions, has raised doubts about the sexualized interpretation of Ọ̀yọ́ history. As Matory records, Abimbola questions "whether the verb *gùn* carries the implications of the English verb to mount.... Concomitantly, he believes that I [Matory] exaggerate the gender correlates of Spirit possession (*gigun*) in the Ọ̀yọ́-Yorùbá context."[115] From the perspective of the present work, sexuality, like gender, is considered to be a social and historical construct. Therefore, in order to determine if a sexualized interpretation is applicable to the Old Ọ̀yọ́ setting, it becomes necessary to define what is normally anamale and anafemale in the culture, noting the historical time period and the changes through time.

The case of hair adornment springs to mind. Ṣàngó priests were noted for their hairstyle — a cornrowed hairdo traditionally called *kòlésè.* Ṣàngó worship was the official religion of the Ọ̀yọ́ court. This hairstyle is often interpreted by scholars as a sign that the priests were trying to enact femaleness. For example, Babayemi writes that for male worshipers to be accepted, "they must dress up their hair as women." While there is a contemporary notion that hair-"doing" and adornment are associated with only females, that notion is recent, not timeless, and is by no means universal — witness the elaborate hairstyles of many of the Èsìẹ stone figures.

In Ogbómọ̀ṣọ́, I conducted interviews with the Àwíṣẹ Ẹlẹ́sìn Ìbílẹ̀, chief Ọyátọ́pẹ́ (practitioner of indigenous religion), who is also the priest of Ọya (the female god).[116] His hair was in braids, and he told me that priests of Ọya, just like Ṣàngó priests, after initiation are never to cut their hair; therefore, for ease of grooming, they put it in braids. The emphasis here is not on braids but on never cutting the hair. Consequently, it is possible that the focus of many scholars on braids is a misguided emphasis in terms of deciphering meaning. The real issue is not why the priests wear braids but why they do not cut their hair.

Nevertheless, hairstyle does have significance in Ọ̀yọ́ history. The ilàrí were a special class of bureaucrats and messengers for aláàfin named for their hairstyle. According to Johnson, "the term Ìlàrí denotes parting of the head, from the peculiar way their hair is done. They are of both sexes and number some hundreds, even as many as the King [aláàfin] desires." It is also common in current times to see male rulers and chiefs in Eastern Yorùbáland with cornrowed hair at certain festivals. Consequently, any analysis of hairstyle in Yorùbá society cannot assume gender. Such an enterprise is best done within the context of the symbolism and metaphysics of hair and the orí (head) upon which it stands.[117] This interpretation must also acknowledge the cultural locality and the socioreligious context. For instance, the genesis of the ceremonial coiffure differs from that of the religious coiffure. There are also different styles of cornrows — the kòlẹ́sẹ̀ may have a different symbolism from the ṣùkú style, for example. In light of a host of complexities, it is difficult to sustain the view that male cornrowing is a sign of transvestitism.

Finally, it is proper to assess the existence of institutions like the orò that function today as male-exclusive institutions — when orò rituals are in process in some Ọ̀yọ́ towns, women are confined to their compounds. In light of my thesis that indigenous cultural norms were traditionally gender-free, the most pertinent questions are: What is the origin of the orò institution, and when did it emerge in Ọ̀yọ́? What is the nature of women's exclusion, taking into account the various permutations of the various identities commonly submerged under the concept of women? For example, a restriction on childbearing anafemales has a different meaning than a universal one. If orò is an old institution, did its character change over time? What are its implications with regard to access and the exercise of power for different sections of the population? These are all empirical questions that cannot be answered by simply declaring that orò is off-limits to women. Indeed, from the evidence that we have at this time, we can say that both *orò* and *ògbóni,* another contemporary institution in Yorùbá polities, are relatively new, being nineteenth-century additions to the sociopolitical structure of Ọ̀yọ́. Two historians, B. A. Agiri and J. A. Atanda, have researched the institutions of *orò* and *ògbóni,* respectively. They have also touched upon the linkages of these institutions with the Egúngún cult, which is thoroughly Ọ̀yọ́ and plays a central role in the government of Ọ̀yọ́. According to Agiri, "in the case of Oyo, . . . available evidence suggests that the *Orò* was introduced there during the nineteenth century by the Jabata immigrant group. Here, the paramouncy of the egúngún has never been in doubt. . . . The egúngún are associated with the important religious matters of state."[118] *Obìnrin* do participate in Egúngún, and the most important official (the *ato*) is an anafemale. The marginalization of the *orò* in Ọ̀yọ́ politics is in sharp contrast to the centrality of both the Egúngún and Ṣàngó cults. The marginality of *orò* suggests its newness and foreignness in the Ọ̀yọ́ cultural milieu. The more interesting question then would be how to comprehend the existence in one and the same polity of the dominant Ṣàngó cult, which is controlled by the mothers of the palace, and the *orò,* which purports to exclude women, a gender bias that is said to embrace even the all-powerful *ayaba* (mothers of the palace). Atanda in his consideration of the *ògbóni* cult, which is usually coupled with *orò,* criticizes the interpolation of institutions in New Ọ̀yọ́ into Old Ọ̀yọ́ practices, something Morton Williams[119] had done in his speculations. Atanda concludes:

> Whatever the case, the point being emphasized is that Ogboni cult became a factor in the government of Oyo only with the foundation of the new capital in the nineteenth century. There is therefore no basis for the present tendency of talking of the role of the cult in the government of the Old Oyo Empire which came to an end at the beginning of the nineteenth century and before the cult was introduced into the Oyo polity by Aláàfin Atiba. In other words, the error should be avoided of interpolating what is a nineteenth century phenomenon into the earlier history of Oyo.[120]

There is no question that the nineteenth century was a period of rapid and monumental changes in Ọ̀yọ́, primarily because of the civil wars and their permutations with the increasingly dominant and multivaried presence of Europeans in the society. The impact of the changes of that period are still being felt and acted out; the nature and type of institutional transformations that took place are still not completely understood. The gendering of Ọ̀yọ́ institutions and the attendant patriarchalization are the most important for this study. In the nineteenth century, gender categories and consequent androcentrism became apparent in some of the discourses, institutions, and interpretations of history. In the next chapter, I focus on the period of colonization, that is, the formal establishment of British rule that instituted in a more systematic fashion the gender-biased trends that emerged in the nineteenth century.

Chapter 4

Colonizing Bodies and Minds

GENDER AND COLONIALISM

●●

THEORISTS OF COLONIZATION like Frantz Fanon and Albert Memmi tell us that the colonial situation, being a Manichaean world,[1] produces two kinds of people: the colonizer and the colonized (also known as the settler and the native), and what differentiates them is not only skin color but also state of mind.[2] One similarity that is often overlooked is that both colonizers and colonized are presumed male. Colonial rule itself is described as "a manly or husbandly or lordly prerogative."[3] As a process, it is often described as the taking away of the manhood of the colonized. While the argument that the colonizers are men is not difficult to sustain, the idea of the colonized being uniformly male is less so. Yet the two following passages from Fanon are typical of the portrayal of the native in the discourses on colonization: "Sometimes people wonder that the native rather than give his wife a dress, buys instead a transistor radio."[4] And, "The look that the native turns on the settler's town is a look of lust, a look of envy; it expresses *his* dreams of possession — all manner of possession: to sit at the settler's table, to sleep in the settler's bed, with *his wife* if possible. The colonized man is an envious man."[5] But what if the native were female, as indeed many of them were? How is this feeling of envy and desire to replace the colonizer manifested or realized for women? Or, for that matter, does such a feeling exist for women?

The histories of both the colonized and the colonizer have been written from the male point of view — women are peripheral if they appear at all. While studies of colonization written from this angle are not necessarily irrelevant to understanding what happened to native females, we must recognize that colonization impacted males and females in similar and dissimilar ways. Colonial custom and practice stemmed from "a world view which believes in the absolute superiority of the human over the nonhuman and the subhuman, the *masculine* over the *feminine* . . . , and the modern or progressive over the traditional or the savage."[6]

121

Therefore, the colonizer differentiated between male and female bodies and acted accordingly. Men were the primary target of policy, and, as such, they were the natives and so were visible. These facts, from the standpoint of this study, are the justification for considering the colonial impact in gender terms rather than attempting to see which group, male or female, was the most exploited. The colonial process was sex-differentiated insofar as the colonizers were male and used gender identity to determine policy. From the foregoing, it is clear that any discussion of hierarchy in the colonial situation, in addition to employing race as the basis of distinctions, should take into account its strong gender component. The two racially distinct and hierarchical categories of the colonizer and the native should be expanded to four, incorporating the gender factor. However, race and gender categories obviously emanate from the preoccupation in Western culture with the visual and hence physical aspects of human reality (see above). Both categories are a consequence of the bio-logic of Western culture. Thus, in the colonial situation, there was a hierarchy of four, not two, categories. Beginning at the top, these were: men (European), women (European), native (African men), and Other (African women). Native women occupied the residual and unspecified category of the Other.

In more recent times, feminist scholars have sought to rectify the male bias in the discourses on colonization by focusing on women. One major thesis that emerged from this effort is that African women suffered a "double colonization": one form from European domination and the other from indigenous tradition imposed by African men. Stephanie Urdang's book *Fighting Two Colonialisms* is characteristic of this perspective.[7] While the depth of the colonial experience for African women is expressed succinctly by the idea of doubling, there is no consensus about what is being doubled. From my perspective, it is not colonization that is two, but the forms of oppression that flowed from the process for native females. Hence, it is misleading to postulate two forms of colonization because both manifestations of oppression are rooted in the hierarchical race/gender relations of the colonial situation. African females were colonized by Europeans as Africans and as African women. They were dominated, exploited, and inferiorized as Africans together with African men and then separately inferiorized and marginalized as African women.

It is important to emphasize the combination of race and gender factors because European women did not occupy the same position in the colonial order as African women. A circular issued by the British colonial government in Nigeria shows the glaringly unequal position of these two groups of women in the colonial system. It states that

"African women should be paid at 75% of the rates paid to the European women."[8] Furthermore, whatever the "status" of indigenous customs, the relations between African men and women during this period can be neither isolated from the colonial situation nor described as a form of colonization, particularly because African men were subjects themselves.[9] The racial and gender oppressions experienced by African women should not be seen in terms of addition, as if they were piled one on top of the other. In the context of the United States, Elizabeth Spelman's comment on the relationship between racism and sexism is relevant. She writes: "How one form of oppression is experienced is influenced by and influences how another form is experienced."[10] Though it is necessary to discuss the impact of colonization on specific categories of people, ultimately its effect on women cannot be separated from its impact on men because gender relations are not zero-sum — men and women in any society are inextricably bound.

This chapter will examine specific colonial policies, practices, and ideologies and ascertain how they impacted males and females in different ways. In this regard, the gender identity of the colonizers is also important. At the level of policy, I shall look at administrative, educational, legal, and religious systems. It will become clear that certain ideologies and values flowed out of these policies and practices, and in an often unstated, but no less profound, way they shaped the behavior of the colonized. Colonization was a multifaceted process involving different kinds of European personnel, including missionaries, traders, and state officials. Hence, I treat the process of Christianization as an integral part of the colonial process. Finally, colonization was, above all, the expansion of the European economic system in that "beneath the surface of colonial political and administrative policy lay the unfolding process of capital penetration."[11] The capitalist economic system shaped the particular ways in which colonial domination was effected.

The State of Patriarchy

The imposition of the European state system, with its attendant legal and bureaucratic machinery, is the most enduring legacy of European colonial rule in Africa. The international nation-state system as we know it today is a tribute to the expansion of European traditions of governance and economic organization. One tradition that was exported to Africa during this period was the exclusion of women from the newly created colonial public sphere. In Britain, access to power was gender-based; therefore, politics was largely men's job; and colonization, which is fundamentally a political affair, was no exception. Although both African men and women as conquered peoples were excluded from the higher echelons of colonial state structures, men were represented at the lower levels of government. The system of indirect rule introduced by the British colonial government recognized the male chief's authority at the local level but did not acknowledge the existence of female chiefs. Therefore, women were effectively excluded from all colonial state structures. The process by which women were bypassed by the colonial state in the arena of politics — an arena in which they had participated during the precolonial period — is of particular interest in the following section.

The very process by which females were categorized and reduced to "women" made them ineligible for leadership roles. The basis for this exclusion was their biology, a process that was a new development in Yorùbá society. The emergence of women as an identifiable category, defined by their anatomy and subordinated to men in all situations, resulted, in part, from the imposition of a patriarchal colonial state. For females, colonization was a twofold process of racial inferiorization and gender subordination. In chapter 2, I showed that in pre-British Yorùbá society, anafemales, like the anamales, had multiple identities that were not based on their anatomy. The creation of "women" as a category was one of the very first accomplishments of the colonial state.

In a book on European women in colonial Nigeria, Helen Callaway explores the relationship between gender and colonization at the level of the colonizer. She argues that the colonial state was patriarchal in many ways. Most obviously, colonial personnel was male. Although a few European women were present in a professional capacity as nurses, the administrative branches, which embodied power and authority, excluded women by law.[12] Furthermore, she tells us that the Colonial Service, which was formed for the purpose of governing subject peoples, was

> a male institution in all its aspects: its "masculine" ideology, its military organisation and processes, its rituals of power and hierarchy, its strong boundaries between the sexes. It would have been "unthinkable" in the belief system of the time even to consider the part women might play, other than as nursing sisters, who had earlier become recognised for their important "feminine" work.[13]

It is not surprising, therefore, that it was unthinkable for the colonial government to recognize female leaders among the peoples they colonized, such as the Yorùbá.

Likewise, colonization was presented as a "man-sized" job — the ultimate test of manhood — especially because the European death-rate in

West Africa at this time was particularly high. Only the brave-hearted could survive the "white man's grave," as West Africa was known at the time. According to Callaway, Nigeria was described again and again as a man's country in which women[14] (European women) were "out of place" in a double sense of physical displacement and the symbolic sense of being in an exclusively male territory. Mrs. Tremlett, a European woman who accompanied her husband to Nigeria during this period, lamented about the position of European women: "I often found myself reflecting rather bitterly on the insignificant position of a woman in what is practically a man's country. . . . If there is one spot on earth where a woman feels of no importance whatever, it is in Nigeria at the present day."[15] If the women of the colonizer were so insignificant, then one could only imagine the position of the "other" women, if their existence was acknowledged at all.

Yet on the eve of colonization there were female chiefs and officials all over Yorùbáland. Ironically, one of the signatories to the treaty that was said to have ceded Ìbàdàn to the British was Lànlátù, an *iyálóde*, an anafemale chief.[16] The transformation of state power to male-gender power was accomplished at one level by the exclusion of women from state structures. This was in sharp contrast to Yorùbá state organization, in which power was not gender-determined.

The alienation of women from state structures was particularly devastating because the nature of the state itself was undergoing transformation. Unlike the Yorùbá state, the colonial state was autocratic. The African males designated as chiefs by the colonizers had much more power over the people than was vested in them traditionally. In British West Africa in the colonial period, (male) chiefs lost their sovereignty while increasing their powers over the people,[17] although we are to believe that their powers derived from "tradition" even where the British created their own brand of "traditional chiefs." Martin Chanock's astute comment on the powers of chiefs in colonial Africa is particularly applicable to the Yorùbá situation: "British officials, . . . where they came across a chief, . . . intended to invest *him* retroactively not only with a greater range of authority than he had before but also with authority of a different type. There seemed to be no way of thinking about chiefly authority . . . which did not include judicial power."[18] Thus male chiefs were invested with more power over the people while female chiefs were stripped of power. Through lack of recognition, their formal positions soon became attenuated.

At another level, the transfer of judicial power from the community to the council of male chiefs proved to be particularly negative for women at a time when the state was extending its tentacles to an increasing number of aspects of life. In pre-British Yorùbá society, adjudication of disputes rested with lineage elders. Therefore, very few matters came under the purview of the ruler and the council of chiefs. But in the colonial administration, the Native Authority System, with its customary courts, dealt with all civil cases including marriage, divorce, and adultery.

It is precisely at the time that the state was becoming omnipotent that women were excluded from its institutions. This omnipotence of the state was a new tradition in Yorùbá society, as it was in many African societies. The omnipotence of the state has deep roots in European politics. Fustel De Coulanges's analysis of the Greek city-states in antiquity attests to this fact:

> There was nothing independent in man; his body belonged to the state, and was devoted to its defence. . . . If the city had need of money, it could order the women to deliver up their jewels. Private life did not escape the omnipotence of the state. The Athenian law, in the name of religion, forbade men to remain single. Sparta punished not only those who remained single, but those who married late. At Athens, the state could prescribe labor, and at Sparta idleness. *It exercised its tyranny in the smallest things;* at Locri the laws forbade men to drink pure wine; at Rome, Miletus and Marseilles, wine was forbidden to women.[19]

Remarkably, Edward Shorter, writing about European societies, echoes De Coulanges's earlier observations: "Traditional European communities regulated such matters as marital sexuality or the formation of the couple. What may be startling, however, is the extent to which these affairs were removed from informal regulation by public opinion and *subjected to public policy.*"[20] To mention a few examples: there was a "fornication penalty" against women who were pregnant out of wedlock — no bridal crowns for pregnant brides; and before a man was allowed to join a guild, the guild insisted "not only that [the] man himself not be illegitimate (or even conceived before marriage), but that his parents be respectably born as well."[21] Above all, the community had the power to halt marriages.[22] We must not forget that in Europe at this time women were largely excluded from formal public authority; therefore, the public policy referred to by Shorter was male-constituted. No doubt, some of these matters were regulated by African societies, but the regulation was in the hands of the lineage and possibly nonfamilial opinion. Consequently, the probability that any one category of people, such as anafemales, could have been excluded from the decision-making process of the family was much less than in Europe.

It was into this unfortunate tradition of male dominance that Africans were drafted — this was particularly disadvantageous to women because marriage, divorce, and even pregnancy came under the purview of the state. Given the foregoing, it is clear that the impact of colonization was profound and negative for women. Appraisals of the impact of colonization that see certain "benefits" for African women are mistaken in light of the overarching effect of the colonial state, which effectively defined females as "women" and hence second-class colonial subjects unfit to determine their own destiny. The postindependence second-class status of African women's citizenship is rooted in the process of inventing them as women. Female access to membership in the group is no longer direct; access to citizenship is now mediated through marriage, through the "wifization of citizenship."

Yet a group of scholars maintains that colonization was of some benefit to African women. Let us consider two scholars who hold that, in some way, African women in relation to African men benefited from colonial rule. According to Jane Guyer, the idea that African women experienced a decline in status under European rule is misrepresented; in reality, according to her, the status gap between men and women actually narrowed due to a "decline in men's status."[23] For one thing, Guyer assumes that gender identities existed for males and females as groups. Furthermore, this is obviously another way of expressing the male-biased notion that colonization is experienced as loss of manhood by the colonized, thereby projecting the erroneous belief that females had nothing (or nothing as valuable) to lose. This is a narrow interpretation of the effect of colonization in terms of something intangible (called manhood). The colonized also lost their capacity to make their own history without foreign interference; they lost their labor and their land; many lost their lives; and because the colonized comprised both males and females, women, too, evidently suffered these losses. Furthermore, an analysis of the notion of manhood, which is usually left undefined, suggests that it is a masculinized version of the concept of the self. Ashis Nandy has written about the colonial experience as the loss of self for the native.[24] From Nandy's more inclusive standpoint, we can begin to analyze the experience of females on the same terms as that of males.

Nina Mba is another scholar who sees some advantages for African women in colonization. In her study of the effects of British rule on women in southwestern Nigeria, she concludes that the colonial marriage ordinance increased women's legal status because it enhanced women's right to marital property.[25] This view is inaccurate for a number of reasons. To start with, her assumption of the status of wives as identical with the "status of women" leads to her inability to grasp the fact that in the cultures of southwestern Nigeria, the rights of anafemales as wives, as daughters, and as sisters derived from different bases. For example, lack of access to their husband's property did not constitute secondary status for "women" because as daughters and sisters they had rights to both lineages — that is, to their father's, their mother's, and their brothers' properties. In the past, conjugal ọkọ could not inherit their aya's property either. So the apparent provision of "marital property" rights in colonial law was not necessarily a good thing for women because the constitution of a new category of property called marital property meant that wives lost their independent property rights and that, by the same token, husbands could now take over their wives' property. Moreover, the positioning of wives as the beneficiaries of husbands also meant that the rights of some other women, such as mothers, sisters, and daughters, were abrogated as well. We must also remember that many Nigerian societies had polygamous marriage systems, which raises the complex question as to which wives inherited what property, given that some wives had been married to the same husband longer than others. Mba does not deal with any of these issues. Finally, her faith in the legal system as a way of "improving women's status" is unwarranted given that the same colonial system had constituted women into second-class subjects. Legal systems do not work in a vacuum, and men, for reasons that will be discussed later, were in a better position to take advantage of the newfangled legal systems. In sum, the idea that women, or for that matter any category of people among the colonized, benefited from colonial rule does not reflect reality.

Upgrading Males: Sex Discrimination in Colonial Education

The introduction of Christianity and Western education was critical to the stratification of colonial society along both class and gender lines. The initial disadvantage of females in the educational system is arguably the main determinant of women's inferiority and lack of access to resources in the colonial period and indeed in the contemporary period. How did this happen? In the first half-century of British colonization in Yorùbáland, Christianity and Western education were inseparable because they were the monopoly of Christian missionaries. The school was the church, and the church was the school. From the point of view of missionaries, the process of Christianizing and educating the African heathens was to be a process of Europeanization. The goal of the missionaries was to transform African societies, not preserve them.

As envisaged by the missionaries, the African family system was to be targeted for reform and, in turn, to be the vehicle for the "civilization" of these societies. One missionary in Yorùbáland was to betray this bias when he posed the question: "Is it proper to apply the sacred name of a home to a compound occupied by two to six or a dozen men each perhaps with a plurality of wives?"[26] "Spiritual rebirth" and the reconstruction of African societies were intertwined in the minds of the missionaries.

To this end, schools were established to facilitate evangelization. Possibly the most important rationale for the establishment of schools in Yorùbáland during this early period of missionary work is summarized in Baptist missionary T. J. Bowen's book published in 1857:

> Our designs and hopes in regard to Africa, are not simply to bring as many individuals as possible to the knowledge of Christ. We desire to establish the Gospel in the hearts and minds and social life of the people, so that truth and righteousness may remain and flourish among them, without the instrumentality of foreign missionaries. This cannot be done without civilization. To establish the Gospel among any people, they must have Bibles, and therefore must have the art to make them or the money to buy them. They must read the Bible and this implies instruction.[27]

Two important points stand out. First, the European missions needed African missionaries for the purpose of Christianizing their own kind. This is not surprising in that during this period, West Africa was still known as the white man's grave because few Europeans could survive in the environment. Therefore, it was imperative to make use of African personnel if Christianity was to be firmly planted. Second, the ability to read the Bible was seen as critical to the maintenance of individual faith. In light of the foregoing, it is not surprising that males were the target of missionary education. They were seen as potential clerks, catechists, pastors, and missionaries in the service of the church. There was no place for women in these professions except as wives, as helpmates to their husbands, which indeed was the role of the few women missionaries.

In 1842, the very first school was established in Badagri by the Wesleyan mission. By 1845, the Church Missionary Society (CMS) had established a boarding school for boys. Abẹ̀òkúta, further inland, was to become the base and education capital of Yorùbáland. By 1851, three thousand Yorùbá emigrants commonly called Sàró,[28] many of them Christians, had settled in this town. One of the most prominent among them was Samuel Ajayi Crowther, who was to become the first African Anglican bishop. Immediately after they arrived in Abẹ̀òkúta,

Crowther and his wife established two schools, one for boys and one for girls. We are told that Mrs. Crowther's sewing school was very popular, that "even the *babalawos* [diviner-priests] brought their little girls to Mrs. Crowther for instruction."[29] Separate-sex practices were established early, as was reflected even in the curriculum of schools that were coeducational. Ajayi summarizes the timetable of the CMS schools in 1848 as follows:

9.0 a.m.:   Singing, Rehearsals of Scripture Passages, Reading one chapter of Scripture, Prayers.

9.15–12 noon: Grammar, Reading, Spelling, Writing, Geography, Tables [except Wednesday, when there was Catechism in place of Grammar].

2.0–4.0 p.m.:   Ciphering [i.e., Arithmetic], Reading, Spelling, Meaning of Words.

4.0 p.m.:   Closing Prayers.[30]

He adds: "This was more or less repeated every day except Friday, which was devoted to rehearsals of Scripture passages, revision and examinations. Girls followed a similar curriculum, but with important changes. In the afternoon session, from Monday to Thursday, they had Sewing and Embroidery."[31]

Although males were the primary focus of missionary education, it is clear that the education of females was not irrelevant to the missionaries' scheme. In fact, they had a vested interest in producing mothers who would be the foundation of Christian families. They were clearly concerned that the home influence "could be destroying the good seed sown in school."[32] The case of the Harrisons and their female wards demonstrates the thinking of missionaries on what this "home influence" looked like. Mr. and Mrs. Harrison kept the female pupils away from their mothers, who were presumed to be trying "to keep their daughters down to their old bad ways."[33] T. H. Popleslour, a missionary and educator, underlined the importance of the family in the education of the child:

The instruction at school comprehends [*sic*] but a part in education. That in the mouldering [*sic*] of a useful and Christian character the life outside the school must always be taken into consideration in the influences operating for good or ill...The parents can play an important part (if they are Christians). How can a heathen who sees no evil in lying, stealing, deception, fornication... teach morality? How can they teach their children the fear of God?[34]

For the Christian missions, both girls and boys needed to be educated, but for different places in the new society the colonizers were in the process of fabricating. Thus, priority was given to male education, and provisions were made for some form of higher education for males in some places.

In the memoirs of Anna Hinderer we are able to see up close the gender bias in the ways in which the missionaries trained their Yorùbá wards. David and Anna Hinderer were Anglican missionaries who together spent more than seventeen years in Yorùbáland beginning in 1853. In Anna's memoirs, entitled *Seventeen Years in Yorùbá Country,* we get a feel for what life was like in nineteenth-century Ìbàdàn. On arriving in Ìbàdàn, the Hinderers readily found a friend in a prominent chief who immediately sent his two children — a boy and a girl — to live with them to acquire an education. Within a short time, they had sixteen children, males and females, as pupils — including children of other prominent people and a few enslaved children who had been redeemed by the missionaries.[35]

However, as in the case of Anglican schools, the Hinderers had a sex-differentiated curriculum. Mrs. Hinderer tells us that apart from the regular "four Rs"[36] that all the children were taught every day from 9 A.M. until noon, the girls were instructed in sewing and embroidery from noon until 2 P.M.[37] It is only in light of this practice that we understand a statement made by Mrs. Hinderer that seems to cast a shadow on the academic ability of the girls. Commenting on the preparation for the baptisms in 1859, she said, "Their [the children's] preparation and examination has been extremely interesting to my husband; the boys seem to have grasped the root of the matter."[38] Her observation is not surprising considering that the boys had at least an extra two hours of preparation every day while the girls were learning to sew and embroider.

Apart from the day-to-day example of separate spheres for Mr. and Mrs. Hinderer, there were more subtle ways in which gender-biased messages were inculcated into the children. For instance, when Mrs. Hinderer received a parcel of "goodies" from England, she gave "each of the girls one of the nice little handkerchiefs, and a pretty pin to fasten it, to their very great delight; and they looked so neat and tidy the next Sunday at church. The boys had their share of guns and tops, but a pencil and piece of paper is their crowning pleasure."[39] The message was plain: the boys were educated to become clerks, catechists, pastors, missionaries, diplomats, and even politicians. The role of the girls was to look dainty and attractive, ready to become wives and helpmates of these potentially powerful men.

In fact, we have enough information about what some of these pioneering pupils became when they grew up to demonstrate the effectiveness of their gendered training and expectations. Susanna, one of the foundation pupils, became Mrs. Olubi, the wife of Olubi, the Hinderers' very first ward. Anna Hinderer wrote of her: "Mrs. Olubi had four children who kept her very busy."[40] The specter of housewifery for women had appeared on the Yorùbá landscape, contrasting with the traditional Yorùbá practice of all adults (anamale and anafemale) being gainfully employed. In sharp contrast, Susanna's husband, Olubi, became one of the most powerful men in nineteenth-century Yorùbáland. As an officer of the Anglican Church and as a diplomat, he negotiated treaties among the warring Yorùbá states and the British. Of course, unlike his wife, Olubi and some of the other male students had had the benefit of higher education at the CMS training mission in Abẹ́òkúta. There were no such schools for girls until much later. What about the brother/sister duo, children of the prominent Ìbàdàn chief who were also foundation pupils of the Hinderers? Akinyele, the boy, spent fifty-five years as a teacher and pastor and is remembered for his contribution in establishing the Anglican church in Ògbómọ̀ṣọ́, another Yorùbá town. His sister, Yejide, is remembered through her children and does not seem to have established herself in a profession. Konigbagbe, one of the other girls, fared better. She became a teacher, but disappears early from the record.[41] One wonders whether her disappearance had to do with the fact that she got married and took her husband's name: a new "tradition" that was adopted by African families as they became Europeanized.

The disparity between the number of boys and girls in school was glaring by the turn of the century and was already a personal problem for educated men who were seeking Western-educated wives. As early as 1902, the main item on the agenda at the reunion of St. Andrews College, Ọ̀yọ́, a premier higher institution for men, was "Where shall we get our wives from and how should they be trained?"[42] By 1930 there were thirty-seven thousand boys, but only ten thousand girls, in approved mission schools. By 1947, the number of girls had increased to thirty-eight thousand, but this was a mere 25 percent of the total number of children in school.[43]

The reason for this gender gap in education is usually attributed to "tradition," the idea that parents preferred to educate their sons instead of daughters.[44] It is not very clear to me, in the Yorùbá case, what particular tradition created this problem. The only writer I have come across who offers some specifics about how "tradition" could have been an obstacle to education did not limit the problem to females. According to T. O. Ogunkoya, in mid-nineteenth-century Abẹ́òkúta, "The Ifá Priests (diviner-priests) had circulated it abroad that any black man who touched a book might be so enfeebled as to become impotent whilst a woman might become barren. If by 1903, men had successfully crossed the hurdle, it was not yet for women."[45] Whatever the historicity of this assertion, the fact that men soon transcended the barriers suggests there were factors at work other than "tradition." How, then, do we account for the persistent underrepresentation of females in the school system? Historical evidence does not support the conjecture that parents initially preferred to send sons to school over daughters. There is nothing to suggest that at the inception of the schools, whether in Badagri, Lagos, Abẹ́òkúta, or further inland in Ìbàdàn, pupils were overwhelmingly boys. Apart from enslaved children who became pupils after they were redeemed by the missionaries themselves, there does not seem to be any set pattern (gendered or not) in the circumstances of the children. Chief Ogunbonna in Abẹ́òkúta was said to have sent his daughter to one of the mission houses because her mother had died and there was nobody to take care of her.[46] Chief Olunloyo in Ìbàdàn sent a son and daughter to live with the Hinderers because he was fascinated by the "magic" of writing.[47] Another young girl ended up with the Hinderers because she took a fancy to Mrs. Hinderer and insisted on going home with her.[48] Even the much-maligned Ifá priests were said to have been eager to send their daughters to a girls' school founded by the wife of Yorùbá missionary Samuel Crowther in Abẹ́òkúta in 1846.[49] Other ways in which pupils were recruited at first included redeeming enslaved children and receiving "pawns."[50] There is no indication that one sex predominated in any of these categories.

It is clear that, initially, the response of Yorùbá parents to schooling for children was not that favorable. They were reluctant to lose the services of their children, both male and female, on the farms and in the markets. Therefore, the missions had to find incentives to get parents to send their children to school. Thus, in Ìjàyè, both the Baptist and CMS paid pupils to come to school. Even in the coastal areas like Lagos and Badagri, inducements had to be provided. Free gifts from Europe were one such inducement.[51] As time went on, there were complaints from parents that schoolchildren had become lazy and disrespectful to elders. The preference for boarding schools was partially related to the desire of parents to pass the cost of raising their "unproductive" children to missionaries if schooling was to deprive them of the services of these children. This situation was soon to change as parents realized the value of education in salaried employment and important positions that the educated came to occupy. None of this was available to females. It is no wonder, then, that parents subsequently were not as eager to educate their daughters as their sons. Western schools were very appropriate for educating boys for their future roles, but the training of girls for the adult life mapped out by the European missionaries and colonial officials did not require that kind of education.

By the 1870s, among the Lagos elite — the Sàró particularly — the mothers had found a good reason for educating their daughters. Namely, educated women were sought after for marriage by educated men. Consequently, the creation of female secondary schools by the Methodist, Anglican, and Catholic missions was due to the effort of women's organizations. They used their privileged positions as wives and daughters of prominent men to establish schools for girls.[52] In Victorian Lagos, some of the up-and-coming Yorùbá professional men were beginning to realize what an educated woman could do for their status and career in colonial society. Kristin Mann, in her pioneering study of marriage in colonial Lagos, shows that educated women were in demand for marriage.[53] Not surprisingly, the ideal for such women was to become housewives. Therefore, they had to find men financially capable of entering what came to be known as "ordinance marriages."[54] No doubt, the Lagos elite families spent considerable sums of money to educate their sons in England for the preferred professions of medicine and law. But, in a sense, the education of daughters was paramount because the only outlet for girls was to "marry well." The greatest fear of Sàró families was the real possibility that their daughters would make a "bad marriage," meaning the traditional form of Yorùbá marriage, which permits a man to marry more than one wife.[55]

By 1882, when the colonial government got involved in education (which up until that time had been monopolized by the Christian missions), there was already a constituency of Africans, at least in Lagos, demanding education for all children. In 1909, King's College, a high school for boys, was established by the colonial government. It was not until 1927 that Queen's College, its female counterpart, was founded. Its founding was a tribute to the tenacity of the Lagos elite women who, in their zeal to convince the government that there was a need for female education, raised £1,000 for the purpose.[56] The attitude of colonial government toward female education was undergoing some improvement. In 1929, E. R. J. Hussey, one of the most outstanding British directors of education in colonial Nigeria, advocated that more schools be built based on the Queen's College model because he "felt it was only when African women were holding positions of importance in the country that the population as a whole could be led to value as good an education for their girls as they did for their boys."[57] Hussey's linking of education and employment was insightful. But apparently this view was not representative of colonial ideology or policy on education and employment. For instance, in 1923, when the Lagos Women's League appealed to the colonial government for the employment of women in the civil service, the response of the chief secretary was: "It is doubtful whether the time has arrived when women could be employed generally in the clerical service in substitution for men."[58] As late as 1951, a circular on the employment of women in the civil service stated: "Only in exceptional circumstances should a woman be considered for appointment to senior grade posts." The exceptions were cases involving well-qualified women who would be unlikely to "control...staff or labor not of their own sex."[59] This is one of the most explicit statements of colonial policy on gender hierarchy. In other words, regardless of qualifications, merit, or seniority, *women were to be subordinated to men in all situations.* Maleness was thus projected as one of the qualifications for employment in the colonial senior civil service. The promotion of a sex as social identity and as a determinant of leadership and responsibility is in stark contrast to the seniority system that was the hallmark of precolonial Yorùbá social organization. Men were to become the "inheritors" of the colonial state. In many ways, women were dispossessed; their exclusion from education and employment was profound and proved devastating over time. Men had more than a head start, not only in numbers but in what Western education and values came to represent in African societies. The ability to negotiate the "modern" world, which led to wealth, status, and leadership roles, was increasingly determined by access to Western education and its use for advancement.

Perhaps the most damaging lasting effect of the association of men with education, gainful employment, and leadership may be its psychological effect on both men and women. This is reflected both structurally and ideologically in the school systems. The notion that females are not as mentally capable as males is commonplace among some of the Western-educated in contemporary Nigerian society. It is part of the colonial legacy. For example, Dr. T. Solarin, one of the most prominent educators in Nigeria, has touched on the problem of sex inequality in education. Mayflower, the high school he founded, became coeducational in 1958. Initially, there was a lot of resistance from male students who felt that girls would not perform as well as boys in school because of their mental inferiority.[60] Dr. Solarin was to betray the same kind of thinking. Commenting on the differential achievements of men and women, he pointed out that Europe had produced women like Joan of Arc and Madame Curie, but "Africa of all continents had sat ever so long and so cruelly on its womanhood."[61] His sympathy for African women notwithstanding, it is remarkable that, based on the Western standards of achievement that he was invoking, Africa has not produced men of the stature of Madame Curie either. Discounting our history, Dr. Solarin failed to deduce this fact, believing the Western-propagated notion that African women are the most oppressed in the world. This example illustrates the degree to which ideas about racial superiority of Europeans and patriarchy are intertwined in the minds of the colonized — Solarin assumed that in Europe, women were treated as equal to men, in spite of all the evidence to the contrary. One wonders what his reaction would have been to the fact that despite Madame Curie's exceptional achievement of two Nobel prizes, she was not admitted into the French Academy of Sciences because of her sex.[62]

Masculinizing the Òrìṣàs: Sex Bias in Godly Places

The introduction of Christianity, which is male-dominant, was another factor in the process of establishing male dominance in Yorùbá society. Christian missions in Africa have been rightly described as the hand-maidens of colonization. Like John the Baptist, they prepared the way. They did so in Yorùbáland, just as in other parts of Africa. Christianity arrived in Yorùbáland in the 1840s, decades before most of the area was brought under British rule. The major missionary groups were the Church Missionary Society (CMS) (from Britain), the Wesleyan Methodists, the Southern Baptists (from the United States), and the Catholics. The CMS was the largest and most significant in the early period. The first mission stations were established in Badagri and Abẹ́òkúta, but they soon expanded to towns such as Ìjàyè, Ògbómòṣọ́, Ọ̀yọ́, and Ìbàdàn.

In general, Christian missionaries were well received by the various Yorùbá states. In fact, there was competition among them to secure the presence of missionaries within their borders. Although Yorùbá religion always had room for the adoption of new gods, the reason Yorùbá rulers sought European missionaries was political, not religious. Yorùbá rulers needed the presence and skills of missionaries in order to secure access to trade with the Europeans on the coast and to enhance their position in the power struggle among Yorùbá states during this time period. Abẹ́òkúta, which became the center of missionary activities in Yorùbáland, enjoyed the patronage of Europeans, including their military support. The first Christian community in Yorùbáland was founded in Abẹ́òkúta. Initially, the community was made up mostly of Sàró, but with time they were able to recruit converts from the local population. From the records, it is not very clear what sort of people were drawn to Christianity and what number of males and females converted. Among the Igbó of southeastern Nigeria, social outcasts and slaves, that is, marginalized persons, were the first converts. In Yorùbáland, probably because of the presence of an already Christianized Yorùbá population — the Sàró — the pattern appears to have been different.

Men seem to have been the primary targets for evangelization, a fact borne out in the debate over polygamy. The most serious and most enduring conflict between the church and its Yorùbá converts was the Yorùbá custom of multiple marriage. It became the most explosive factor in the relationship between Yorùbá would-be Christians and the evangelists. For the missionaries, having multiple wives was not only primitive but against God's law; polygamy was adultery, pure and simple.[63] Therefore, the minimum a Yorùbá convert was expected to do before being baptized was to divest himself of all but one of his wives. J. F. A. Ajayi has noted that it is remarkable that the missions were so dogmatic in their opposition to polygamy but were tolerant of slavery. The following quote, attributed to the secretary of the CMS, shows this: "Christianity will ameliorate the relationship between master and slave; polygamy is an offense against the law of God, and therefore is incapable of amelioration."[64]

From the perspective of this study, what is equally interesting is how women appear in this debate. One would have thought that since Yorùbá men were the ones who had multiple conjugal partners and thus fell outside the Christian ethos, the woman would have been the natural target for Christianization. Not so. What we find is this recurring question: Should the church baptize the wife of a polygamist?[65] The fact that the question arose at all shows that women were not treated as individual souls for the purpose of salvation. Their individual faith was secondary to the more important question of whose wives they were. Regardless of the fact that salvation was to be constituted by an individual coming to Christ, women were not viewed as individuals — they were seen only as wives. Yorùbá missionary Ajayi Crowther was quick to point out to the church that "the wife of a polygamist was an involuntary victim of a social institution and should not be denied baptism because of that."[66] But were women victims of polygamy or victims of the church during this period? My point is that if a polygamist became a Christian, it was only then that the question arose as to which wives were to be discarded and which children were bastards. Women and children were to be penalized for a cultural conflict that was not of their own making. In fact, they were being penalized for being good cultural citizens. The implication of conversion was not lost on the Yorùbá, yet the church failed to address this thorny issue. The admonition of some of the Yorùbá missionaries that polygamy should be tolerated but progressively reformed fell on deaf ears.

By 1891, various conflicts between the Yorùbá Christian community and the missions resulted in secession. In popular discourse, there is the claim that the intolerance of the church for polygamy was one of the main reasons for the break. In 1891, the first African church independent of the missions was founded in Lagos. J. B. Webster, in his pioneering study of independent churches in Yorùbáland, however, asserts that the emergence of indigenous churches in Yorùbáland was a tribute to how committed the Yorùbá had become to Christianity.[67] From my standpoint, this Yorùbá commitment to Christianity was necessarily a commitment to Judeo-Christian patriarchy, and this represented a bad omen for women.

Nevertheless, a new era was dawning in the history of the church in Yorùbáland. In the mission churches, women had been taken for granted; they had been excluded from the clergy and had had no official role whatsoever. But with the founding of the independent churches, women began to assume roles that were more prominent and that were more in tune with the traditional representation of anafemales in Yorùbá religion. As a matter of fact, quite a number of these churches were established by women. The most prominent of them was cofounded by Abíọ́dún Akínṣòwọ́n in 1925, but there were many others.[68] Women also played important roles in the day-to-day running of the churches and as prophets.

Although women's role in the independent churches was more noticeable than in the European mission churches, it could never parallel the representation of anafemales in the indigenous Yorùbá religion. J. D. Y. Peel, in his monumental study of independent churches in Yorùbáland, argues that although the independent churches gave more scope for leadership to women, a "line is...drawn at women heading whole organizations and dominating the men as a group."[69] He claims that in the case of Abíọ́dún Akínṣòwọ́n, men were not prepared to let her be the overall leader of the organization. What is curious about this assertion is that Peel does not give us any evidence other than the "claim" of some men. In fact, on closer reading of Peel's study, one finds little logical support for this interpretation. If it is true that men did not want female leaders, then why did churches that were publicly acknowledged (by both men and women) as the brainchildren of women succeed in attracting both male and female members? This question is not addressed by Peel. There is a certain degree of male bias in the way questions are posed in his study. Another glaring example of this is Peel's analysis of the background of church founders as if they were all male. In spite of the fact that he documents a number of churches founded by women, in his analysis of the social background of church founders his major question was posed thus: "What sort of men were the founders of the Aladura (independent) churches in these years?"[70] He goes on to examine various factors such as town of origin, occupation, and education. Gender was not made an issue because the maleness of church founders was taken for granted.

The case of Madame Ọlátuñríé, another prominent female leader, calls into question Peel's assertion of men's reluctance to accept female leadership. According to Peel, there was a leadership tussle in the church between Madame Ọlátuñríé and a man, Mr. Ṣóṣan. She had declared that through a vision, God had made her the head of the church, and, for all intents and purposes, the church accepted her as the leader. But Peel tries to minimize her victory over Mr. Ṣóṣan by summing it up in this way: "Luckily, owing to the *modesty* of Ṣóṣan (the man), who was chairman, a split was averted and she was given a charismatic position over him as Ìyá Aláköso (Mother Superintendent)."[71] From this passage, we do not get a clear picture that the woman had become the effective head of this church; it is only much later in the study that we see a statement that Mr. Ṣóṣan succeeded Ọlátuñríé many years later,[72] which would suggest that he indeed had wanted to be the leader and had lost the power struggle years earlier. The men in these churches may well have been sexist, but what is interesting is that some of the female leaders presented did not seem to have internalized the notion that they should have lesser places in the church than men. Madame Ọlátuñríé and Abíọ́dún Akínṣọ̀wọ́n attest to this fact. When the latter declared herself the sole leader of the church she cofounded, she was challenged by two men in the organization and was urged to accept the position of "leader of women." She rejected it, and her response is instructive: "Were there not prophetesses in the Bible, . . . and had not Queen Victoria ruled the British Empire?"[73] The truth of Abíọ́dún's statement notwithstanding, both the Bible and Victorian England promoted patriarchy, and Yorùbá society had been drawn into their orbits. Christianity had become another vehicle for promoting male dominance, and its impact was deeply felt beyond the boundaries of the church.

It is impossible to minimize the impact of Christian missions in Yorùbáland. We can pursue different angles on the role of these missions: their role in the "making of a new elite"[74] or their role in facilitating colonization or even their role in the awakening of cultural nationalism. Of particular interest here is the way in which Christianity led to the reinterpretation of Yorùbá religious system in a male-biased fashion by theologians and churchmen.

An upshot of the Christianization of Yorùbá society was the introduction of notions of gender into the religious sphere, including into the indigenous religious system. In traditional Yorùbá religion, anasex-distinctions did not play any part, whether in the world of humans or in that of the gods. Like other African religions, Yorùbá religion had three pillars. First, there was Olódùmarè (God — the Supreme Being). Olódùmarè did not have a gender identity, and it is doubtful that s/he was perceived as a human being before the advent of Christianity and Islam in Yorùbáland. Second, the òrìṣà (gods) were the manifestations of the attributes of the supreme being and were regarded as his/her messengers to humans. They were the most obvious focus of Yorùbá worship. Though there were anamale and anafemale òrìṣà, as in other institutions this distinction was inconsequential; therefore, it is best described as a distinction without difference. For example, both Ṣàngó (the god of thunder) and Ọya (the female river god) were known for their wrath. Furthermore, a census of the òrìṣà to determine their sex composition is impossible since the total number of òrìṣà is unknown and is still expanding. In addition, not all the òrìṣà were thought of in gendered terms; some were recognized as male in some localities and female in others. Third, there were the ancestors, both male and female, venerated by members of each lineage and acknowledged yearly in the Egúngún masquerade: a cult of ancestor veneration. In the world of humans, the priesthood of various gods was open to both males and females. In general, the singular predictor of who worshiped which òrìṣà was lineage membership and town of origin. From the foregoing, it is clear that Yorùbá religion, just like Yorùbá civic life, did not articulate gender as a category; therefore, the roles of the òrìṣà, priests, and ancestors were not gender-dependent.

Following the adoption of Christianity and the acquisition of writing among the Yorùbá, there seems to have been an attempt by scholars and Yorùbá churchmen to reinterpret the religion using the male bias of Christianity. The founding of Yorùbá indigenous churches represented a process of Yorùbánizing Christianity,[75] but the other process that came out of the Yorùbá Christian community was what can be called the Christianization of Yorùbá religion. A major contribution of the Christian missions in Nigeria was the reduction of indigenous languages into writing. Samuel Ajayi Crowther, a Yorùbá missionary, was instrumental in this process. By 1861, the Bible had been translated into Yorùbá, and the new Christian elite in Yorùbáland set to work codifying the customs, traditions, and religion of the people. However, their vision was often seriously colored by Christianity. This is particularly noticeable regarding sex. There tended to be a male bias in the language and interpretations of Yorùbá traditions. In the hands of Yorùbá Christians, laypersons, theologians, and church leaders, the pillars of Yorùbá religion tended to be masculinized. Olódùmarè began to look like "our Father in heaven"; the female òrìsà, when they were recognized, began to look less powerful than the male òrìsà in some nebulous way; and "our ancestors" become our forefathers.

An example of this masculinization of Yorùbá religion can be seen in the work of two scholars in a more recent period. E. Bolaji Idowu, a scholar and churchman, in his study of Yorùbá religion depicts the Yorùbá perception of the supreme being: "Their picture of *Olódùmarè* is, therefore, of a personage, venerable and majestic, aged but not aging with a grayness which commands awe and reverence. He speaks, He acts, He rules."[76] Apart from the gender bias inherent in the use of the English third-person masculine singular pronouns, the picture of the Yorùbá supreme being that emerges is decidedly male and quite biblical. Idowu does not tell us how he arrived at this picture. J. O. Awolalu, another Yorùbá theologian, goes a step further in the description and characterization of the supreme being based on Yorùbá names for the supreme being: "He is Holy and Pure, that is why the Yorùbá refer to him as *Oba Mímọ* — The Pure King, *Oba tí kò léérí* — the King without blemish, *Alálàfunfun Òkè* — the One Clothed in White Robes, who dwells above."[77] These names of the supreme being, which Awolalu uses as evidence, have been influenced by Christianity and Islam, as other writers have noted, but neither Idowu nor Awolalu dated the appearance of these names in Yorùbá society. More importantly, there is no evidence that the Yorùbá thought of the Supreme Being as human.

The implications of replacing female symbols with male ones and transforming gender-neutral gods into male gods in African religions are yet to be analyzed. However, the work of feminist theologians regarding Judeo-Christian patriarchy's effect on women in the West is indicative of what is in store for African women as the patriarchalizing of their religions continue. In regard to Judeo-Christian religions, Carol Christ asserts: "Religions centered on the worship of a male God create 'moods' and 'motivations' that keep women in a state of psychological dependence on men and male authority, while at the same time legitimating the *political* and *social* authority of fathers and sons in the institutions of society."[78] The organization of religion in any given society, including religious symbols and values, reflects the social organization. Therefore, as African women are increasingly marginalized in society, it is not surprising that they are shortchanged in religious systems as well. The ramifications of patriarchalized religions may be greater in Africa than in the West because religion permeates all aspects of African life; the notion of a nonreligious space even today is questionable.

No Woman's Land

Another landmark of European penetration of indigenous societies, whether in Africa or in the Americas, was the commercialization of land. Land became a commodity to be bought and sold. The focus of this section is to analyze the effect of the commodification of land and how females were shortchanged in the transition from collective rights of access to private ownership.

In nineteenth-century Yorùbáland, as in most parts of Africa, land was not a commodity to be individually owned, bought, and sold. The following statement from the memoirs of Anna Hinderer, a European missionary living in Ìbàdàn at the time, shows the Yorùbá conception of property and ownership: "When Mr. Hinderer, on first settling at Ìbàdàn, asked what price he must pay for some land..., the chief said laughing, 'Pay! Who pays for the ground? All the ground belongs to God; you cannot pay for it.'"[79] If there was any claim to land, it was lineage-based and communally based.[80] Land was never sold — it was given to newcomers either by the *oba* or by representatives of lineages. The lineage was the landholding unit, and all members of the family, male and female, had rights of usage. As Samuel Johnson noted, "No portion of such farms can be alienated from the family without the unanimous consent of all the members thereof."[81]

Use rights to land were universal. However, in recent literature on women and development, attempts have been made to reinterpret women's use rights as inferior to men's rights in some way. For example, M. Lovett states that in many precolonial societies in Africa, "women possessed no independent, autonomous rights to land; rather their access was mediated through men."[82] This interpretation of the precolonial right of access to land through lineage membership (by birth) as access through the father, and access to land through marriage as access through the husband, shifts the focus of discussion from rights as communally derived and guaranteed to rights as based on the individual. In this way, the concept of individualism is transposed onto societies where communal rights superseded the rights of individuals. Furthermore, such a statement misses the point, in that it interpolates the relative scarcity of land in the colonial period, when land had become commodified and therefore valuable and more restricted, to the precolonial period, when it was plentiful. Statements like Lovett's also go astray by failing to understand that even in traditional African societies in which women gained access to land through marriage, such access was secure because it was guaranteed by the community. Moreover, one's right to be a member of the lineage was derived not from being the son or daughter of one's parents but from being born into the lineage. One must remember that *the lineage was conceived as being composed of the living, the dead, and the unborn*. Marriage, being an interlineage affair, meant that the lineage (not just the particular husband) guaranteed the right to land.

In the Yorùbá case, *obìnrin* and *okùnrin* members of the family had the same routes of access; membership in the lineage was based on birth, not marriage — thus, anafemales marrying into a lineage had no rights to the land of their husbands' lineage. Their right to land was held and guaranteed by the lineage of their birth. G. B. A. Coker, writing on the rights of Yorùbá lineage members to immovable property such as land, states: "The rights of the members of a family are equal *inter se,* and it is not possible to have interests differing in quality and quantity."[83] Colonial anthropologist P. C. Lloyd, writing on Yorùbá society in a sim-, ilar vein, asserts: "The rights of management [of family lands] can only be exercised by the family acting as a corporate group and not by any individual member, unless he [or she] is so authorized."[84] To assume, as writers like Lovett have, that men (as a group) had a supervisory right that women (as a group) did not have is to misrepresent the facts. In precolonial Yorùbáland, the rights of the individual derived from group membership. This is an expression of the classic African conception of the individual in relation to the community, ever so beautifully expressed by the dictum, "We are, therefore I am," in contradistinction to the Europe-identified Cartesian pronouncement, "I think, therefore I am."

Furthermore, in the Yorùbá case, if corporate land was to be partitioned, it was not done on the basis of anasex-distinction. As I noted earlier, Yorùbá did not make a social distinction between anafemale and anamale members of the family. To pose questions about the quality of male versus female rights is to assume individual rights to land, which is the cornerstone of Western notions of property ownership. More importantly, it is to assume that females have a gender identity that assured or jeopardized their access to land. As I showed in the previous chapter, Yorùbá anafemales' rights as offspring (members of the lineage) were different from their rights as in-marrying females. Thus, the duality and divergence of African female identity as members of the lineage through birth (offspring) and members of the lineage through marriage were, in fact, the first casualty of the European notion of "the status of women" (the idea that all women had one common condition).

This Yorùbá "no man's land" system of land tenure thus started to undergo transformation in the colonial period, to the detriment of women. Their land rights were affected by a number of developments, best illustrated by the case of Lagos, which was occupied by the British in 1861. Changes there were indicative of what was to take place in other Yorùbá towns following European rule.

Land sales evolved quite early in Lagos because of the presence of European merchants and a Westernized class of Yorùbá — the Sàró. Land grants to European merchants from the ọba of Lagos were understood as outright sales. In the case of the Sàró, their Western education and values predisposed them to the buying and selling of land. More directly, the system of crown grants of land was used in which local "owners of property held their land as a grant from the British Crown."[85] For example, an ordinance was issued in 1869 that provided for property ownership for any person who "had been in occupation either by *himself* or his subtenant."[86] This Crown grant system served to propagate further the idea of land for sale. The idea that persons occupying land had a right of ownership must have turned many a family property into private property, usually male-owned. First, the movement from collective ownership of land to private and individual ownership was stacked against women because by colonial definition (as the wording of the ordinance suggests) only men could be individuals. Second, given that marriage residence in Yorùbáland was in general patrilocal, it is not likely that a woman occupied land *"by himself."* I should be quick to note that the apparent disadvantage in this case stemmed not from the Yorùbá tradition of patrilocality but from the colonial law that occupation of land constituted ownership, thereby abrogating the precolonial rights of access conferred by birth. After all, the idea that a man occupied land by himself and not on behalf of the lineage was a result of the new dispensation and could only be sustained by the European idea of a male household head whose authority was absolute. More significantly, relative to men, many women lacked both cultural capital and currency that had become necessary for accumulation in Victorian Lagos.

Social historian Kristin Mann is correct when she articulated that in Victorian Lagos,

> the ability to read and write in English ensured the early educated Christians advantages in a community where the government and private citizens increasingly wrote down, in the language of colonial rulers, important communications and commercial and legal

transactions....Illiterate merchants soon found they had to hire literate clerks.[87]

Among the Sàró, the number of educated women was far less than men; and besides, the Victorian values of such women meant that they saw the business of acquiring property and breadwinning as properly within the sphere of men. Nevertheless, Sàró women benefited from their privileged status, and in fact some of them took advantage of their education. The situation in Abéòkúta was almost identical to that of Lagos, as the former was the other locality where the Sàró were concentrated. The sale of land in Abéòkúta became so rapid and generated so many problems that in 1913 the council issued an order limiting sale to indigenes of the town.[88]

The production of cash crops such as cocoa proved to be another factor that increased the value of land. In gender terms, it is also important because it generated new wealth from which women were by and large marginalized. This process can be seen further inland. In Ìbàdàn, Ife, and Ondo, the commercialization of land and its rapid sale were due to the expansion of cocoa cultivation. Though the British did not introduce cocoa into Yorùbáland, they quickly recognized the potential of its exploitation for the benefit of the colonial government. They promoted its spread and subsequently monopolized its marketing. The major impact of cocoa cultivation on women was that they were marginal to the biggest opportunity for gaining wealth that opened up during this period. According to Sara Berry, the pioneers of the cocoa cultivation were Yorùbá men who had been exposed to Christianity.[89] The literature has assumed a link between women's marginality in cocoa production and their lack of association with farming in the precolonial period. However, in chapter 2, I demonstrated that the evidence shows that farming was not a gender-defined occupation in precolonial Yorùbáland. Even if we accept the notion of a gender division of labor, the disadvantage of women still needs to be accounted for considering that even in societies where females were recognized as farmers and took part in the cocoa boom, as among the Ashanti of Ghana, women did not seem to do as well as men during the colonial period; despite the claim that Yorùbá women had been dominant in trade, this did not guarantee their continued dominance in the colonial period. No comparable opportunity for accumulating wealth opened up to women. Therefore, we begin to see a gender gap in access to wealth. This gap was heightened because cocoa production gave men an advantage in trade and provided them with capital. Again, this fact shows that the polarization of trade and farming as distinct occupational types is misleading.

The individuation of land ownership and the scarcity attendant upon commercialization did not augur well for women's rights. Simi Afonja has documented that in Ondo since the colonial period, women's rights have been abrogated, especially in the case of children who want to enforce their rights of access based on their mother's membership in a lineage.[90] Jane Guyer found that in another Yorùbá locality, as a result of the value placed on land used to grow cocoa, patrilineages were unwilling to pass it down through females. They preferred to pass this land through males in the second generation, though they remained willing to pass food-crop land through both male and female members of the lineage.[91]

Perhaps the most serious development resulting from land sale was the ideology explaining the new reality of land sales and abrogation of women's rights as "our custom" rather than as a "tradition" that developed in the colonial period. Gavin Kitching, in his discussion of the impact of the European land-tenure system on the Kikuyu of Kenya, points out that it was in the colonial period that Africans started to conceptualize their land-use patterns in terms of Western notions of land purchase, sale, and tenancy.[92] Such developments were also evident in Yorùbáland. Fadipe notes that by the 1930s, there existed an erroneous belief in some Yorùbá localities that "the sale of land has been a long tradition among them."[93] In the same way, the marginalization of females from family land has also been presented as a "long tradition." Simi Afonja cites a seventy-year-old man in the town of Ife who stated that "it was unheard of for the commoner women to own landed property and houses in the past."[94] However, Afonja did not raise the next logical question as to which "past" he was referring to, particularly because private property in land and houses for any person was unknown in Yorùbáland until the nineteenth century in Lagos and Abẹ́òkúta and much later in the hinterland.

Making Customary Law Customary

The process of reinventing the past to reflect the present is critical to my analysis of gender-formation in colonial Yorùbáland. In the previous chapter, I showed the way it operated with regard to the writing of history. The treatment of land sale and property ownership was another example of this process, and there were still other institutional sites in which this process was glaring. The making of customary law also illustrates how traditions were reinvented in this period. In the process of the constitution of customary law, women were excluded; their rights steadily eroded as new customs were fashioned mainly to serve male interests. Customary law is a contradiction in terms because there was nothing "customary" in the way it came into being. Here I am making a distinction between the recording of customary norms and mores as laws, on the one hand, and the construction of new traditions as customary law, on the other. The ultimate source of the "new customary law" was not custom but the British colonial government. As part of the colonial administrative machinery, it set up a native court system in which civil cases were to be adjudicated as long as the law applied was "not repugnant to justice, equity and good conscience."[95] Male local rulers became salaried officials of the colonial government, and one of their functions was to "adjudicate" customary law. The dual nature of colonial-initiated customary law as something new and something old (its appeal to the Yorùbá past for legitimacy) is captured by T. M. Aluko's description of a native court in Idasa, a fictional town in colonial Yorùbáland:

> At last they saw the Court House from a distance. The father approached it with awe and diffidence, the son with curiosity and excitement. It had traditional mud walls but was plastered and white-washed both inside and out. The thatched roof had recently been replaced by corrugated-iron sheets, a sign that justice was at the vanguard of the march of civilization in this important town.[96]

That justice had a house all its own was a new tradition in Yorùbáland, and this realization is the reason the father approached it with "awe and diffidence" and the son with "curiosity and excitement."

The establishment of native courts in Yorùbáland was not about taking preexisting courts and updating them, as legal scholars tend to explain — it was the development of a new way of thinking about justice and a new place for administering it. In pre-British Yorùbáland, judicial power inhered in various courts (in the sense of a quorum), not just the council of chiefs. But the colonial government imposed a European view of justice that would be in the hands of male chiefs to the exclusion of all other groups. The exclusion of female officials was one of the sure signs that custom had nothing much to do with the fashioning of "customary court." The aláké (ruler) of Abéòkúta (a Yorùbá polity) was to acknowledge the glaring omission of women when during discussion of marriage and divorce in 1937 he lamented that the women of Egbaland (Abéòkúta) had not even been consulted on a matter that concerned them so closely.[97] As Martin Chanock argues, "from the British point of view, . . . the customary law would have been what the chiefs [male chiefs] did in their courts, while what happened outside the courts was 'extra-legal.' But in real village life there was no such clear-cut distinction between the realms of public and private."[98] Nina Mba exhibits this Western point of view when she states that in precolonial Yorùbáland "the dissolution of a marriage was extra-judicial: It was effected *merely* by the mutual consent of the parties involved."[99] She suggests that this was a simple and nonjudicial way of settling conflicts, a curious notion in light of the fact that the "parties involved" in a Yorùbá marriage could include a large number of people, since marriage was an interlineage affair. Why lineage adjudication of marriage is extrajudicial is unclear except, of course, if one accepts the colonial definition of the public and private spheres.

Another way the colonial government tailored the making of customary law was through the administration of native law and custom by the higher courts, which meant that such administration was in the hands of colonial officials born and bred in England, although they were supposed to be assisted by indigenous assessors in the person of "traditional chiefs." Consequently, it was the English judicial approach that was applied. The use of the "repugnancy law" led to the abolition of some customary laws.[100] A good example of colonial construction of customary law is cited by Coker. Analyzing a case on Yorùbá women's property rights, he writes: "Evidence was taken first from both parties in the case, and secondly from chiefs summoned as expert witnesses. The learned Chief Justice [an Englishman], who heard the matter, preferred the evidence of the Lagos chiefs to the evidence given by the Yorùbá (hinterland) chiefs."[101] Although they used chiefs as assessors, the British officials reserved the right to dispense with their evidence, as shown by this example. The criterion for selecting which sets of evidence were more "customary" than the other sets was not clear. Therefore, the process was fraught with misinterpretation and misrepresentation, if not outright nonsense, as exemplified in this pronouncement attributed to the Honorable Justice Paul Graham, in reference to a case about Yorùbá women's property rights in colonial Lagos:

> The defendant called as witness an old man.... The evidence he gave was a perfectly clear *reductio ad absurdum* of the defendant's case.... I have heard a good deal of nonsense talked in the witness box about Yorùbá custom but seldom anything more ridiculous than this. Even the defendant's counsel himself had to throw over this witness.[102]

How the British judges distinguished custom from the process of "customizing" newfangled social practices is not always that obvious, although it was quite clear that personal and sectional interests were being promoted that did not augur well for both tradition and women. As Coker concludes in regard to rights of Yorùbá females in family property:

> It should be borne in mind that although it has been suggested that under native law and custom in olden days the rights of females were restricted, there seems to be no authority for this suggestion, for the cases did not contain any instance in which such a proposition of native law and custom had been propounded by independent assessors. Any suggestion on those lines could only have come from the parties themselves, and especially from the *party who stands to win if such propositions were accepted as law.*[103]

The issue of interested parties was the crux of the matter. Unfortunately for women, they were marginalized by the process through which flexible customary rules were encoded into legal principles after "the nonsense" and the "biased" had been supposedly weeded out. Customs are produced through repetition. The constant challenge to female rights during this period created an impression that such rights were newly created. Furthermore, the appearance of women in the court system as mere litigants, never assessors or judges, served to propagate the idea that men are the custodians of tradition and women its hapless victims.

The Wages of Colonization

Central to colonial rule was the question of how to extract wealth from the colonies for the benefit of the occupying European powers. To this end, by the turn of the century, the British colonial administration started to build a railway line that would link various parts of their three colonies that were to become Nigeria. For this study, the railways are important because railway service pioneered wage labor and proved to be the largest employer of labor in colonial Nigeria. Women were largely excluded from the wage-labor force (although there have been relatively large improvements since independence, female representation in the formal sector remains much lower than that of men).

By 1899, over ten thousand men were employed in the construction of the railways. Later, more men were employed to operate the system. Most of the original workers were Yorùbá. According to W. Oyemakinde, unlike other parts of Nigeria and indeed other areas of Africa, there was no labor shortage for the construction of the railways in Yorùbáland because there was already in existence a "floating population" of men.[104] These were displaced persons who had been enslaved in the wake of the Yorùbá civil wars in the nineteenth century. This population was easily recruited as labor by the colonial government. However, despite the presence of females among this population, and in spite of the fact that some of the initial work on the railways involved head-loading supplies, which was no different from what males and females did in the nineteenth century, women were not employed in any considerable numbers. It is not clear what happened to the "floating" female population.

More importantly, the introduction of capitalist relations in the form of wage labor was a novelty in the Yorùbá economy and was to have major repercussions, particularly in the definition of work. All through the nineteenth century, in spite of the expansion of trade with Europe, no free-market developed in Yorùbáland as regards labor. In fact, domestic slavery (as distinct from the Atlantic slave trade) expanded during this period due to the increased demand for labor, as trade with Europe in agricultural produce expanded. Oyemakinde notes that in colonial Yorùbáland wage labor became the avenue for former slaves to buy their freedom.[105] The implications of this statement are far-reaching in light of the fact that females did not have access to wages. Does it then mean that female enslavement was prolonged? This is an interesting question that cannot be answered in this study. Historical studies of slavery and the slave trade in Africa remain trapped in Eurocentric concerns and misrepresentations.

Apart from access to cash, which wage labor meant for men, there were other more subtle but equally profound effects. Because men were paid a wage, their labor acquired exchange value while women's labor retained only its use value, thereby devaluing work that became associated with women. Walter Rodney's analysis of work in the colonial situation is elucidating:

> Since men entered the money sector more easily and in greater numbers than women, women's work became greatly inferior to that of men within the new value system of colonialism: men's work was "modern" and women's work was "traditional" and "backward." Therefore, the deterioration in the status of African women was bound up with the consequent loss of the right to set indigenous standards of what work had merit and what did not.[106]

This gender distinction was to lead to the perception of men as workers and women as nonworkers and therefore appendages of men. Women's work became invisible. Yet in reality the starvation wages that men were paid by the colonial government were insufficient to reproduce the family, and women's labor remained as necessary as ever for the survival of the community. It is well documented that African men, unlike their European counterparts, were paid a single and not a family wage. In fact, by 1903, the initial attraction of wage work on the railways in Nigeria gave way to a labor shortage and trade union organization by disgruntled workers.[107]

In addition, wage labor involved migration away from places of origin to centers of government and commerce that were developing all over the colony at the time. It meant that women moved with their husbands away from kin groups. The case of Madame Bankole, a subject in an ethnographic study of Yorùbá migrant families, is not atypical:

> In 1949 she married...another Ijebu man who was a supervisor in the telegraph office and had recently been widowed. He was transferred frequently from place to place, and she went with him, changing her trade each time. From Warri in the western Niger delta she transported palm oil to Ìbàdàn and re-sold it there to retailers. Then from Jos and Kano she sent rice and beans to a woman to whom she sublet her...stall, and received crockery in return that she sold in the North. She also cooked and sold food in the migrant quarters of those towns. From 1949 to 1962 she moved around with him.[108]

What is most striking about Madame Bankole's experience is her resourcefulness and entrepreneurial spirit, responding to the market and her situation. But on a more subtle note, Madame Bankole had become a wife, an appendage whose situation was *determined* by her husband's occupation. Although she retained one of the dominant indigenous occupations of Yorùbáland, the focus of her existence appears to have shifted from trade to marriage as an occupation. The combination of male wage labor and migration produced a new social identity for females as dependents and appendages of men. Regardless of the fact that in precolonial Òyó the position of an *aya* was junior to that of her conjugal partner, the perception of an *aya* as a dependent and an appendage was a new one. For example, in spite of the fact that Madame Bankole was not dependent in economic terms, there is a perception of her dependency built into the new family situation. The anafemales had moved from being *aya* to *wife*.

A corollary of women's exaggerated identity as wives was that other identities became muted. As couples moved away from kin groups, women's identity as offspring (daughters) and members of the lineage became secondary to their identities as wives. Though Madame Bankole retained a dominant precolonial occupation in Yorùbáland (i.e., trading), the fact that she had to fold up shop whenever her husband's job demanded shows that she and her occupation were secondary. The family itself was slowly being redefined as the man plus his dependents (wife/wives and children) rather than as the "extended" family, including siblings and parents. The emergence of men as apparent sole breadwinners was to shape the kind of opportunities and resources that were made available by both the colonial and the neocolonial state that followed. For example, the reason why men had more educational opportunities is often ascribed to the notion that they were the "breadwinners." The symbolism of bread is particularly apt since both bread and the male as sole breadwinner are colonial infusions into Yorùbá culture. The definition of men as the "breadwinners" resulted in discrimination against women in the taxation system, which has continued to the present. Women cannot claim any exemptions for children as long as the fathers of such children are still alive. As Fola Ighodalo notes, one of the first female permanent secretaries in the Nigerian civil service said about the tax regulation: "This particular regulation has completely disregarded the social circumstances of Nigeria where polygamy is a way of life and under which many women have to carry solely the responsibility for the maintenance, education and every care of their children."[109]

The notion that only men really work shows up in the compilation of national statistics on labor force participation. The percentage of women in the formal sector remains small.[110] This is accounted for by the fact that most women are self-employed and their engagements are not defined as work, despite their participation in the cash economy. It is important to point out that I am not referring here to their contribution of goods and services in the home but employment outside the home as traders and farmworkers, to give two examples. From the standpoint of national statistics-accounting, Madame Bankole was unemployed.

Becoming Women, Being Invisible

We can discern two vital and intertwined processes inherent in European colonization of Africa. The first and more thoroughly documented of these processes was the racializing and the attendant inferiorization of Africans as the colonized, the natives. The second process, which has been the focus of this chapter, was the inferiorization of females. These processes were inseparable, and both were embedded in the colonial situation. The process of inferiorizing the native, which was the essence of colonization, was bound up with the process of enthroning male hegemony. Once the colonized lost their sovereignty, many looked to the colonizer for direction, even in the interpretation of their own history and culture. Many soon abandoned their own history and values and embraced those of the Europeans. One of the Victorian values imposed by the colonizers was the use of body-type to delineate social categories; and this was manifested in the separation of sexes and the presumed inferiority of females. The result was the reconceptualization of the history and customs of the natives to reflect this new race and gender bias of the Europeans. Thus, in Yorùbá society we see this demonstrated in the dialogue on women between two male characters in T. M. Aluko's novel set in colonial Yorùbáland: "This woman, Sister Rebecca, is a good woman. But you cannot always rely on the evidence of a woman, ... 'Daughter of Eve, Tempter of Adam' — Jeremiah dug up woman's unenviable ancestry."[111]

There is no question in the mind of this character that Eve was the legitimate "ancestress" of Yorùbá women. Why and how? These questions are not raised precisely because the character — reflecting the attitude of many people — believes that the colonized had become part and parcel of the history of the colonizer, and as such there was only one set of ancestors for both native and colonizer (though there were different ancestors [i.e., Adam and Eve] for males and females, in keeping with the Victorian notion of separation of the sexes). The point about the natives' loss of control over their history has been succinctly made by Albert Memmi when he notes that "the most serious blow suffered by the colonized is being removed from history."[112] In a similar vein, Frantz Fanon calls on the native to "put an end to the history of colonisation . . . and to bring into existence the history of the nation — the history of decolonisation."[113] Fanon's rallying call very clearly situates the question of resistance and the necessity and possibility of the colonized transforming the state of things.

For African women, the tragedy deepened in that the colonial experience threw them to the very bottom of a history that was not theirs. Thus, the unenviable position of European women became theirs by imposition, even as European women were lifted over Africans because their race was privileged. More specifically, in the Yorùbá case, females became subordinated as soon as they were "made up" into women — an embodied and homogenized category. Thus by definition they became invisible. The precolonial Yorùbá seniority system was displaced by a European system of hierarchy of the sexes in which the female sex is always inferior and subordinate to the male sex. The ultimate manifestation of this new system was a colonial state that was patriarchal and that has unfortunately survived the demise of "the empire." Whatever the values, history, and world-sense of any cultural group in Africa, the colonial government held political control and "the specifically symbolic power to impose the principles of the construction of reality."[114] The reality created and enforced was the inferiority of Africans and the inferiority of females until the colonized chart their own reality.

Germane to the emergence of both men and women as identifiable and hierarchical categories is the creation of separate spheres of operation for the sexes. A new public sphere was created just for males. The creation of a public sphere in which only men could participate was the hallmark and symbol of the colonial process. This gender-based division into spheres was not, however, the only segmentation of society going on at the time. In fact, what we see in Africa in the colonial and neocolonial periods is the reality of a number of public spheres. In an essay on the nature of the state in postcolonial Africa, Peter Ekeh posits the existence of two public realms as a legacy of colonization.[115] The first he designates the primordial-public, as it is based on primordial groupings, sentiments, and activities. The other, the civic-public, is associated with colonial administration and is based on civil structure, the military, the police, and the civil service.[116] For Ekeh, the difference between the two has to do with their moral bases: the primordial-public being moral and the civic-public being amoral. From the standpoint of the present work, an important distinction between the two publics that is often overlooked is that the civic-public is male-dominant and the primordial-public is gender-inclusive. These two ways of labeling the colonial segmentation of society thus point in the same direction. As I have shown, the exclusion of women officials from the structures of the colonial state overrode the precolonial practice of politics being the province of all adults. In precolonial Yorùbáland, anafemales had not been excluded from leadership positions, but this changed drastically in the colonial period.

The indigenous, primordial realm did not collapse into the civic-public realm; it continued to exist orally and in social practice. However, it tended to be subordinated to the newer civic-public realm because most of the resources and wealth of the society were concentrated in the state arena. The two realms were not rigidly separate. In fact, they flowed into each other precisely because the actors were one and the same, particularly after the departure of the colonizers. The European colonial officials during the colonial period did not directly participate in the primordial-public realm, but their control of state power often determined what went on in that realm. Further, different groups of people were articulated into these two realms differently. The Western-educated, emergent elite tended to be affected more directly by the civic-public realm because they were the "inheritors" of the colonial state, with all its privileges and ideologies. Consequently, we tend to find ideas of male superiority and African inferiority more prevalent within this privileged class — they were (and are) in closer and more extended contact with the civic-public sphere. The civic-public realm expanded in the sense that more people were drawn directly into it, and its greatest manifestation was in the Western educational system that was a bequest of the colonial experience. In the section on education, I showed what a determinant education was in the stratification of colonial society. In the arena of education, there is still a perception within certain sections of the population that females are not as capable as their male counterparts.

Today, the participation of females in this privileged system remains very low, a fact that is of itself perceived as evidence of their inability to function in this "all-male world." Seemingly paradoxically, it is precisely the women who are embedded in this realm who realize their subordination. Nevertheless, there are certain class privileges that accrue to both men and women of this most patriarchalized class — the elite. Therefore, it is important that even as we acknowledge the construction of women as a homogenized, subordinated group by the colonizer, we recognize the class hierarchy that cross-cut the gender hierarchy that developed in the colonial period. Ultimately, the process of gender-formation is inseparable from that of institutionalizing race and class hierarchies.

The paradox of the imposition of Western hegemony on African women is that the elite women who derive class privileges from the legacy of the colonial situation appear to suffer from the ill-effects of male dominance the most. For the women in the lower classes, their experience of male dominance is muted, probably because it is overshadowed by socioeconomic disadvantages. Obviously, socioeconomic disadvantage and gender subordination are intertwined, feeding on each other. But it appears that the difference between the experiences of the elite and lower-class women of male dominance is important as a determinant of their consciousness and hence what sorts of action they take (or do not take) against the system. This distinction is particularly important in the contemporary period.

One important concern in this study is the role of intellectuals in the construction of reality. In the colonial period, it was not only colonial officials and policies that were determinant. Western writers have also played a role in the construction of reality, which in turn determines our views of what we see or do not see on the ground. Note that the apprehension process now privileges the visual. One very concrete example of the invisibility of African women (or is it an example of the blindness of researchers?) is illustrated by the experience of R. S. Rattray, an eminent colonial anthropologist of the Ashanti of Ghana. In 1923, Rattray, after many years of studying the Ashanti, was surprised to "discover" the important "position of women" in the state and family. Puzzled that after many years of being the expert on the Ashanti this most significant fact had escaped him, he asked the Ashanti elders why. In his words:

> I have asked the old men and women why I did not know all this — I had spent many years in Ashanti. The answer is always the same: "The white man never asked us this; you have dealings with and recognize only the men; we supposed the *European considered women of no account*, and we know you do not recognize them as we have always done."[117]

In Yorùbáland, the transformation of *obìnrin* into women and then into "women of no account" was at the essence of the colonial impact as a gendered process. Colonization, besides being a racist process, was also a process by which male hegemony was instituted and legitimized in African societies. Its ultimate manifestation was the patriarchal state. The specificities of how Yorùbá anafemales were "rendered of no account" have been the focal point of this chapter. However, the recognition of the profound impact of colonization does not preclude the acknowledgment of the survival of indigenous structures and ideological forms. Colonial and neocolonial Yorùbá society was not Victorian England in gender terms because both men and women actively resisted cultural changes at different levels. Indigenous forms did not disappear, though they were battered, subordinated, eroded, and even modified by the colonial experience. It is important to note that gender hierarchies in Yorùbá society today operate differently than they do in the West. Undoubtedly, there are similarities founded on the fact that in the global system, white males continue to set the agenda of the modern world and white women because of their race privileges, are the second most powerful group in this international program. Recall the UN conferences on women. In the West, to paraphrase Denise Riley, the challenge of feminism is how to proceed from the gender-saturated category of "women" to the "fullness of an unsexed humanity."[118] For Yorùbá *obìnrin*, the challenge is obviously different because at certain levels in the society and in some spheres, the notion of an "unsexed humanity" is neither a dream to aspire to nor a memory to be realized. It exists, albeit in concatenation with the reality of separate and hierarchical sexes imposed during the colonial period.

Chapter 5

The Translation of Cultures

ENGENDERING YORÙBÁ LANGUAGE, ORATURE,
AND WORLD-SENSE

• •

Our [Yorùbá] translators in their zeal to find a word expressing the
English idea of sex rather than age, coined the . . . words arakonrin,
i.e., the male relative; arabinrin, the female relative; these words
have always to be explained to the pure but illiterate Yorùbá man.
— SAMUEL JOHNSON, *The History of the Yorùbás*

Our [i.e., English] common stock of words embodies all distinctions men have found worth drawing, and the connections they
have found worth marking, in the lifetimes of many generations.
— JOHN LANGSHAW AUSTIN, *Philosophical Papers*

THE PRECEDING CHAPTERS have repeatedly demonstrated that at
many levels, questions of language and translation are central
to this study.[1] Western feminist theorists have underscored the
importance of language in the construction of gender. In the English-
speaking West, feminists have shown the connections between the
male-centeredness of the language and women's secondary status in their
societies.[2] Language is a social institution and at the level of the individual affects social behavior. A people's language reflects their patterns of
social interactions, lines of status, interests, and obsessions. That much
is apparent in the above epigraph by Austin; if English makes much of
gender differences, it is because these are the distinctions that the society
found worth drawing. If Yorùbá society did not make gender distinctions and instead made age distinctions, as the Johnson quote suggests
it did, then for the Yorùbá, the age distinctions were the ones worth
drawing, at least until the British showed up on our doorstep. It is significant that in spite of the fact that Johnson was conscious of Yorùbá
non-gender-specificity, his reference to the Yorùbá man in his example,
rather than a non-gender-specific Yorùbá person, could be read as the

157

privileging of the male, as in Austin's usage of the English word "men." (Feminist linguists have argued convincingly that the so-called generic use of "man" in English is not actually generic but one more way of promoting the male as norm through language.)[3] The question that this raises is this: In a milieu in which these two interacting languages — Yorùbá and English — articulate different cultural values, how do we distinguish the Yorùbá gender-freeness from the English male-as-norm in the speech and writing of Yorùbá bilinguals? This question is of special significance when we look at literature and cultural translation.

Richard Gilman, writing on the importance of language in society, summarizes the relationship between language and gender:

> The nature of most languages tells us more about the hierarchical structure of male-female relationships than all the physical horror stories that could be compiled.... That our language [English] employs the words *man* and *mankind* as terms for the whole human race demonstrates that male dominance, the *idea* of masculine superiority, is perennial, institutional, and rooted at the deepest level of our historical experience.[4]

It is not surprising, therefore, that in a society where gender is a primary organizing principle, gender distinctions are reflected in the language.

As I have shown in chapter 2, Yorùbá is a non-gender-specific language: Yorùbá names and pronouns do not make gender distinctions. The third-person pronouns ó and wón are used for both males and females; the former is used in reference to a person who is in a junior or equal position to the speaker; the latter, the formal pronoun, is used for older persons and those of a higher status. The absence of gender-specific categories in the language is a reflection of the degree to which sex differences in Yorùbáland do not form the basis of social categories. Therefore, the lack of Yorùbá words translatable as the English "son," "daughter," "brother," or "sister" reflects the absence of social roles based on such gendered kinship terms. The word omo is used to refer to male and female offspring. Ègbón and àbúrò are the words denoting siblings, regardless of sex, the distinction being between younger and older siblings. It is seniority that is linguistically coded in Yorùbá.

Yet Yorùbá and English have been in close contact over the last one hundred and fifty years. Because of colonization and the imposition of English as the lingua franca of Nigeria, many Yorùbás are now bilingual. The impact of English on Yorùbá continues to be felt through loanwords, translation of Yorùbá culture into English, and the adoption of Western values. The role of the educational establishment is crucial in this process. Schooling and academic scholarship represent the most systematic ways in which Yorùbá society and discourse are being gendered. The focus of this chapter is to investigate the impact of English on Yorùbá language, literature, and society as concerns questions of gender.

It is perhaps not surprising that among students of Yorùbá culture, the fact of the gender-freeness of the language is no secret. What is puzzling, however, is the failure of many scholars to examine the meaning and implications of this fact in their own work. A few examples will suffice. Having read the work of Ayodele Ogundipe, a Yorùbá scholar of orature, literary critic Henry Louis Gates Jr. correctly surmised that "metaphysically and hermeneutically, at least, Foaçuten and Yorùbá discourse is truly genderless, offering feminist literary critics a unique opportunity to examine a field of texts, a discursive universe, that escaped the trap of sexism inherent in Western discourse."[5] Scholars of Yorùbá language and culture have tended not to grasp the full significance of Yorùbá gender neutrality, even when this fact is acknowledged. Gates himself is not free of this contradiction since he is quick to add a disclaimer that in recognizing Yorùbá genderlessness, he is not attempting to show that there is no sexism in the society but just that the "Yorùbá discursive and hermeneutical universes are not" gender-biased.[6] Since language is part of social behavior, it is impossible to separate Yorùbá discourse and social behavior, as Gates suggests.

Ayo Bamgbose, the foremost Yorùbá linguist, writes: "A statement about gender in Yorùbá is ... without any real basis in the language. Rather, it should be seen as a statement about English structure transferred into Yorùbá."[7] However, in Bamgbose's discussion of the novels of D. O. Fagunwa, the pioneer Yorùbá-language novelist, he singles out "women" as one of the themes without raising any questions, regardless of his earlier assertion about the absence of gender categories in Yorùbá. To discuss "women" as a theme is to make a stereotypical gender statement, such as, "They [women] stay with a man when the going is good." Furthermore, Bamgbose goes on to discuss another theme in the novels that he calls "man and other creatures."[8] Interrogating Fagunwa's novel, he observes that "man is shown as the enemy of other creatures. . . . Mammals, birds, snakes, fishes . . . all hate men, the reason for this being man's cruelty."[9] It would seem at first as if his use of "man" in this passage can be read to include females, but apparently not, since he goes on to make the following statement: "These comments [about man] are, of course, exaggerated when taken as referring to men in general, but it is true that these traits are to be found in varying degrees at least in some men."[10] This statement, in conjunction with his earlier pronouncements, at the very least creates confusion about the notion of gender in Yorùbá and its usage by Bamgbose.

Similarly, in a comprehensive study of *oríkì* (praise poetry), a Yorùbá oral genre, Karin Barber reaches the following conclusion: "Unlike in many traditional African cultures, the Yorùbá world is not dichotomized into clearly distinct male and female sectors. The rigid pairs of correspondences that appear in so many accounts of African cosmology are not on view here. The house is not divided, nor is the mental world carved into male and female domains."[11] Central to Barber's study, however, is the idea that there is such a social category as "women" in Yorùbáland — as the subtitle of her book, *Oriki, Women, and the Past in a Yoruba Town*, shows. Her analysis of *oríkì* is in fact predicated on the assumption that it is a women's genre. There is a contradiction in recognizing a social category "women" constituted on the basis of anatomy and at the same time acclaiming that the Yorùbá world is not gendered. Barber's association of the *oríkì* with "women" is related to the special role of "wives"[12] in using praise poetry to affirm and promote the lineage of their husbands. The Yorùbá category *ọkọ* includes what in English a married woman would call husband and sisters-in-law; therefore, it is not gender-specific but denotes lineage membership. The contradiction, then, in these scholarly pronouncements on Yorùbá world-sense is a result of the failure to recognize the fundamental distinction between the social identity of anafemales as both *ìyàwó*[13] and *ọkọ*, with all its implications for social roles, access, and even questions of place and identity. From this standpoint, it is a mistake to lump females together in a category called "women" based on their anatomy, as if their anatomy defined their social roles. Females, like males, have multiple shifting roles from one moment to the next and from one social setting to another. To say that *oríkì* is performed by wives has a different meaning from saying that it is performed by women, because in any particular gathering in Yorùbáland, not all the females are wives; there would, in fact, be other females who are defined as "husbands" in relation to the praise-singing wives. To generalize the "wife" role to all females (which is what labeling them "women" does) is to distort the Yorùbá reality. The problem, as I pointed out earlier, is not unrelated to the fact that scholars tend to focus on the couple and their children as the unit of analysis, thereby seeing females solely in the role of *ìyàwó* and males only as *ọkọ*, since upon marriage, many brides move in with their conjugal family. Again, a close look at Bamgbose's discussion of the theme of women in Fagunwa will show that the stereotypical portrayal of females disproportionately focuses on them in their role as wives. This does not do justice to their other defined roles. Witness: "They [women] stay with a man while the going is good."[14] Or: "The downfall of the hero's father in almost all the novels is due mainly to the accumulation of wives.... One woman, plenty of happiness; two women, two troubles."[15] It appears as if "wife" is used in these writings as a synonym for "woman," as if Yorùbá society is like Western societies where, until recently, the social identity of a wife was total, defining the woman. No single role defines *obìnrin* in Yorùbáland. If any role looms large, it is motherhood, not wifehood, but motherhood itself is not one thing; rather, it suggests a multiplicity of possibilities for social categorization.

Undoubtedly, shifts in institutions and social organization have occurred in Yorùbáland since British colonization, and any discussion of Yorùbá world-sense and social hierarchies has to acknowledge these changes. Such analysis must specify the historical time period and the dialectics of indigenous constructions and "imposed adoptions." The dialectics of the indigenous world-sense and imposed or adopted Western values and institutions represent the challenge of interpreting social processes in our societies in the contemporary period. It is against this background that the significance of literary critic Olakunle George's reading of D. O. Fagunwa's first novel, *Ogboju ode ninu igbo irunmale,* can be appreciated. George argues convincingly that at the level of language, the effect of European colonization cannot be reduced to the adoption of the foreign language by the colonized. Equally important is the impact of the colonial experience on the "indigenous linguistic — which is to say, conceptual — universe of the colonized."[16] George postulates that Fagunwa's choice of the Yorùbá language as his artistic medium should not be automatically interpreted to mean that he was espousing Yorùbá values in opposition to English values. In fact, for George, "Fagunwa demonstrates an unapologetic hybridity and hybridization of epistemic inheritances.... The epistemic terrain within which he operates valorizes Western modernity as sincerely — at least — as he urgently seeks to reclaim the Yorùbá traditional system."[17] One cannot agree with George that Fagunwa was influenced by the West, but it is arguable that these effects should be used to then define his work as hybrid. To label Fagunwa a hybrid is to erase his Yorùbá center.

More essential for my argument in this book is the fact that there is, unquestionably, a certain reality to language in and of itself. Therefore, Fagunwa's choice of Yorùbá as the language of his craft has important ramifications beyond the binary opposition between the indigenous and the foreign, and the dialectics of their articulation. For one thing, at the level of the politics of language in the colonial situation, Fagunwa puts himself on the side of Yorùbá and at the service of Yorùbá language — a Yorùbá institution. His contribution to the culture cannot be overemphasized.

Without any doubt, languages in contact do impact one another, and in that sense no language is an island. For example, in the case of Yorùbá, English is not the only language from which there has been extensive borrowing; Hausa has been an older source of Yorùbá vocabulary. The more important question, however, is the nature of contact, since this has enormous effect on the direction, amount, and content of exchange. In fact, the choice of calling these linguistic intrusions a borrowing or an imposition rests on the social context of contact. Yorùbá people were colonized by the British. As such, imposition is the more accurate description of this particular situation, at least in the original instance. Furthermore, in the milieu in which two interacting languages like Yorùbá and English espouse different cultural values, it becomes clear that the question of translation and borrowing is not an innocuous one of language-contact but a serious one of colonial impact and its negative implications for the culture at the receiving end.

A deeper problem associated with the imposition of European values on Yorùbá culture through translation has been noted by other scholars. Literary critic Olabiyi Yai perceives the unreflecting translations of Yorùbá into English as essentially a failure to acknowledge the epistemological differences between the two cultures.[18] This, according to Adeleke Adeeko, results in an "uncritical insistence by scholars upon finding Yorùbá equivalents of English terms [as if they defined human constants]."[19] This problem is not new, as the 1877 epigraph from Samuel Johnson at the beginning of this chapter shows.

Translating Cultures

Commenting on the musical quality of Yorùbá language, Ulli Beier correctly notes that when Yorùbá is translated into English, "*poetry* is what is left out."[20] I have asserted that *gender* is what is added. Apart from creating new Yorùbá words, Yorùbá have borrowed words extensively from English. A look at Crowther's *Grammar and Vocabulary of Yorùbá*, published in 1852, shows some twenty loanwords from English. One hundred and thirty years later, Adebisi Salami put the number of English loanwords in Yorùbá at two thousand, conservatively.[21] The borrowing has continued apace, particularly with regard to so-called technical and scientific terms. There have also been gender borrowings, the most notorious being two little words that can be found in the remotest parts of Yorùbáland today, even among monolingual Yorùbá speakers: *mà* (as in "madam") and *sà* (as in "sir"). These two gender-specific words are used to show respect to the senior (in terms of status or age) whom the speaker is addressing. They were popularized in the school yard and were originally used to address school teachers. Today, they are a universal way of showing deference. One suspects that the attraction of these words for Yorùbá speakers lies not so much in their gender-specificity as in their ability to code seniority linguistically. Similarly, the use of *brǫdá* (senior male relative) and *sìstá* (senior female relative) speaks to this Yorùbá concern. Interestingly, in Yorùbá, a tonal language, the seniority inheres not so much in the use of the word but in the tone with which it is said. Thus, for example, one might say in Yorùbá: *Sístà mi ni* (This is my junior sister) or *Sìstá mi ni* (This is my senior sister). The words in the two sentences are essentially the same; the difference in meaning is carried by the tonal combinations indicated by the different accents. Though the Yorùbá interest in denoting seniority is maintained even in the assimilation of these English words, their gendered uses are no less significant. The use of these paired items (*mà/sà* or *brǫdá/sìstá*) draws attention to the sex of the addressee or the character in question in a way that is completely new in Yorùbá discourse.[22]

A gender word that has been widely adopted and used in a very sexist way is "madam." It has become an address form for women in positions of authority over the speaker. In the domestic setting, the "master's wife" is called "madam" by the domestic servants; students use the term to address a female professor; and those lower down in an office hierarchy will use the word in addressing a senior female secretary or office worker. Madam is also used as a sign of respect for an older woman who is not a relative. It is an all-purpose term. The problem is that it is often used for female bosses in lieu of *ǫgá* or *ààrę*, which were the common Yorùbá non-gender-specific terms for "boss" or "senior" or "leader." *Ǫgá* and *ààrę* are increasingly associated with male authority.[23] Furthermore, terms of authority and leadership like "president" or "director" are increasingly used for males only; females in such positions are labeled "madam." Therefore, we can begin to talk about the linguistic genderization of authority in Yorùbáland. This is happening through the adoption of English-derived words and through the genderization of Yorùbá words that were once non-gender-specific.

The problem of imposing gender on Yorùbá discourse is particularly acute in the translation of Yorùbá literature into English. Yet the simple fact that gender is not linguistically coded in Yorùbá does not seem to be taken into account in the translations of Yorùbá oral and written literature — for instance, as noted earlier, the Yorùbá nonspecific pronouns "o" and "wǫn" are translated as "he"/"they" in English, as if they were equivalents. The Yorùbá word *ènìyàn*, meaning "humans," is routinely translated as "man," and the Yorùbá word *ǫmǫ*, meaning "child" or "offspring," is routinely translated as "son." At the very

least, one would expect that translators would offer a disclaimer similar
to the one Oyekan Owomoyela gives in his book on Yorùbá proverbs:

> A word on my use of personal pronouns. Yorùbá pronouns are
> gender neutral. In using them, therefore, one does not run the risk
> of unintended sexism as one does with English pronouns. I have
> found it somewhat clumsy to use the combination "he or she," or
> "he/she," or "him or her." ... I hope my readers will accept the use
> of masculine pronouns with universal application in the non-sexist
> spirit in which I use them.[24]

This is a rare acknowledgment of the imposition of the sexism of English
on Yorùbá literature through translation. Nevertheless, Owomoyela's
acceptance of English categories is not a solution. His male identity is
on the side of privilege, so it is not surprising that he underestimates the
distortion this adoption imposes. The issue goes beyond awkwardness;
it is about accuracy. Using masculine pronouns when maleness is not
specified communicates inaccurate information. More serious is the fact
that accepting the English categorization erases the Yorùbá gender-free
framework.

More fundamental in Yorùbá discourse is the problem of "thinking in
English" in the case of Yorùbá bilinguals, even as we speak and engage
in Yorùbá. This problem is revealed in the title of an essay that purports
to talk about oral poets in Yorùbá society: "The Yorùbá Oral Poet and
His Society."[25] Even if this usage can be excused by the idea that the
English male pronoun is generic and therefore unmarked, the following
usage, which comes from the same essay, cannot: "The Yorùbá oral poet
is not a tool but a man."[26] At the very least it adds confusion as to the
identity of oral poets, whom the author admits in his essay are both
males and females. Another example of this confusion in translation due
to the gender gap between Yorùbá and English is found in Oludare Olajubu's review of a book about Yorùbá myths. He states that there are
many Yorùbá tales known as *sèniyàn seranko,* which should translate
as "be-human, be-animal" but which Olajubu translates as "be-man-be-
animal."[27] Clearly, the emphasis in Yorùbá is on a human being turning
into an animal, but the implication of his translation is of a male person
turning into an animal. The Yorùbá word *èniyàn* does not mean "man";
it stands for human beings in general.

Many of the collectors and translators of Yorùbá oral literature are
trained as literary critics, and thus the major tool of their trade is
language; therefore, one cannot excuse their lack of attention to such
a critical factor in their rendering of Yorùbá into English. Thus constructions like this one, from another Yorùbá scholar, are preferable:

"Yorùbá oral poets not only sought to explain the world,...*they* also stoked the embers of curiosity in children."[28] Obviously, English can be used in a less-gendered fashion. The training of scholars of Yorùbá is part of the problem and this fact has also been noted as a reason for the privileging of written literature over oral. The observations of Olabiyi Yai are relevant: "Critics of oral poetry are almost invariably trained in the criticism of written poetry before specializing in oraliture. This seemingly harmless chronological inversion is consecrated as logical to the extent that written literature criticism serves as the bedrock to oral poetry criticism, the latter being perceived as its appendage."[29] Written literature in Yorùbáland is mostly literature written by Yorùbás in English, and even Yorùbá-language literature is influenced by English. This is because most (if not all) of the writers are Yorùbá/English bilinguals who are trained first and foremost in English. As a result, the gender bias carried in English is transferred into Yorùbá literature.

Scholarship on language and gender goes beyond the analysis of the structure of language. Feminists are also concerned with gender differences in language use, and some have argued that the difference between men's and women's speech is related to the sexism of the English language. In the United States, for example, some scholars have argued that men and women speak different "genderlects."[30] There is not enough evidence regarding non-Western societies to warrant such a decisive conclusion. However, anthropologists have also concerned themselves with the relation between gender and speech and have articulated a way of conceptualizing it in a subfield known as the ethnography of speaking. According to Joel Sherzer, "The ethnography of speaking is concerned with language use in social and cultural context.... [It] is also concerned with the ways in which forms of discourse and patterns of speaking are related to the various roles in a society, such as those of men and women."[31] He goes on to suggest that gender distinction in language in industrialized societies is, on the one hand, related to surface grammar, manner of speaking, who uses certain categories of words more than others, and so on. On the other hand, he says that in nonindustrialized societies, it is related to verbal genre, defined as the "culturally recognized, routinized and sometimes though not necessarily overtly marked and formalized forms and categories of discourse."[32] Against this background and given the gendered approach to Yorùbá orature by scholars like Barber, one should pose the question: Is there a gender basis to the performance and classification of Yorùbá oral genre?

Scholars who have attempted to classify Yorùbá oral genre have concluded that Yorùbá poetry is classified not so much by its contents or structure but by the *group* to which the reciter belongs and the techniques of recitation he (or she) employs. Thus a number of genres have been identified and studied.[33] They include:

- *Ìjálá:* poetry of hunters and devotees of Ògún chanted at social gatherings.

- *Ìwì:* poetry chanted by members of the Egúngún cult — that is, masquerade.

- *Ìyèrè ifá:* chants performed by diviner-priests.

- *Oríkì:* praise poetry, an everyday genre chanted most notably by wives of the lineage and professional praise-singers.

- *Ìtàn:* stories told by lineage elders about town and family on special occasions or when the need arises.

- *Ẹkún ìyàwó:* (or *rárà ìyàwó*): laments of a bride chanted on the eve of the wedding.

- *Èṣù-pípè:* chants performed by the devotees of the divinity Èṣù.

- *Ṣàngó-pípè:* chants performed by the devotees of the divinity Ṣàngó.

- *Ògún-pípè:* chants performed by the devotees of the divinity Ògún.

- *Ọya-pípè:* chants performed by the devotees of the divinity Ọya.

- *Òwe:* proverbs used in everyday speech by anybody.

- *Àlọ́ àpamọ̀:* riddles told for entertainment by both children and adults.

- *Àlọ́:* folk tales.

Most of the genres are performed by lineage, occupational, and/or religious groupings. *Ìjálá, ìwí, ìyèrè ifá, Ṣàngó-pípè, Ọya pípè,* and *Èṣù pípè* all fall into this category. Because religion and occupations are lineage-based in Yorùbáland, access to each genre is shaped by factors other than sex. From an ethnography-of-speaking perspective, it appears that a genre like *ẹkún ìyàwó* (the lament of brides) can be classified as a women's genre, particularly because laments are associated with women in the cross-cultural literature.[34] Such a classification would be mistaken, however, because *ẹkún ìyàwó* is related to the social role of a bride (not her anatomy) as someone who must leave her natal family to go and live as a stranger in the husband's compound. It is a once-in-a-lifetime performance for each bride, and both old men and women are involved in teaching the bride in preparation for this public performance. If a female never becomes a bride, then she has no occasion to perform this oral poetry. Further, because the content of one Yorùbá oral genre is indistinguishable from another, the occasion of the performance, rather than content, becomes the distinguishing characteristic. As Olajubu puts it: "All the major forms of Yorùbá poetry draw from a common source of praise names, proverbs, and wise sayings; they employ the same pattern of poetic language."[35] Most Yorùbá verbal genres draw from the *oríkì,* classified as a genre in its own right. But scholars have also noted the difficulty of distinguishing the *oríkì* from other genres because of its ubiquity. Barber calls *oríkì* a "master discourse" due to its "manifold realisations...in daily life";[36] other verbal genres are composed mainly of it. To paraphrase Barber, *oríkì* are composed for innumerable subjects of all types — human, animal, and spiritual — and they are performed in different modes or genres. They are a central component of almost every significant ceremony in the life of the compound and town and are constantly in the air in the form of greetings, congratulations, and jokes.[37] The ubiquitousness of the *oríkì* and the infinite number of uses to which it is put make it difficult to understand what Barber means when she all but labels it a women's genre in her study of the form in Òkukù town. Similarly, the concern in the field of ethnography of speaking with identifying verbal genres as men's or women's is related to the constitution of men and women as a priori categories based on their anatomy, which is not necessarily a universal way of structuring the social world.

In Yorùbáland, we cannot speak of gender roles; instead today we can speak of the roles of *oko, aya,* brides, younger siblings, mothers, Ifá priests, or Ògún devotees, for example. Distinctions in speech and verbal genre are related more to social roles than bioanatomical differences. Speech in Yorùbáland cannot be characterized by the gender of the speaker. Rather, the position from which one speaks determines of the mode of address and choice of pronouns. For example, because Yorùbá language is particular about seniority, only seniors can address someone with a given name in speech, and they also can use *o,* which is the informal pronoun. Similarly, *ìyàwó,* being juniors, must address their particular conjugal partner using *e,* the pronoun denoting seniority. However, since nobody is permanently in a junior position, from one moment to the next, or from one speaker to the next, the position changes — the speech of any individual is fluid and shifting, reflecting the position in a particular social interaction at a moment in time. The speech of males and females exhibits the same kind of characteristics because both have opportunities to be senior and junior, depending on with whom they are interacting. Whether the time has come for distinguishing male and female speech in Yorùbá language is an empirical question that calls for research. The preoccupation in recent times with labeling texts male or female may be necessary in some cultures, but what makes a particular text gendered should be explained, not assumed. Is it that a text is female or in a women's genre because only (and all) females have knowledge of it? Or because in the particular society only females are allowed to perform it? Or because of some other criteria? The point is that the conditions of this sort of categorization must be explicitly laid out.

"Doing Gender": A Research Hazard

This section reviews a study of Yorùbá oral tradition that raised interesting questions about gender and language and offers a case study of the way Western gender predilections are imposed on Yorùbá culture. The study is entitled "Esu Elegbara: The Yorùbá God of Chance and Uncertainty: A Study of Yorùbá Mythology," by Ayodele Ogundipe. It is a study of Èṣù, the Yorùbá "god of uncertainty," through praise poetry, narratives, and myths collected from devotees of the god. The study is of interest for the following reasons:

1. The anatomic-sex-specificity (or lack thereof) of Èṣù has been critical to many scholarly interpretations of the place of the divinity in Yorùbá religion and thought. Ogundipe's contribution is to go beyond gender assignations and show that in the indigenous construction of Èṣù, the divinity is as often represented as female as male. Consequently, she convincingly demolished the idea that Èṣù is a phallic divinity.

2. The data for the study were collected from two groups of Èṣù devotees — the Lagos group, which was male, and the Ìbàdàn group, which was female. This should afford us the rare opportunity of finding out whether there are any gender effects on the devotees' knowledge, mode of worship, and the way they are presented by the researcher.

3. The author, a Yorùbá woman, makes the claim that her gender and age affected her ability to gather data. She did not, however, analyze the impact of this claim in any systematic fashion.

The data for the study were collected in the late 1960s from the Èṣù devotees in Lagos and Ìbàdàn. Ogundipe claims that there were "certain parts of [the] Èṣù shrine into which women were not allowed."[38]

She feels that the all-male group in Lagos was reluctant to discuss some matters in her presence because of her female gender and young age. She explains this situation: "Although women are not excluded from Yorùbá cults, female participants who hold significant positions are usually advanced in years."[39] Her own study contradicts this pronouncement. If indeed in the cult of Èṣù worship in Yorùbáland "women" were not allowed to go near the shrine, why was there an all-female group in Ìbàdàn, with its own shrine and which was no less devoted to Èṣù worship than the Lagos group? Ogundipe does not tell us that the two groups were devotees of different gods — it was the same Èṣù. Unfortunately, she does not set the sex restriction in Lagos against her own findings. One wonders why. Her statement that "women are not excluded" but that only elderly women could hold leadership positions has the following implications: religious cults are male-founded in Yorùbáland, and women are included or excluded. This is erroneous, given her finding that there are all-male, all-female, mixed-sex, and what-have-you religious cults in Yorùbáland. Moreover, recruitment into religious cults is generally lineage-based. At the level of the individual, it is related to personal problems in the family that may lead to the worship of one divinity or another. For example, two of Ogundipe's Lagos male informants had become Èṣù devotees because they were consecrated to the cult by their mother, who had made such a vow to Èṣù. In contrast, the leader of the group in Ìbàdàn said she had inherited Èṣù worship from her mother, who herself had been an "*Èṣù* devotee *lati orun wa,* meaning 'right from heaven.' "[40] In other words, her mother was born into the cult. Indigenous Yorùbá religion has no gender restriction on either cult founding or cult membership. In fact, some scholars of Yorùbá alternative churches have suggested that this influence may have been operative in the founding of the Aladura sect; many of its churches were founded by females in spite of the male dominance in Christianity.[41] Ogundipe's observation that female leaders of cults are advanced in years is always read backward to mean younger females are restricted because of menstruation. This assumption has not been tested and is not supported by any kind of data. It has not been demonstrated that there are menstrual taboos in indigenous Yorùbá cults, and in some of the Yorùbá Christian churches in which such restrictions have been identified, it would be worthwhile to investigate the influence of world religions (Islam and Christianity) that have such restrictions. Finally, I think it is disingenuous to point out that "women" in leadership positions tend to be elderly. In general, the same seems to be true of the male leadership.

A continued review of the study suggests that Ogundipe uncritically

accepts the pronouncements about sex from some of her male informants and discounts contrary information from the female devotees and
her own findings. This privileging of males may not be unrelated to her
own biases and assumptions, which are founded on her academic training and Christian background, both of which are Western and both of
which are important sources of gender distinctions. (This is not peculiar
to Ogundipe — a majority of African scholars have a similar background.) There is clearly a male bias in the way she writes about the two
groups of Èṣù devotees. This is particularly apparent in her biography of
the different informants. One must remember that her primary interest
was to acquire their knowledge of Èṣù through the oral poetry and prose
of the cult. In her short biography of the female informants, she says of
Mutiu Adeleke: "Of all the women, ... Mutiu was certainly the pretti-
est. A stunning looking woman in her mid-forties ... An unconventional
woman, in spite of her good looks..."[42] About Ajisafe Mosebolatan,
an elderly devotee in her sixties or seventies: "The women said she was
quite a beauty when she was younger, but I found that hard to believe
because she looked so aged and wrinkled when I met her."[43] Apart from
the fact that one wonders what this kind of "beauty pageant" information has to do with the women's devotion to their god, one is puzzled
as to what kind of questions from the researcher prompted the women's
statements about Ajisafe's faded beauty. In writing about the men, no
such information is offered, even when Ogundipe focuses on their physical appearance. Of Gbadamosi Àkànní, a male "informant," she states:
"Of medium build and height, he seemed taller than he actually was
because he carried himself very straight."[44] Bola Esubiyi, another male,
was "a short dark man in his late fifties," and Moses Olojede "was a
dark, wiry man."[45] Of course, she does not volunteer any information
as to who was the darkest and the most handsome of the three, as she
did with the females.

The way in which she describes the dancing abilities of two informants, one male and one female, both of them coincidentally named
Bola, is interesting. Of Bola Esubiyi (the male), she writes, "He was
a skilled dancer."[46] Of Bola Esubunmi (the female), she writes, "Bola
was a magnificent dancer. During one of the festivals she danced up a
storm."[47] One gets the impression that dancing comes *naturally* to the
female, but the male had to cultivate it. This interpretation smacks of the
gender distinction that some feminists have noted in Western cultures in
which females are associated with nature and males with culture.

The problem of gender bias continues in her description of the leaders of the two groups. Let us compare the information she presents
about them:

Baderinwa Esunbunmi (the female). Baderinwa Esunbunmi held sway among the devotees of Ìbàdàn. A tall, massive woman in her late 60s, Baderinwa was certainly the grand dame of the group. Everyone else in the group was *cowed* by her.... Baderinwa was a regal woman with dark gleaming skin and piercing red eyes.[48]

The Elegushe (male). The Elegushe is a traditional title borne by Mr. J. O. Buraimoh, a tall, gaunt man well into his 70s who had a clean shaven head and a fastidiously clean appearance. Mr. Buraimoh had a most intimidating presence. His luminous eyes looked at one...[49]

The description of the Elegushe is reverential; he is portrayed appropriately as the leader of a religious cult. In contrast, Baderinwa is presented as if she was the leader of a social club. One wonders whether her dark, gleaming skin was one of her qualifications for leadership as the "grand dame" of the group. Even when Ogundipe is discussing an obviously similar attribute of the two leaders, it is presented as negative in the female and positive in the male. When Ogundipe writes that "the group was cowed" by Baderinwa, one gets the impression that she actively sought to bully the group. The Elegushe, in contrast, effortlessly "had a most intimidating presence." His eyes were "luminous" while hers were "piercing red."[50]

Ogundipe's treatment of the female devotees is even less reverential, if not downright disrespectful. For instance, this surfaces when the researcher asked Baderinwa (whom she had earlier described as a prosperous trader, a woman of means living in a large house, a mother of five children) whether she was married. It is difficult to imagine how Ogundipe, herself a young Yorùbá woman who presented herself as a cultural insider, could have said, "Are you married?" to Madam Baderinwa, who was said to be at least the same age as the researcher's mother. There is no indelicate way of doing this in Yorùbá. To crown it all, in reporting Baderinwa's reaction to this question, Ogundipe writes she "simply giggled."[51] For a woman who was described as sixty-something, massive, a prosperous trader, a woman of means, the mother of five children, the verb "giggle" seems totally out of place. Baderinwa was no school girl; she was a sixty-something leader of a religious cult.

Individually, the female devotees are presented differently than the men. Collectively, there are also differences, particularly in how they are named. The Lagos informants, the male group, are referred to variously as the "Iddo group," "elders," "members," "Esu devotees," and "the group." The all-female Ìbàdàn group are simply called "women": "The women had taken to keeping religious objects indoors.... The women engaged in different kinds of livelihood.... The women's group at Ol-unloyo's compound..."[52] On the one hand, when Ogundipe visited the female leader, she would send her children out to fetch the other "women." On the other hand, in Lagos, when she visited the house of the male leader, "important members of the group were then sent for."[53] From this presentation, one gets the distinct impression that the female devotees were first and foremost women and that this was the basis of their coming together as a group rather than the fact that they worshiped together as members of a religious cult. The constant reference to them as women instead of as Èṣù devotees suggests that they met primarily to socialize and only as an afterthought engaged in Èṣù worship; this, of course, casts a shadow on the seriousness of their religious devotion. Ogundipe does not give us any facts about their behavior, which suggests that the female devotees were less devoted to their god. On the contrary she writes: "Baderinwa had a very esoteric knowledge of Esu worship. She always prepared herself ritually as did the other women, before each interview. One could not just walk in and start a discussion of Esu. There were sacrifices to be offered and sometimes ritual cleansing to be performed before any serious discussion could take place."[54]

Ogundipe works as a vector of Western gender norms, injecting them into her study. Maria Black and Rosalind Coward have posited that "women's exclusion as representatives of a generalized humanity [in the English language] is not a product of a semantic rule." Instead, it is due to the fact that "the attributes of the male can in fact disappear into a 'non-gendered subject.' Women, on the other hand, never appear as non-gendered subjects."[55] Ogundipe has transferred this problem of sex bias in the English language and society to her subjects. She presents the female devotees as having a gender identity; the male devotees are prototypical Èṣù worshipers, hence, the nongendered references to them. Yet she does not give any information about the behavior of the female devotees that warrants the difference in representation.

No doubt Ogundipe felt closer to and freer and hence more familiar with the "Ìbàdàn group," probably because of her own consciousness of sex as a possible source of identity. She mentions a couple of times that both she and the Lagos male informants felt uncomfortable during her interviews because of her young age and female sex. I believe this representation tells us about the researcher's background and biases. In addition to the Western gender-biased intellectual and religious grounding, there seems to have been a class bias also. Members of the Lagos group, apart from being male, appeared to be better-off economically and more cosmopolitan; some of them were in fact literate and could speak English.[56]

Ogundipe's conscious and unconscious biases notwithstanding, she is able to challenge convincingly the view of some scholars of Yorùbá religion that Èṣù is a phallic deity. She is particularly critical of Westcott, whom she accuses of imposing Western values on Yorùbá data. She is worth quoting at some length. For her, Westcott's interpretation of Èṣù as a phallic symbol "demonstrates the author's agility with Freudian and western psychoanalytical associations as well as her western intellectual preoccupation with reading phallic interpretations into anything with more length than girth."[57]

She continues:

> As male or female in sculpture, Èṣù usually wears an elaborately long hairstyle, ... occasionally stylized as a phallus. As a male, Èṣù usually wears a pubic apron or trousers; as a female, the female breasts are prominent. Èṣù is also variously portrayed with a pipe in his mouth, club in his hand, sucking his thumb, or blowing a whistle.[58]

Ogundipe herself is not totally free of Western associations, however, even as she correctly concludes that Èṣù's depiction in Yorùbá religion is both male and female. She writes: "Although his masculinity is depicted as visually and graphically overwhelming, his equally expressive femininity renders his enormous sexuality *ambiguous,* contrary, and genderless."[59] The point, however, is not that Èṣù's sexuality is ambiguous or that the god is androgynous, but that Èṣù's anasex is *incidental* to the conception, function, role, and powers of the god. It is precisely because the Yorùbá world-sense labels no attributes as masculine or feminine that it is possible for Èṣù to be depicted as both without any contradictions or mental gymnastics. Consequently, Ogundipe completely misses the point and imposes a Western gender framework when she writes: "Figuratively, Èṣù is female when he is positive, attentive, conforming, predictable, and gentle; he is male when he is negative, inattentive, nonconforming, unpredictable, and ruthless."[60] This is a clear genderizing of Yorùbá discourse unsupported by either her data or even the portrayal of other divinities in Yorùbá culture. Her interpretation is based on the binary opposition between male and female attributes in the West: that is, if males are one thing, then females are the opposite. For example, they cannot both be strong — if men are strong, then women must be weak. In Yorùbáland, both males and females have common attributes. Yorùbá does not make gender assignations of character or personality.

Let us look at the representation of another Yorùbá divinity — Ọya, the Yorùbá female river god (not goddess, because the term òrìṣà in Yorùbá is not gendered). She is usually portrayed as fearsome and ruthless; one of the lines from her praise poetry reads, "*Obìnrin gbona, ọkùnrin sa*" (literally: females will hit the road, and males will run; everybody flees when she appears).[61] This hardly supports the Western idea of femininity. Judith Gleason, in a study of mighty Ọya, notes that the Yorùbá conception of the god suggests a "type of energy that our [Western] culture does not see as feminine."[62]

Yorùbá genderlessness is not to be read as androgyny or ambiguity of gender. It is not genderless in terms of a presence of both male and female attributes. Instead it is genderless because human attributes are not gender-specific. Bioanatomical differences are a source of neither distinction nor identity in Yorùbáland. The *orí*, the metaphysical head and the fountainhead of individual fate and identity, is without sex. Anasex differences are *incidental* and do not define much. As I noted earlier, the fact that Yorùbá society is interpreted on the basis of Western languages and conceptualizations in and of itself introduces a certain measure of genderization. For example, the observation that Yorùbá discourse is genderless necessarily imposes a gendered way of seeing and hearing Yorùbá. After all, how do you say "genderless" in Yorùbá? It is not a Yorùbá category and only has meaning in a discourse that is in the process of making Yorùbá fit the Western dominant pattern.

Karin Barber correctly concludes that the Yorùbá world is not dichotomized into male and female spheres.[63] But the Yorùbá world today is not isolated from other worlds, particularly the Western world. In fact, the point that Ogundipe's study makes so poignantly is that the Yorùbá world is increasingly part and parcel of the Western world, and our interpretations of it cannot escape this fact.

Yorùbá: A Genderless Language in a Genderful World

Yorùbá is changing, and like many African languages, it is changing rapidly — a result, in part, of the imposition of European languages and structures on African societies. One of the most notable changes in Yorùbá culture is the growing importance of gender categories in language, literature, and society. The role of scholars and bilinguals has been singled out in the process. However, the question of biases in language is not only one of language use; how statements are heard is equally important. In other words, what the members of an audience bring to the situation constitutes part of the meaning of a particular

qnestrez

utterance. If they are gender-conscious, then they will tend to "hear" gender distinctions in speech. Gender is a way of both seeing and hearing the world. For example, I have noticed that it is difficult for many Westerners to conceive of female ọkọ (commonly rendered as "husband") without thinking of homosexuality or transvestitism. On the contrary, in Yorùbáland females as ọkọ are taken for granted, their role being seen as social and not sexual. In a gender-saturated world that extends far beyond and out of control of the Yorùbá, it is not surprising that Yorùbá non-gender-specificity could be interpreted as the male-as-norm of the English language. Yorùbá scholars have to be explicit about questions of gender in translation — we cannot, for example, wait for the non-gender-specific third-person pronoun to appear before we use English in a less male-dominant fashion, as indeed people are beginning to do in the United States (although it is an uphill task and their success is questionable).

Perhaps one should note that the feminist search for a genderless language is often presented as capable of fulfillment only out of this world, in the world of science fiction. But Douglas R. Hofstadter suggests such a fulfillment on the terrestrial plane: "I know of no human being who speaks non-sexist as their native tongue. It will be very interesting to see if such people come to exist. If so, it will have taken a lot of work by a lot of people to reach that point."[64] I, like millions of other Yorùbá, speak a nonsexist language. For us, however, what needs to be documented is not how we came to speak this nonsexist language but how we are increasingly speaking a "sexist" one — a process that I have attempted to document. It should be noted that there are other languages besides Yorùbá that at one time at least could be characterized as genderless. But are such languages heard as such? Genderlessness in language is not necessarily a futuristic undertaking; sadly, it could well be passé.

The Same and Different Worlds of Gender

Western discourses, feminist and nonfeminist alike, assume that all societies perceive the human body as gendered and then organize men and women as social categories based on this assumption. A major contribution of feminist discourse has been that it made explicit the gendered and male-dominant nature of all forms of Western institutions and discourses. Before feminist inquiries, scholarship and science in particular were held to be disembodied/objective, that is, not culture-bound. But I have argued in this book that not all societies use the "evidence" of the body to constitute gender categories. There are other categories that

imagine inworld of a gendered world

① argument

are constituted using the perception of the body, and there are many categories that appear to ignore the body. After all, even in the West, despite the deeply held assumption of gendered human bodies, the body is assumed to constitute evidence for another category—race. Gendered bodies are neither universal nor timeless. Yorùbá social categories were not based on anatomical differences.

Nevertheless, scholars deploy Western categories and theories across cultures without examining their ethnocentric foundations. Gendered bodies have been assumed for both Yorùbáland and other African societies. This study argues not only that this is a mistake but that it is also an obstacle to the pursuit of knowledge, and this has ramifications for the conduct of research and policy formulation.

From the perspective of doing research, the assumption of women as a social category prevents us from asking the "right" questions about any given society, since questions are already conceptualized a priori. It prevents us, as knowledge-seekers, from asking first-order, foundational questions generated from the evidence of particular societies. Instead what we find are canned questions based on Western experiences masquerading as universals. Ultimately, this is not about which questions are asked but whose questions and why.[65]

Perhaps some of the pitfalls of propagating the Western viewpoint as the universal can be illustrated by examining the way in which the United Nations has been constituted and the policies that it pursues. Sue Ellen Charlton, in a book on women and Third World development, asserts that "the dependency triad describes the situation that exists in virtually every country in the world, one in which women are dependent upon men in formal politics at the local, national and international levels."[66] But this statement is true only because both formal politics and women as a political category are products of an international system that was created and continues to be dominated by the West. The United Nations is emblematic of this Western dominance. The activities and policies of the United Nations around the question of women as a globally victimized category have made possible the conception of "women" as a recognizable, victimized sociopolitical category. The Western feminist movement has been globalized, and international feminists have created a set of discourses and practices about gender and a climate of opinion worldwide around which Western ideas about "women" are institutionalized and exported to every nook and cranny of the world. Therefore, in a sense, the division of the world into local, national, and international levels is a false one because of the interrelationships among the different levels.

In fact, the UN Women's Decade captured the paradox of women as both a local and a global category and helped illuminate the way "she" is deployed at the different levels. The United Nations declared 1975 the International Women's Year. A world conference was held in Mexico, during which 1975 to 1985 was inaugurated as the Women's Decade. A follow-up conference was held in Copenhagen in 1980, and, finally, in 1985, the end of the Women's Decade was marked by a conference in Nairobi. The importance of the Women's Decade has to do with the way it unequivocally put "women" as a victimized category on the world's agenda. Womanhood has been pathologized, at a global level, and the concerns of the feminist international have underlined this globalization of what was once a local Western preoccupation. Germaine Greer, the Australian feminist, was right when she declared in 1975:

> The decision to have a women's year was simply a belated recognition of the fashionableness of feminism in the West, whose lifestyles dominate the UN self-image. . . . International Women's Year is a single extension of Madison Avenue feminism: the agricultural laborers of Asia and Africa might as well lay down their hoes and light up a Virginia Slim.[67]

More than that, the focus on women by the United Nations represented a convergence of interests among Western feminists, Western governments and the United Nations. The feminists' concern with women's control of reproduction coincided with the interests of Western governments and the United Nations to control population growth in the Third World. The women's conference of 1975 was essentially a continuation of the UN population conference held in Bucharest the previous year. The divergence of opinion between Western feminists and Third World feminists at these conferences about what constitutes women's issues and priorities underscores the difficulty of conceiving a sociopolitical category of "women" at the global level.

The UN Women's Decade is particularly significant because it institutionalized and systematized on a worldwide basis a particular Western way of viewing the human body. Colonization set this process in motion; Western feminism contributed to it; and the United Nations through its policies and declarations elevated it to a norm, particularly at the level of formal politics and governments. Western ideas about gender have also trickled down to the remotest parts of the world. In Africa the actions of international organizations are noteworthy for proliferating these structures and processes through the creation of local women's organizations (NGOs [nongovernmental organizations]) and for using gender constructs as a policy tool. How these interact with indigenous constructions is an empirical question that depends on the issues and the context, but it is impossible to deny the influence of the West in shaping local discourses and practices about gender.

The greatest impact of these Western ideas regarding the primacy of gender is that they have made it difficult to present alternative ways of looking at anatomic sex-distinctions without pathologizing the female. In the wake of the conflicts and controversies between Western and non-Western women during the UN Women's Decade conferences, one recurring question was: What is a central concern for women worldwide? Aline K. Wong, a Singaporean scholar, correctly asserted: "I think it is, what do women want *to be* as women?"[68] But much more than that, one should ask why this category, "women," has been singled out and what is the makeup of such a group. Unfortunately, these are not questions that are asked before the construct "women" is imposed transculturally. Research questions lead to particular answers; the fact that the parameters of many Western discourses, including feminism, are preset limits the questions that can be posed.

The goal of my research has been to get beyond the preset parameters so that one can ask first-order questions about Yorùbá society. The task has not been straightforward because I have had to elucidate why, in the first place, gender categories are being investigated for Yorùbáland and why Yorùbá anafemales were assumed to be subordinated and victimized even before research was done in their society. Questions such as, Why are women victimized or subordinated? and, What is the gender division of labor? are not first-order questions in regard to Yorùbáland because both of these questions assume gender. Foundational questions for one interested in social organization might be, What is the Yorùbá conception of difference? Is the human body used as evidence in this conceptualization? A researcher curious about difference and hierarchy might ask, What constitutes difference in Yorùbáland? (It is by no means obvious that all societies will agree on what constitutes sex-differences — for example, in the West, hormones and chromosomes are part of the distinction, but in many other societies such conceptualizations are absent.)

Researchers need to interrogate their own standpoints and biases as they pose questions, collect data, and interpret evidence. For a start, all scholars should take seriously Linda Nicholson's admonition that "it is time that we [Westerners] explicitly acknowledge that our claims about women are not based on some given reality but emerge out of our own places within history and culture; they are political acts that reflect the contexts we emerge out of and the futures we would like to see."[69] The present book has cleared the way for asking first-order, foundational questions about gender and difference in Yorùbá society. It has shown that our interest in gender in Yorùbáland cannot be divorced from the West's domination of both the constitution of the academy/ scholarship and the sociopolitical and economic world spheres. Ultimately, this study raises the question of whether it is possible to have independent research questions and interests given the Western origins of most disciplines and the continued Western dominance of the world, for now.

Notes

<hr />

Preface

1. Dorothy E. Smith, *The Everyday World as Problematic: A Feminist Sociology* (Boston: Northeastern University Press, 1987), 30.

2. Judith Lorber, *Paradoxes of Gender* (New Haven: Yale University Press, 1994), 13.

3. Michel Foucault, *The History of Sexuality,* vol. 1, *An Introduction* (New York: Random House, 1990), 69.

4. Shelly Errington, "Recasting Sex, Gender, and Power," in *Power and Difference: Gender in Island Southeast Asia,* ed. Jane Atkinson and Shelly Errington (Stanford, Calif.: Stanford University Press, 1990), 33.

5. For a history of the emergence of and shifts in the category "women" in Britain, see Denise Riley, *Am I That Name? Feminism and the Category of Women in History* (Minneapolis: University of Minnesota Press, 1988).

6. Standard Yorùbá as it is spoken today derives mostly from the Ọ̀yọ́ dialect.

7. For a delineation of the term "Old Ọ̀yọ́," see chap. 2, n. 1, below.

8. Lorber, *Paradoxes of Gender,* 10.

9. Keletso Atkins, *The Moon Is Dead! Give Us Our Money! The Cultural Origins of an African Work Ethic, Natal, South Africa 1843–1900* (London: Heinemann, 1993), 67.

Chapter 1: Visualizing the Body

1. Compare Thomas Laqueur's usage: "Destiny Is Anatomy," which is the title of chapter 2 of his *Making Sex: Body and Gender from the Greeks to Freud* (Cambridge, Mass.: Harvard University Press, 1990).

2. Elizabeth Spelman, *Inessential Woman: Problems of Exclusion in Feminist Thought* (Boston: Beacon Press, 1988), 37.

3. J. Edward Chamberlain and Sander Gilman, *Degeneration: The Darker Side of Progress* (New York: Columbia University Press, 1985), 292.

4. Naomi Scheman, *Engenderings: Constructions of Knowledge, Authority, and Privilege* (New York: Routledge, 1993), 186.

5. Elizabeth Grosz, "Bodies and Knowledges: Feminism and the Crisis of

181

Reason," in *Feminist Epistemologies,* ed. Linda Alcoff and Elizabeth Potter (New York: Routledge, 1994), 198; emphasis added.

6. Scheman, *Engenderings.*

7. See, for example, the following for accounts of the importance of sight in Western thought: Hans Jonas, *The Phenomenon of Life* (New York: Harper and Row, 1966); Donald Lowe, *History of Bourgeois Perception* (Chicago: University of Chicago Press, 1982).

8. Compare the discussion in Nancy Scheper-Hughes and Margaret Lock, "The Mindful Body: A Prolegomenon to Future Work in Medical Anthropology," *Medical Anthropology Quarterly,* n.s., 1 (March 1987): 7–41.

9. The work of Sander Gilman is particularly illuminating on European conceptions of difference and otherness. See *Difference and Pathology: Stereotypes of Sexuality, Race, and Madness* (Ithaca, N.Y.: Cornell University Press, 1985); *On Blackness without Blacks: Essays on the Image of the Black in Germany* (Boston: G. K. Hall, 1982); *The Case of Sigmund Freud: Medicine and Identity* (Baltimore: John Hopkins University Press, 1993); *Jewish Self-Hatred: Anti-Semitism and the Hidden Language of the Jews* (Baltimore: John Hopkins University Press, 1986).

10. See, for example, the following: Linda Nicholson, "Feminism and Marx," in *Feminism as Critique: On the Politics of Gender,* ed. Seyla Benhabib and Drucilla Cornell (Minneapolis: University of Minnesota Press, 1986); Michele Barrett, *Women's Oppression Today* (London: New Left Books, 1980); Heidi Hartmann, "The Unhappy Marriage of Marxism and Feminism: Towards a More Progressive Union," in *Women and Revolution: A Discussion of the Unhappy Marriage of Marxism and Feminism,* ed. Lydia Sargent (Boston: South End Press, 1981).

11. Bryan Turner, "Sociology and the Body," in *The Body and Society: Explorations in Social Theory* (Oxford: Blackwell, 1984), 31.

12. Ibid.

13. Troy Duster, *Backdoor to Eugenics* (New York: Routledge, 1990).

14. Ibid.

15. Michael Omi and Howard Winant, *Racial Formation in the United States from the 1960s to the 1980s* (New York: Routledge, 1986). Compare also the discussion of the pervasiveness of race over other variables, such as class, in the analysis of the Los Angeles riot of 1992. According to Cedric Robinson, "Mass media and official declarations subsumed the genealogy of the Rodney King Uprisings into the antidemocratic narratives of race which dominate American culture. Urban unrest, crime, and poverty are discursive economies which signify race while erasing class" ("Race, Capitalism and the Anti-Democracy," paper presented at the Inter-disciplinary Humanities Center, University of California–Santa Barbara, winter 1994).

16. Duster (*Backdoor*) points to the widely held notion that diseases as well as money "run in families."

17. Compare Cornel West's concept of racial reasoning in *Race Matters* (New York: Vantage, 1993).

18. Cited in Stephen Gould, *The Mismeasure of Man* (New York: Norton, 1981), 19.

19. Ibid.

20. A recent anthology questions the dominant self-representation of Jews as "the People of the Book" and in the process attempts to document a relatively less common image of Jews as "the People of the Body." The editor of the volume makes an interesting point about "the [Jewish] thinker" and his book. He comments that the thinker's book "is evocative of…wisdom and the pursuit of knowledge. In this way, the image of the Jew (who is always male) poring over a book is always misleading. He appears to be elevated in spiritual pursuit. But if we could peer over his shoulders and see what his text says, he may in fact be reading about matters as erotic as what position to take during sexual intercourse. What is going on in 'the thinker's' head or more interestingly in his loins?" (Howard Elberg-Schwartz, "People of the Body," introduction to *People of the Body: Jews and Judaism from an Embodied Perspective* [Albany: State University of New York Press, 1992]). The somatocentric nature of European discourses suggests that the phrase the "People of the Body" may have a wider reach.

21. Attention to the body has not been smooth-sailing in feminism either. See Elizabeth Grosz, *Volatile Bodies: Toward a Corporeal Feminism* (Bloomington: Indiana University Press, 1994).

22. Virginia Woolf had summed up the feminist position succinctly: "Science it would seem is not sexless; she is a man, a father infected too" (quoted in Hillary Rose, "Hand, Brain, and Heart: A Feminist Epistemology for the Natural Sciences," *Signs* 9, no. 1 [1983]: 73–90). See also the following: Sandra Harding, *The Science Question in Feminism* (Ithaca, N.Y.: Cornell University Press, 1986); idem, ed., *The Racial Economy of Science* (Bloomington: Indiana University Press, 1993); Donna J. Haraway, *Primate Visions: Gender, Race, and Nature in the World of Modern Science* (New York: Routledge, 1989); and Margaret Wertheim *Pythagoras' Trousers: God Physics and the Gender Wars* (New York: Random House, 1995).

23. Dorothy E. Smith, *The Everyday World as Problematic: A Feminist Sociology* (Boston: Northeastern University Press, 1987), 30.

24. R. W. Connell, *Masculinities* (London: Polity Press, 1995), 53.

25. Susan Okin, *Women in Western Political Thought* (Princeton, N.J.: Princeton University Press, 1979); Elizabeth Spelman, *Inessential Woman: Problems of Exclusion in Feminist Thought* (Boston: Beacon Press, 1988).

26. Quoted in Laqueur, *Making Sex,* 54.

27. Ibid.

28. Lorna Schiebinger, *The Mind Has No Sex? Women in the Origins of Modern Science* (Cambridge, Mass.: Harvard University Press, 1989), 162.

29. For an account of some of these dualisms, see "Hélène Cixous," in *New French Feminisms: An Anthology,* ed. Elaine Marks and Isabelle de Courtivron (Amherst, Mass.: University of Massachusetts Press, 1980).

30. Gould, *Mismeasure of Man, 20.*

31. Laqueur, *Making Sex*.

32. See Suzanne J. Kessler and Wendy McKenna, *Gender: An Ethno-methodological Approach* (New York: John Wiley and Sons, 1978).

33. For elucidation, see Jane F. Collier and Sylvia J. Yanagisako, eds., *Gender and Kinship: Essays toward a Unified Analysis* (Stanford, Calif.: Stanford University Press, 1987).

34. Linda Nicholson has also explicated the pervasiveness of biological foundationalism in feminist thought. See "Interpreting Gender," in *Signs* 20 (1994): 79–104.

35. Kessler and McKenna, *Gender*.

36. In the title of this section, I use the term "sisterarchy." In using the term, I am referring to the well-founded allegations against Western feminists by a number of African, Asian, and Latin American feminists that despite the notion that the "sisterhood is global," Western women are at the top of the hierarchy of the sisterhood; hence it is actually a "sisterarchy." Nkiru Nzegwu uses the concept in her essay "O Africa: Gender Imperialism in Academia," in *African Women and Feminism: Reflecting on the Politics of Sisterhood*, ed. Oyèrónké Oyěwùmí (Trenton, N.J.: African World Press, forthcoming).

37. Lorber, *Paradoxes of Gender*, 17–18.

38. Ibid.

39. See Ifi Amadiume, *Male Daughters, Female Husbands: Gender and Sex in an African Society* (London: Zed Books, 1987), for an account of this institution in Igboland of southeastern Nigeria. See also Melville J. Herskovitz, "A Note on 'Woman Marriage' in Dahomey," *Africa* 10 (1937): 335–41, for an earlier allusion to its wide occurrence in Africa.

40. Kessler and McKenna, *Gender*, 24–36.

41. Serena Nanda, "Neither Man Nor Woman: The Hijras of India," in *Gender in Cross-cultural Perspective*," ed. Caroline Brettell and Carolyn Sargent (Englewood Cliffs, N.J.: Prentice Hall, 1993).

42. Gayle Rubin, "The Traffic in Women," in *Toward an Anthropology of Women*, ed. Rayna R. Reiter (New York: Monthly Review Press, 1975).

43. Kessler and McKenna, *Gender*, 7; Laqueur, *Making Sex*.

44. Judith Butler, *Gender Trouble: Feminism and the Subversion of Identity* (New York: Routledge, 1990), 7.

45. In her study (*Male Daughters*) of the Igbo society of Nigeria, anthropologist Ifi Amadiume introduced the idea of "gender flexibility" to capture the real separability of gender and sex in that African society. I, however, think that the "woman to woman" marriages of Igboland invite a more radical interrogation of the concept of gender, an interrogation that "gender flexibility" fails to represent. For one thing, the concept of gender as elaborated in the literature is a dichotomy, a duality grounded on the sexual dimorphism of the human body. Here, there is no room for flexibility.

46. The "race and gender literature" is grounded on notions of differences among women.

47. See, for example, Holly Devor, *Gender Blending: Confronting the Lim-*

its of Duality (Bloomington: Indiana University Press, 1989); Rebecca Gordon, "Delusions of Gender," *Women's Review of Books* 12, no. 2 (November 1994): 18–19.

48. Kathy Ferguson, *The Man Question: Visions of Subjectivity in Feminist Theory* (Berkeley: University of California Press), 7.

49. My use of the nineteenth century as a benchmark is merely to acknowledge the emerging gender configurations in the society; the process must have started earlier, given the role of the Atlantic slave trade in the dislocation of Yorùbáland.

50. See chapter 2 for a full account of Yorùbá world-sense as it is mapped onto social hierarchies.

51. This is not an attempt on my part to partake of some of the reductionist discussion about the "orality" of African societies in relation to "writing" in the West; nor is it the intention of this book to set up a binary opposition between the West and Yorùbáland, on the one hand, and writing and orality, on the other, as some scholars have done. There is a huge literature on writing and orality. A good entry point into the discourse, though it is an overly generalized account, is Walter Ong, *Orality and Literacy: The Technologizing of the Word* (New York: Methuen, 1982). For a recent account of some the issues from an African perspective, see Samba Diop, "The Oral History and Literature of Waalo, Northern Senegal: The Master of the Word in Wolof Tradition" (Ph.D. diss., Department of Comparative Literature, University of California–Berkeley, 1993).

52. See Wande Abimbola, *Ifa: An Exposition of the Ifa Literary Corpus* (Ìbàdàn: Oxford University Press, 1976).

53. Amadou Hampate Ba, "Approaching Africa," in *African Films: The Context of Production,* ed. Angela Martin (London: British Film Institute, 1982), 9.

54. Lowe, *History of Bourgeois Perception,* 7.

55. Evelyn Fox Keller and Christine Grontkowski, "The Mind's Eye," in *Discovering Reality: Feminist Perspectives on Epistemology, Metaphysics, Methodology, and Philosophy of Science,* ed. Sandra Harding and Merrill B. Hintikka (Boston: Reidel, 1983), 208.

56. Ibid.

57. Jonas, *Phenomenon of Life,* 507.

58. Keller and Grontkowski, "The Mind's Eye."

59. Nancy Chodorow, *Feminism and Psychoanalytic Theory* (New Haven: Yale University Press, 1989), 216.

60. See Amadiume, *Male Daughters;* and Valerie Amos and Pratibha Parma, "Challenging Imperial Feminism," *Feminist Review* (July 1984): 3–20.

61. Catherine Coles and Beverly Mack, eds., *Hausa Women in the Twentieth Century* (Madison: University of Wisconsin Press, 1991), 6.

62. Claire Robertson, *Sharing the Same Bowl: A Socioeconomic History of Women and Class in Accra, Ghana* (Bloomington: Indiana University Press, 1984), 23.

63. Ibid., 25.

64. For example, Bessie House-Midamba and Felix K. Ekechi, *African Market Women's Economic Power: The Role of Women in African Economic Development* (Westport, Conn.: Greenwood Press, 1995); Gracia Clark, *Onions Are My Husband: Accumulation by West African Market Women* (Chicago: University of Chicago Press, 1994).

65. I mean this in the sense of being reactive; I do not mean it in the Marxist sense of being retrogressive, although such a reading too is possible.

66. On the Ìbàdàn school of history, see Arnold Temu and Bonaventure Swai, *Historians and Africanist History: A Critique* (London: Zed Press, 1981). The UNESCO series on African history was also a response to the charge that Africans are people without history.

67. See the following volumes for some of the debates: Paulin J. Hountondji, *African Philosophy: Myth and Reality* (London: Hutchinson, 1983); Kwasi Wiredu, *Philosophy and African Culture* (New York: Cambridge University Press, 1980); P. O. Bodunrin, *Philosophy in Africa: Trends and Perspectives* (Ile-Ife, Nigeria: University of Ife Press, 1985); Tsenay Serequeberhan, ed., *African Philosophy* (New York: Paragon House, 1991).

68. In general, sociology of knowledge speaks to the issues of knowledge-formation, social identity, and social interests. According to Karl Mannheim, "persons bound together in groups strive in accordance with the character and position of the groups to which they belong to change the surrounding world. ... It is the direction of this will to change or to maintain, this collective activity, which produces the guiding thread for the emergence of their problems, their concepts, and their forms of thought" (*Ideology or Utopia?* [London: Routledge and Kegan Paul, 1936], 3).

69. See Hountondji, *African Philosophy,* as an example of an antinativist orientation.

70. An example of a nativist response is Oyekan Owomoyela, "Africa and the Imperative of Philosophy: A Skeptical Consideration," in *African Philosophy,* ed. Tsenay Serequeberhan (New York: Paragon House, 1991).

71. Abiola Irele, "In Praise of Alienation," in *The Surreptitious Speech: Presence Africaine and the Politics of Otherness, 1947–1987,* ed. V. Y. Mudimbe (Chicago: University of Chicago Press, 1992); emphasis added.

72. Quoted in Christopher Miller, *Theories of Africans: Francophone Literature and Anthropology in Africa* (Chicago: University of Chicago Press, 1990), 18.

73. Samuel Johnson, *The History of the Yorubas* (New York: Routledge and Kegan Paul, 1921), vii.

74. Nkiru Nzegwu, "Gender Equality in a Dual-Sex System: The Case of Onitsha," *Canadian Journal of Law and Jurisprudence,* 7, no. 1 (January 1994): 88, 91.

75. Tola Pearce, "Importing the New Reproductive Technologies: The Impact of Underlying Models of Family, Females and Women's Bodies in Nigeria" (paper presented at the World Institute for Development Economics Research

Conference, "Women, Equality and Reproductive Technology," Helsinki, August 3–6, 1992).

76. N. A. Fadipe, *The Sociology of the Yoruba* (Ìbàdàn, Nigeria: Ìbàdàn University Press, 1970).

77. Johnson, *History of the Yorubas.*

78. Molara Ogundipe-Leslie, *Re-creating Ourselves: African Women and Critical Transformations* (Trenton, N.J.: African World Press, 1994), 212. For further discussion of *ilémosú,* see the next chapter.

79. E. Bolaji Idowu, *Olodumare: God in Yoruba Belief* (London: Longman, 1962).

80. Johannes Fabian, *Time and the Other: How Anthropology Makes Its Object* (New York: Columbia University Press, 1983).

81. Here I am thinking specifically of the Indian subcontinent.

82. Serequeberhan, *African Philosophy,* xviii.

83. It is obvious that their qualification for membership rests on Western credentials. This too is a fundamental issue that needs to be problematized given their nationalist concerns.

84. This was an acronym that developed in the 1980s out of the cultural wars/canon wars, which was a struggle over what should constitute the "canon" in the humanities in universities in the United States. For some of the relevant issues, see Henry Louis Gates Jr., *Loose Canons: Notes on the Culture Wars* (New York: Oxford University Press, 1992).

85. Here I am alluding to the tradition of the founding fathers, who constituted the primary concerns of each discipline way before Africans, members of a dominated group, could participate. In women studies the same tradition is maintained with founding mothers.

86. Robert Bates, V. Y. Mudimbe, and Jean O'Barr, eds., *Africa and the Disciplines* (Chicago: University of Chicago Press, 1993).

87. I am alluding to "Hottentot Venus," the African woman who was exhibited in Europe in the nineteenth century, her buttocks being the curiosity. See Sander Gilman, "Black Bodies, White Bodies," in *Race, Writing, and Difference,* ed. Henry Louis Gates Jr. (Chicago: University of Chicago Press, 1985). Gilman notes that the lines of discovery from the secrets possessed by "Hottentot Venus" to twentieth-century psychoanalysis runs reasonably straight (257).

88. Given the role of anthropology as the handmaiden of colonization, it is surprising that this issue is underanalyzed by the editors of the volume.

89. Kwame Anthony Appiah, "Out of Africa: Topologies of Nativism," *Yale Journal of Criticism,* 12, no. 1 (fall 1988): 153–78.

90. I want to acknowledge Nkiru Nzegwu especially here, for her contribution in our many discussions of the issue of the subversion of matrilineal principle as an erasure of Akan cultural norms.

91. This section, in particular, benefited from the many discussions I had with Nkiru Nzegwu.

92. Appiah, "Out of Africa."

93. Ali A. Mazrui's notion of Africa's triple heritage seems to suffer from the

same kind of diminution of Africa. See Mazrui, *The Africans: A Triple Heritage* (New York: Little Brown and Co., 1986).

94. See Ulli Beier, *Yoruba Myths* (New York: Cambridge University Press, 1980); Wande Abimbola, "Ifa as a Body of Knowledge and as an Academic Discipline," *Journal of Cultures and Ideas*, 1, no. 1 (1983): 1–11.

95. V. Y. Mudimbe, *Parables and Fables: Exegesis, Textuality, and Politics in Central Africa* (Madison: University of Wisconsin Press, 1991), 24.

96. Ibid., 125.

97. Ibid.

98. V. Y. Mudimbe, *The Invention of Africa: Gnosis, Philosophy, and the Order of Knowledge* (Bloomington: Indiana University Press, 1988), 200.

99. Yorùbá studies encompasses work on Yorùbá peoples in West Africa and in the Yorùbá diaspora, including Brazil and Cuba. Apart from English, it incorporates a number of European languages, including French, Portuguese, and Spanish. Studies in English dominate: that is, most of the scholars do their major work in English. I am most concerned with Yorùbá discourse in English. For definition and issues in Yorùbá studies, see A. I. Asiwaju, "Dynamics of Yoruba Studies," *Studies in Yoruba History and Culture,* ed. G. O. Olusanya (Ìbàdàn: University Press Limited, 1983).

100. Andrew Apter, *Black Critics and Kings: The Hermeneutics of Power in Yoruba Society* (Chicago: University of Chicago Press, 1993).

101. A similar point is made in Oyekan Owomoyela, *Visions and Revisions: Essays on African Literatures and Criticism* (New York: Peter Lang, 1991).

102. Hountondji, *African Philosophy.*

103. Marc Bloch, *The Historian's Craft* (New York: Knopf, 1954), 68–69.

104. Hampate Ba, "Approaching Africa," 8; emphasis added.

105. Idowu, *Olodumare,* 27.

106. Ibid.

107. Ade Obayemi, "The Phenomenon of Oduduwa in Ife History," in *The Cradle of a Race: Ife from the Beginning to 1980,* ed. I. A. Akinjogbin (Lagos: Sunray Publications, 1992), 66; emphasis added.

Chapter 2: (Re)constituting the Cosmology and Sociocultural Institutions of Ọ̀yọ́-Yorùbá

1. Old Ọ̀yọ́ refers to Ọ̀yọ́-ile (Ọ̀yọ́ "home"), the original space that was settled. There are many other Ọ̀yọ́ that were occupied at different historical time periods before the establishment of New Ọ̀yọ́ in 1837. The distinction I wish to draw, however, is between New Ọ̀yọ́, which was established in the nineteenth century, and all the previous Ọ̀yọ́. Ọ̀yọ́ was many places, spatially speaking, but my allusion is to one culture and its continuities, despite a lot of movement. This chapter, then, is concerned with the period before the monumental changes of the nineteenth century. According to Robert Smith, "The Oyo of the

alafin are three: Oyo-ile, Oyo-oro, . . . and lastly New Oyo. Although only these three bear the name 'Oyo,' tradition recounts that, since their dispersion from Ile-Ife . . . , the Oyo people have settled in sixteen different places" ("Alafin in Exile: A Study of the Ìgbòho Period in Oyo History," *Journal of African History* 1 (1965): 57–77). For the history and social organization of Ọ̀yọ́, see the following: Samuel Johnson, *The History of the Yorubas* (New York: Routledge and Kegan Paul, 1921); S. O. Babayemi, "The Rise and Fall of Oyo c. 1760–1905: A Study in the Traditional Culture of an African Polity" (Ph.D. diss., Department of History, University of Birmingham, 1979); J. A. Atanda, *The New Oyo Empire: Indirect Rule and Change in Western Nigeria, 1894–1934* (Bristol, England: Longman, 1973); Robert S. Smith, *Kingdoms of the Yoruba* (Madison: University of Wisconsin Press, 1969); Robin Law, *The Oyo Empire c. 1600–c. 1836* (Oxford: Clarendon Press, 1977); Toyin Falola, ed., *Yoruba Historiography* (Madison: University of Wisconsin Press, 1991); Peter Morton-Williams, "An Outline of the Cosmology and Cult Organization of the Oyo Yoruba," *Africa* 34, no. 3 (1964): 243–61.

As to the term "world-sense": it is a more holistic term than "worldview" because it emphasizes the totality and conception of modes of being.

2. Serge Tcherkézoff, "The Illusion of Dualism in Samoa," in *Gender Anthropology,* ed. Teresa del Valle (New York: Routledge, 1989), 55.

3. Gayle Rubin, "The Traffic in Women," in *Toward an Anthropology of Women,* ed. Rayna R. Reiter (New York: Monthly Review Press, 1975).

4. Judith Lorber, *Paradoxes of Gender* (New Haven: Yale University Press, 1994).

5. Simone de Beauvoir, *The Second Sex* (New York: Vintage Books, 1952).

6. Marilyn Frye, *The Politics of Reality* (Trumansburg, N.Y.: Crossing Press, 1983), 165.

7. In his book *Visions and Revisions: Essays on African Literatures and Criticism* (New York: Peter Lang, 1991), Oyekan Owomoyela attempts a gendered reading of this saying. But, in my view, he is just imposing Western gender thinking on Yorùbá (81).

8. See, for example, Thomas Laqueur, *Making Sex: Body and Gender from the Greeks to Freud* (Cambridge, Mass.: Harvard University Press, 1990); and Judith Butler, *Gender Trouble: Feminism and the Subversion of Identity* (New York: Routledge, 1990).

9. Nancy Chodorow, *Femininities, Masculinities, Sexualities: Freud and Beyond* (Lexington: University of Kentucky Press, 1994).

10. For a discussion of sexual dimorphism and the need to integrate biological and social constructs, see Alice Rossi, "Gender and Parenthood," *American Sociological Review* 49, no. 1 (1984): 73–90.

11. The title of a recent book is especially appropriate in this regard; see Elizabeth Grosz, *Volatile Bodies: Toward a Corporeal Feminism* (Bloomington: Indiana University Press, 1994).

12. Diana Fuss, *Essentially Speaking: Feminism and the Nature of Difference* (New York: Routledge, 1989), xi.

13. Suzanne J. Kessler and Wendy McKenna, *Gender: An Ethnomethodological Approach* (New York: John Wiley and Sons, 1978).

14. See, for example, Judith Butler's discussion of sex as fiction in *Gender Trouble*.

15. Johnson, *History of the Yorubas,* 65.

16. Personal communication with Dr. Jakob K. Olupona, historian of Yorùbá religion.

17. Ibid. Johnson claims that during the Egúngún festival, there is an overnight vigil at the graves of the ancestors; it is called *ikúnlẹ̀* because the whole night is spent kneeling and praying (31).

18. Ibid., 65; emphasis added.

19. Ibid., 31.

20. Ifá is one of the most important knowledge systems in Yorùbáland, producing a vast storehouse of information on the society in the divination verses. Ifá is the *òrìṣà* (god) of divination.

21. Wande Abimbola, *Ifa: An Exposition of Ifa Literary Corpus* (Ìbàdàn: Oxford University Press, 1976), 131–32. It is only in the English translation that the anasex of the three friends becomes apparent or constructed.

22. Rowland Abiodun, "Verbal and Visual Metaphors: Mythical Allusions in Yoruba Ritualistic Art of Ori," *Word and Image* 3, no. 3 (1987): 257; emphasis added.

23. Lorber, *Paradoxes of Gender,* 1.

24. Ngugi Wa Thiong'o, *Decolonising the Mind: The Politics of Language in African Literature* (London: James Currey, 1981).

25. Ifi Amadiume, *Male Daughters, Female Husbands: Gender and Sex in an African Society* (London: Zed Books, 1987), makes a similar point about the non-gender-specificity in the Igbó subject pronoun (89).

26. Johnson, *History of the Yorubas,* xxxvii.

27. N. A. Fadipe, *The Sociology of the Yoruba* (Ìbàdàn: Ìbàdàn University Press, 1970), 129.

28. Candance West and Don Zimmerman, "Doing Gender," in *The Construction of Gender,* ed. Judith Lorber and Susan A. Farrell (Newbury Park, Calif.: Sage, 1991).

29. William Bascom, *The Yoruba of Southwestern Nigeria* (Prospect Heights, Ill.: Waveland Press, 1969), 54.

30. J. S. Eades, *The Yoruba Today* (London: Cambridge University Press, 1980), 53.

31. Kathy Ferguson, *The Man Question,* 128.

32. Hugh Clapperton, *Journal of 2nd Expedition into the Interior of Africa* (Philadelphia: Carey, Lea, and Carey, 1829), 1–59.

33. T. J. Bowen, *Central Africa* (Charleston: Southern Baptist Publication Society, 1857), 218.

34. For a discussion of Yorùbá urbanism, see the following: E. Krapf-Askari, *Yoruba Towns and Cities: An Inquiry into the Nature of Urban Social Phenom-*

ena (Oxford: Clarendon, 1969); and Akin Mabogunje, *Urbanization in Nigeria* (London: University of London Press, 1968).

35. For example, Peter C. Lloyd, "The Yoruba Lineage," *Africa* 25, no. 3 (1995): 235–51.

36. Today, they are called *ìyàwó ile*. The term *ìyàwó* seems to have supplanted *aya*. In past usage, *ìyàwó* meant specifically "bride," but now it has been extended to mean "wife."

37. Compare Karen Sacks, *Sisters and Wives: The Past and Future of Sexual Equality* (Urbana, Ill.: University of Illinois Press, 1982).

38. I borrowed the phrase "priority of claim" from Niara Sudarkasa's study of the Awé, a Yorùbá community. My usage differs, however, in that I do not accept that gender is part of its composition. See Niara Sudarkasa, "In a World of Women: Fieldwork in a Yoruba Community," in *The Strength of Our Mothers* (n.p., 1996).

39. See Michelle Rosaldo and Louise Lamphere, eds., *Women, Culture, and Society* (Stanford, Calif.: Stanford University Press, 1974), 19–20.

40. Sandra T. Barnes, "Women, Property, and Power," in *Beyond the Second Sex: New Directions in the Anthropology of Gender*, ed. Peggy Reeves Sanday and Ruth Gallagher Goodenough (Philadelphia: University of Pennsylvania Press, 1990).

41. Jacob K. Olupona, *African Traditional Religions in Contemporary Society* (New York: Paragon House, 1991).

42. S. O. Babayemi, "The Role of Women in Politics and Religion in Oyo" (paper presented at the Institute of African Studies, University of Ìbàdàn, seminar entitled "Women's Studies: The State of the Arts Now in Nigeria," November 1987).

43. Olupona, *African Traditional Religions*, 30.

44. Johnson, *History of Yorubas*, 86.

45. Fadipe, *Sociology of the Yoruba*, 126.

46. Bolanle Awe, *Nigerian Women in Historical Perspective* (Lagos, Nigeria: Sankore, 1992), 58, 65.

47. Niara Sudarkasa, *Where Women Work: A Study of Yoruba Women in the Market Place and at Home*, Museum of Anthropology, Anthropological Papers 53 (Ann Arbor: University of Michigan Press, 1973), 100.

48. Babayemi, "Role of Women," 7.

49. Eades, *Yoruba Today*.

50. Ibid.

51. Felicia Ekejiuba, "Contemporary Households and Major Socioeconomic Transitions in Eastern Nigeria" (paper presented at the "Workshop on Conceptualizing the Household: Issues of Theory, Method, and Application," Boston University).

52. See Fadipe, *Sociology of the Yoruba*, for a comprehensive account of the process.

53. Culled from Dejo Faniyi, "Ekun Iyawo: A Traditional Yoruba Nuptial Chant," in Abimbola, *Ifa: An Exposition*, 685.

54. Abimbola, *Ifa: An Exposition*, 73.

55. Ibid.

56. Fadipe, *Sociology of the Yoruba*, 74.

57. Ibid.

58. Compare Roland Hallgren, *The Good Things in Life: A Study of the Traditional Religious Culture of the Yoruba People* (Loberod: Plus Ultra, 1988).

59. I. O. Oruboloye, *Abstinence as a Method of Birth Control* (Canberra: Department of Demography, Australian National University, 1981); Aderanti Adepoju, "Rationality and Fertility in the Traditional Yoruba Society, South-West Nigeria," in *The Persistence of High Fertility*, ed. John C. Caldwell (Canberra: Department of Demography, Australian National University, 1977).

60. Molara Ogundipe-Leslie, *Re-creating Ourselves: African Women and Critical Transformations* (Trenton, N.J.: Africa World Press, 1994), esp. 69–75.

61. Clothes were stored in boxes, with the most valuable at the bottom. *Sanya* and *alari* are two examples.

62. I have used the more common term "polygamy," not the technical "polygyny."

63. Clapperton, *Journal*.

64. Sudarkasa, *Where Women Work*, 123.

65. Abimbola: *Ifa: An Exposition*, 139.

66. B. W. Hodder, *Markets in West Africa: Studies in Markets and Trade among the Yoruba and Ibo* (Ìbàdàn: Ìbàdàn University Press, 1969), 103.

67. Claude Lévi-Strauss, *Elementary Structures of Kinship* (Boston: Beacon Press, 1969).

68. Rubin, "Traffic in Women."

69. Elizabeth Schmidt, *Peasants, Traders, and Wives: Shona Women in the History of Zimbabwe, 1870–1939* (Portsmouth, N.H.: Heinemann Educational Books, 1992), 17.

70. See John U. Ogbu, "African Bride Wealth and Women's Status," *American Ethnologist 5*, no. 2 (1978): 241–62.

71. Edward Shorter, *A History of Women's Bodies* (New York: Basic Books, 1982), 4; emphasis added.

72. Ibid., xii.

73. See, for example, the introduction to Jane Guyer, *Farm and Family in Southern Cameroon* (Boston: Boston University, African Studies Center, 1984).

74. Bernard T. Adeney, "Polygamy: How Many Wives in the Kingdom of God?" *Transformation: An International Evangelical Dialogue on Missions and Ethics* 12, no. 1 (1995): 5.

75. Abiola Irele, "In Praise of Alienation," in *The Surreptitious Speech: Presence Africaine and the Politics of Otherness, 1947–1987*, ed. V. Y. Mudimbe (Chicago: University of Chicago Press, 1992).

76. This is a reference to the biologically deterministic sociobiological theorists of human life who would have us believe that males are hormone-driven.

77. Since the colonial period, there has been a shift in the establishment of paternity rights. Traditionally, fatherhood was established by being married to

the mother of the child, regardless of who the biological father was. Today, biology is promoted. See Peter Lloyd, "Divorce among the Yoruba," *American Anthropologist*, 70, no. 1 (1968): 67–81.

78. Sudarkasa, *Where Women Work*, 25; Peter Lloyd, "Craft Organization in Yoruba Towns," *Africa* (London) 23, no. 1 (1953): 30–44.

79. B. Belasco, *The Entrepreneur as Cultural Hero: Pre-adaptations in Nigerian Economic Development* (New York: Praeger, 1980), 60.

80. Jane Guyer, "Food, Cocoa, and the Division of Labour by Sex in Two West African Societies," *Comparative Studies in Society and History*, 22, no. 3 (1980): 362; emphasis added.

81. Sudarkasa, *Where Women Work*, 25.

82. See, for example, Funso Afolayan, "Women and Warfare in Yorubaland during the Nineteenth Century," in *War and Diplomacy in Precolonial Nigeria*, ed. Toyin Falola and Robin Law (Madison: African Studies Program, University of Wisconsin, 1992); and T. M. Ilesanmi, "The Yoruba Worldview on Women and Warfare," in *War and Diplomacy*.

83. Smith, "Alafin in Exile," 68.

84. Ibid., 68.

85. J. F. Ade Ajayi and Robert Smith, *Yoruba Warfare in the Nineteenth Century* (Ìbàdàn: Ìbàdàn University Press, 1971).

86. G. J. Afolabi Ojo, *Yoruba Culture: A Geographical Analysis* (London: University of London Press, 1966).

87. Toyin Falola, "Gender, Business, and Space Control: Yoruba Market Women and Power," in *African Market Women's Economic Power: The Role of Women in African Economic Development*, ed. Bessie House-Midamba and Felix K. Ekechi (Westport, Conn.: Greenwood Press, 1995).

88. Ojo, *Yoruba Culture*.

89. B. W. Hodder, *Markets in West Africa: Studies in Markets and Trade among the Yoruba and Ibo* (Ìbàdàn: Ìbàdàn University Press, 1969), 103.

90. Smith, "Alafin in Exile," 70

91. Sudarkasa, *Where Women Work*, 26.

92. Cheikh Anta Diop, *Precolonial Black Africa* (Trenton, N.J.: Africa World Press, 1987), 8.

93. Interview conducted in Ògbómòsó on May 7, 1996. All quotes are from the transcripts of the recording.

94. There is a lot that can be said about contemporary cultural conflict between indigenous institutions and the newly acquired Western and Islamic dispensations, but this is not the place for it.

95. Karin Barber, *I Could Speak until Tomorrow: Oriki, Women, and the Past in a Yoruba Town* (Edinburgh: Edinburgh University Press, 1991), 289.

96. Ibid.

97. There appears to be a linguistic disjuncture in calling this *obìnrin* a *babalawo*, in that the prefix *bàbá* is usually attached to an adult male diviner — *bàbá* being father. A female diviner would probably have *ìyá* (mother) in the

prefix, as in *iyanifa* or *iyalawo*. I do not know if the disjuncture is Barber's or that of her informants.

98. Barber, *I Could Speak,* 289.

99. In a paper on the Suku of Zaire, Igor Kopytoff discusses why women's leadership positions appear to be more prevalent in some non-Western cultures than in the West. He alludes to Benazir Bhutto as an example of such. From the Yorùbá perspective, Bhutto is not an exception — she is merely carrying out the family trade. See Igor Kopytoff, "Women's Roles and Existential Identities," in *Beyond the Second Sex: New Directions in the Anthropology of Gender,* ed. Peggy Reeves Sanday and Ruth Gallagher Goodenough (Philadelphia: University of Pennsylvania Press, 1990).

100. F. J. Pedler, *Economic Geography of West Africa* (London: Green, 1955), 139.

101. Hodder, *Markets,* 103.

102. See Jean Kopytoff, *A Preface to Modern Nigeria: Sierra Leonians in Yoruba 1830–1890* (Madison: University of Wisconsin Press, 1965), 21, for a discussion of the ethnic composition of recaptives.

103. Sudarkasa, *Where Women Work,* 26.

104. Johnson, *History of the Yorubas,* 91.

105. Clapperton, *Journal,* 6.

106. See, for example, Judith Brown, "A Note on the Division of Labor by Sex," *American Anthropologist* 72, no. 5 (1970): 1073.

107. Sudarkasa, *Where Women Work,* 156.

108. Ibid.

109. Felicity Edholm, Olivia Harris, and Kate Young, "Conceptualising Women," *Critique of Anthropology* 3, no. 9 (1978): 119.

110. Ibid., 123.

111. Sudarkasa, *Where Women Work,* 34.

112. R. W. Connell, *Gender and Power* (Stanford, Calif.: Stanford University Press, 1987), 54.

113. Ibid.

114. Jane Guyer, "Food," 363.

115. Shelly Errington, "Recasting Sex, Gender, and Power," in *Power and Difference: Gender in Island Southeast Asia,* ed. Jane Atkinson and Shelly Errington (Stanford, Calif.: Stanford University Press, 1990), 40.

116. See the discussion in Stephen Gould, *The Mismeasure of Man* (New York: Norton, 1981).

117. Frank Sulloway, *Born to Rebel: Birth Order, Family Dynamics, and Creative Lives* (New York: Pantheon Books, 1996).

118. Edholm, Harris, and Young, "Conceptualising Women," 127.

119. This term is from Fuss, *Essentially Speaking.*

Chapter 3: Making History, Creating Gender

1. One of the earliest scholarly engagements with African oral tradition as history is Saburi Biobaku, "The Problem of Traditional History with Special

Reference to Yoruba Traditions," *Journal of the Historical Society of Nigeria* (December 1956): 1.

2. A. I. Asiwaju, "Political Motivation and Oral Historical Traditions in Africa: The Case of Yoruba Crowns," *Africa* 46 (1976): 113–47.

3. Ibid., 116.

4. See Eric Hobsbawn and Terence Ranger, eds., *The Invention of Tradition* (Cambridge: Cambridge University Press, 1983).

5. J. D. Y. Peel, "Making History: The Past in the Ijesha Present," *Man* 19 (1984): 111–32.

6. Ibid., 113.

7. Arjun Appadurai, "The Past as a Scarce Resource," *Man* 16 (1981): 201, 281.

8. For a discussion of the complexity of the notion of "invented tradition," see Gyekye Kwame, *An Essay on African Philosophical Thought* (Philadelphia: Temple University Press, 1995), xxiii–xxxii.

9. Olabiyi Yai, "In Praise of Metonymy: The Concepts of Tradition and Creativity in the Transmission of Yoruba Artistry over Space and Time," in *The Yoruba Artist: New Theoretical Perspectives on African Arts*, ed. Rowland Abiodun, H. J. Drewal, and J. Pemberton III, 107–15 (n.p., 1994).

10. Bolanle Awe, *Nigerian Women in Historical Perspective* (Lagos: Sankore Publishers, 1992), 7.

11. This is my own characterization of the unbridled universalisms of Western feminism.

12. Bolanle Awe, "Writing Women into History: The Nigerian Experience," in *Writing Women's History: International Perspectives*, ed. Karen Offen et al. (London: Macmillan Academic and Professional Publications, 1991).

13. Peel, "Making History," 114–15, discusses the importance of recognizing historical conjunctural features in any analysis of the past.

14. For aspects of his biography, see J. F. Ade Ajayi, "Samuel Johnson: Historian of the Yoruba," and Phillip Zachernuk, "Samuel Johnson and the Victorian Image of the Yoruba," both in *Pioneer, Patriot and Patriarch: Samuel Johnson and the Yoruba People,* ed. Toyin Falola (Madison: African Studies Program, University of Wisconsin, 1993), 33–46.

15. N. A. Fadipe, *The Sociology of the Yoruba* (Ìbàdàn: Ìbàdàn University Press, 1970), 63.

16. The Sàró, also called Akus and recaptives, were liberated slaves who had been settled in the British colony of Sierra Leone. Many originated in Yorùbáland, were sold during the Atlantic slave trade, and were then liberated by the British squadron on the West African coast during the abolitionist phase of British expansion. In 1843, after being Westernized and Christianized, they started emigrating back to Yorùbáland and were to play a decisive role in the penetration of Western values and goods among the Yorùbá. By the middle of the nineteenth century, they had become an elite group in Lagos and Abéòkúta. They represented the internal factor that facilitated the colonization of Yorùbáland. They also brought literacy and Western schooling to Nigeria. Bishop Ajayi

Crowther — the first African Anglican bishop in Africa — was one of them, and he was instrumental in reducing Yorùbá into writing. Indeed, the varied role of individual Sàró and the collective in the history of modern Nigeria cannot be overstated. See Jean Kopytoff, *A Preface to Modern Nigeria: Sierra Leonians in Yoruba 1830–1890* (Madison: University of Wisconsin Press, 1965), for a history.

17. Robin Law, "How Truly Traditional Is Our Traditional History? The Case of Samuel Johnson and the Recording of Yoruba Oral Tradition," *History in Africa* 11 (1984): 197.

18. For a discussion of feedback in other African oral traditions, see David Henige, "The Problem of Feed Back in Oral Tradition: Four Examples from the Fante Coastlands," *Journal of African History* 14, no. 2 (1973): 223–25. For a discussion of Johnson and feedback in Yorùbá history, see B. A. Agiri, "Early Oyo History Reconsidered," *History in Africa* 2 (1975): 1–16.

19. Agiri, "Early Oyo History," 1.

20. Ibid.

21. Law, "How Truly Traditional?" 207–11.

22. Ibid., 209–10.

23. Samuel Johnson, *The History of the Yorubas* (New York: Routledge and Kegan Paul, 1921), 176.

24. Ibid., xxxvii.

25. Robert Smith, "Alafin in Exile: A Study of the Igboho Period in Oyo History," *Journal of African History* 1 (1965): 57–77.

26. Johnson, *History of the Yorubas,* vii; emphasis added.

27. Law, "How Truly Traditional?" 198.

28. Curiously, he does not mention the female *akunyungba* (royal bards) or the *ayaba* (royal consorts) as one of his sources.

29. See Law, "How Truly Traditional?" for some of these disjunctures.

30. Ibid., 213.

31. I want to thank Olufemi Taiwo for his generous contribution of his ideas on this issue.

32. There are no known references to Ọ̀yọ́ written records earlier than the seventeenth or early eighteenth centuries. Invariably, the earliest eyewitness accounts are from Europeans.

33. Law, "How Truly Traditional?" 213.

34. J. A. Atanda, *The New Oyo Empire* (Bristol, England: Longman, 1973).

35. Law, "How Truly Traditional?"

36. Agiri, "Early Oyo History," 5.

37. Johnson, *History of the Yorubas,* 41.

38. Agiri, "Early Oyo History," 5.

39. Smith, "Alafin in Exile," 64.

40. Johnson, *History of the Yorubas,* 47.

41. Ibid., 41.

42. Ibid.

43. Atanda, *New Oyo Empire,* 210; my translation.

44. Johnson, *History of the Yorubas,* 155.

45. Agiri, "Early Oyo History," 9. He argues that Ṣàngó may not have been an individual and that myths about him developed to explain the period of Nupe control over Ọ̀yọ́.

46. Johnson, *History of the Yorubas,* 47.

47. There is another meaning: female royal offspring are sexually free — undomesticatable.

48. Johnson, *History of the Yorubas,* 86.

49. Ibid., xx.

50. Ibid., 173; emphasis added.

51. Ibid.

52. Ibid., 156.

53. Ibid., 155. There is indeed some general confusion in the literature as to the lineage identity (Are they wives or daughters?) of the female officials in Ọ̀yọ́ political hierarchy. The confusion is compounded by the fact that in English, they are called "queens" or "ladies of the palace" (Robert S. Smith, *Kingdoms of the Yoruba* [Madison: University of Wisconsin Press, 1969]).

54. Johnson, *History of the Yorubas,* 63–67. See also S. O. Babayemi, "The Role of Women in Politics and Religion in Oyo" (paper presented at the Institute of African Studies, University of Ìbàdàn, seminar entitled "Women's Studies: The State of the Arts Now in Nigeria," November, 1987).

55. Smith, *Alafin in Exile,* 68; emphasis added.

56. The meaning of the term *baálè* needs further analysis since it is associated with *bàbá* (father).

57. Transcripts of recorded interviews conducted in Ògbọ́mọ̀ṣọ́ on March 3 and 26, 1996. I also have in my possession an autobiographical pamphlet given me by the baálè herself: Oloye Mary Igbayilola Àlàrí (Baálè Máyà, Ayetoro), *Iwe Itan Kukuru Nipa Ilu Máyà.*

58. Law, "How Truly Traditional?" 210.

59. Smith, *Alafin in Exile,* 75 n. 52.

60. J. D. Y. Peel, "Kings, Titles, and Quarters: A Conjectural History of Ilesha I: The Traditions Reviewed in History," *Africa* 6 (1979): 109–52.

61. Asiwaju, "Political Motivation," 113, 120. It should be recalled that according to Johnson, the polity of Ketu was one of the original ones founded by Òdúdúwà's children. In the case of Ketu, however, it is said that because this child of Òdúdúwà was female, the deed of founding passed to her son.

62. Peel, "Kings," 129, 149 n. 70.

63. Johnson, *History of the Yorubas,* 7–8.

64. J. D. Y. Peel, "Making History: The Past in the Ijesha Present," *Man* 19 (1984): 113.

65. Johnson, *History of the Yorubas,* 65.

66. Arnold Temu and Bonaventure Swai, *Historians and Africanist History: A Critique* (London: Zed Press, 1981).

67. P. F. de Moraes Farias, "History and Consolation: Royal Yoruba Bards Comment on Their Craft," *History in Africa* 19 (1992): 263–97.

68. Ibid., 274–75.

69. Ibid., 275.

70. Ibid.

71. Ibid, 277.

72. In the Yorùbá Bible, the same expression is used to indicate that Jesus is the only son of God. The implications of the non-gender-specificity of the Yorùbá term ọmọ to refer to Jesus have not been studied.

73. Bolanle Awe, "Praise Poetry as Historical Data: The Example of Yoruba Oriki," *Africa* 44 (1974): 332.

74. Ibid., 348.

75. Ibid.

76. Karin Barber, "Documenting Social and Ideological Change through Yoruba Personal Oriki: A Stylistic Analysis," *Journal of Historical Society of Nigeria* 10, no. 4 (1981).

77. Adeboye Babalola, *Awon Oriki Borokinni* (Ìbàdàn: Nigerian Publisher Services, 1981).

78. S. O. Babayemi, *Content Analysis of Oriki Orile* (n.p., n.d.), 168, 169.

79. Awe, "Praise Poetry," 340–46.

80. Barber, *I Could Speak,* 198.

81. Ibid., 34.

82. Ibid., 259.

83. Babalola, *Awon Oriki Borokinni,* 7–9.

84. Ibid.

85. Oloye Mary Igbayilola Àlàrí (Baálè Máyà, Ayetoro), *Iwe Itan Kukuru Nipa Ilu Máyà.*

86. Barber, *I Could Speak,* 30.

87. Ibid., 32.

88. Bolanle Awe, "The Iyalode in the Traditional Yoruba Political System," in *Sexual Stratification: A Cross-cultural View,* ed. Alice Schlegel (New York: Columbia University Press, 1977).

89. Johnson, *History of the Yorubas,* 66.

90. Oba Oyèwûmí is my father; I have had numerous conversations on all these questions with him.

91. For the rise and influence of Ìbàdàn, see Bolanle Awe, "The Rise of Ìbàdàn as a Yoruba Power" (Ph.D. diss., Oxford University, 1964).

92. Interview conducted at her residence in Ògbómòsó on July 7, 1996.

93. Awe, "The Iyalode," 157.

94. Ibid., 147, 148.

95. Ibid., 153.

96. Oladipo Yemitan, *Madame Tinubu: Merchant and King-Maker* (Ìbàdàn: University Press Limited, 1987), 47–48.

97. Awe, "The Iyalode," 152.

98. See, for example, the discussion in Atanda, *New Oyo Empire.*

99. Awe, "The Iyalode," 151.

100. M. T. Drewal and H. J. Drewal, "Composing Time and Space in Yoruba Art," *Word and Image: A Journal of Verbal/Visual Enquiry* 3 (1987): 225.

101. Philip Stevens, *Stone Images of Esie, Nigeria* (New York: Africana Publishing Company, 1978).

102. Ibid., 22.

103. Ibid., 65.

104. Ibid.

105. John Berger, *Ways of Seeing* (London: Penguin, 1972).

106. C. O. Adepegba, *Yoruba Metal Sculpture* (Ìbàdàn: Ìbàdàn University Press, 1991), 31.

107. Stevens, *Stone Images,* 65.

108. John Pemberton, "The Oyo Empire," in Henry Drewal et al., *Yoruba: Nine Centuries of Art and Thought* (New York: Harry N. Abrams Inc., 1989), 78.

109. Ibid., 82.

110. Johnson, *History of the Yorubas,* 65.

111. Pemberton, "Oyo Empire," 162.

112. Ibid.

113. Babayemi, "Role of Women."

114. James Matory, "Sex and the Empire That Is No More: A Ritual History of Women's Power among the Oyo-Yoruba" (Ph.D. diss., Department of Anthropology, University of Chicago, 1992), 6.

115. Ibid., 538.

116. Interview conducted in his residence in Ògbómòsó on March 16, 1996. Transcripts of recorded interview available.

117. See Rowland Abiodun, "Verbal and Visual Metaphors: Mythical Allusions in Yoruba Ritualistic Art of Ori," *Word and Image* 3, no. 3 (1987): 257, and the discussion in chapter 2.

118. B. A. Agiri and T. Ogboni, "Among the Oyo-Yoruba," *Lagos Notes and Records* 3 (1972): 53.

119. Peter Morton-Williams, "An Outline of the Cosmology and Cult Organization of the Oyo Yoruba," *Africa* 34, no. 3 (1964): 243–61.

120. J. A. Atanda, "The Yoruba Ogboni Cult: Did It Exist in Old Oyo?" *Journal of Historical Society of Nigeria* 6, no. 4 (1973): 371.

Chapter 4: Colonizing Bodies and Minds

1. This is a bifurcated world — a world cut in two. Abdul Jan Mohammed elaborates the idea of Manichaeanism in the colonial world as "a field of diverse yet interchangeable oppositions between White and Black, good and evil, superiority and inferiority, civilization and savagery, intelligence and emotion, rationality and sensuality, self and Other, subject and object" ("The Economy of Manichean Allegory: The Function of Racial Difference in Colonialist Literature," in *Race, Writing, and Difference,* ed. Henry Louis Gates Jr. [Chicago: University of Chicago Press, 1988], 82).

2. Frantz Fanon, *The Wretched of the Earth* (New York: Grove Weidenfeld, 1963); Albert Memmi, *The Colonizer and the Colonized* (Boston: Beacon Press, 1965).

3. Ashis Nandy, *The Intimate Enemy: Loss and Recovery of Self under Colonialism* (Delhi: Oxford University Press, 1983), 5. Dominance is often expressed in sexual terms; consequently, colonization is seen as a process of taking away the manhood of the colonized, and national liberation seen as a step toward its restoration.

4. Fanon, *Wretched of the Earth*, 63.

5. Ibid., 39; emphasis added.

6. Nandy, *Intimate Enemy*, x; emphasis added.

7. Stephanie Urdang, *Fighting Two Colonialisms: Women in Guinea-Bissau* (London: Zed Press, 1979); Elizabeth Schmidt, *Peasants, Traders, and Wives: Shona Women in the History of Zimbabwe, 1870–1939* (Portsmouth, N.H.: Heinemann Educational Books, 1992), makes the claim that Shona women of Zimbabwe were beholden to two patriarchies — indigenous and European.

8. Cited in Nina Mba, *Nigerian Women Mobilized: Women's Political Activity in Southern Nigeria, 1900–1965* (Berkeley: University of California, Institute of International Studies, 1982), 65.

9. It is misleading to assume that the relationship between African men and women was untouched by colonization. After all, according to Memmi, "I discovered that few aspects of my life and personality were untouched by the fact of colonization. Not only my own thoughts, my passions and my conduct, but the conduct of others towards me was affected" (*Colonizer,* viii).

10. Elizabeth Spelman, *Inessential Woman: Problems of Exclusion in Feminist Thought* (Boston: Beacon Press, 1988), 123.

11. Bill Freund, *The Making of Contemporary Africa* (Bloomington: Indiana University Press, 1984), 111.

12. Helen Callaway, *Gender, Culture, Empire: European Women in Colonial Nigeria* (Oxford: MacMillan Press in association with St. Anthony's College, 1987), 4.

13. Ibid., 5–6.

14. Callaway appears to be impervious to the fact that there were gender distinctions among the Africans, despite the fact that part of her motivation for writing was to restore a gendered analysis of colonization.

15. Quoted in Callaway, *Gender,* 5.

16. Samuel Johnson, *The History of the Yorubas* (New York: Routledge and Kegan Paul, 1921), 656.

17. M. Crowder and O. Ikime, *West African Chiefs* (Ife: University of Ife Press, 1970), xv.

18. Martin Chanock, "Making Customary Law: Men, Women and the Courts in Colonial Rhodesia," in *African Women and the Law: Historical Perspectives,* ed. M. J. Hay and Marcia Wright (Boston: African Studies Center, Boston University, 1982), 59; emphasis added.

19. Fustel De Coulanges, *The Ancient City: A Study on the Religion, Laws*

and Institutions of Greece and Rome (n.p., 1983 [1987]), 293–94; emphasis added.

20. Edward Shorter, *The Making of the Modern Family* (New York: Vintage Books, 1983), 50; emphasis added.

21. Ibid., 51.

22. Ibid., 52.

23. Jane Guyer, *Family and Farm in Southern Cameroon* (Boston: Boston University, African Studies Center, 1984), 5.

24. Nandy, *Intimate Enemy*.

25. Nina Mba, *Nigerian Women Mobilized: Women's Political Activity in Southern Nigeria, 1900–1965* (Berkeley: University of California, Institute of International Studies, 1982), 54.

26. J. F. A. Ajayi, *Christian Missions in Nigeria 1841–1891* (Evanston, Ill.: Northwestern University Press, 1965), 15.

27. T. J. Bowen, *Central Africa* (Charleston: Southern Baptist Publication Society, 1857), 321–22.

28. On the Sàró, see chap. 3, n. 16, above.

29. A. Fajana, *Education in Nigeria 1942–1939: An Historical Analysis* (Lagos: Longman, 1978), 25.

30. Ajayi, *Christian Missions*.

31. Ibid., 139; emphasis added.

32. Fajana, *Education in Nigeria*, 29.

33. Ibid., 37.

34. Quoted in ibid., 30.

35. Anna Hinderer, *Seventeen Years in the Yoruba Country: Memorials of Anna Hinderer* (London: Seeley, Jackson and Halliday, 1877), 69–70.

36. I call it "four Rs" (Religion, Rithmetic, Riting, and Religion) to show it was thoroughly permeated with religious instruction.

37. Hinderer, *Seventeen Years*.

38. Ibid., 206–7.

39. Ibid., 108.

40. The following information is drawn from Kemi Morgan, *Akinyele's Outline History of Ìbàdàn* (Ìbàdàn: Caxton Press, n.d.).

41. Ibid.

42. T. Ogunkoya, *St. Andrews College Oyo: History of the Premier Institution in Nigeria* (New York: Oxford University Press, 1979), 25.

43. Extrapolated from Mba, *Nigerian Women*, 61.

44. For a more recent elaboration of this line of thinking, see Laray Denzer, "Yoruba Women: A Historiographical Study," *International Journal of African Historical Studies* 27, n. 1 (1994): 19.

45. Ogunkoya, *St. Andrews College Oyo*, 25.

46. This is a curious statement considering the large size of Yorùbá families. It may be an indication that the girl's mother had been enslaved, and she was therefore without kin on the mother's side.

47. Hinderer, *Seventeen Years*, 69.

48. Ibid., 151–52.

49. Fajana, *Education in Nigeria*, 25.

50. *Iwofa* in Yorùbá. This is a system of bonded labor in which an individual pledges his or her services or the services of his or her wards to creditors until a loan is repaid. "Pawns" were often children. For discussions of the institution, see Johnson, *History of Yoruba;* and N. A. Fadipe, *The Sociology of the Yoruba* (Ìbàdàn: Ìbàdàn University Press, 1970).

51. Ajayi, *Christian Missions*, 135.

52. Mba, *Nigerian Women*, 62.

53. Kristin Mann, *Marrying Well: Marriage, Status, and Social Change among the Educated Elite in Colonial Lagos* (Cambridge: Cambridge University Press, 1985).

54. Ibid., 77–91.

55. Ibid.

56. Mba, *Nigerian Women*, 62–64.

57. Quoted in ibid., 63.

58. Ibid., 64.

59. Ibid., 63.

60. T. Solarin, *To Mother with Love: An Experiment in Auto-biography,* (Ìbàdàn: Board Publications, 1987), 223.

61. Ibid., 226.

62. See Lorna Schiebinger, *The Mind Has No Sex? Women in the Origins of Modern Science* (Cambridge, Mass.: Harvard University Press, 1989), 10–11.

63. Ajayi, *Christian Missions*, 106.

64. Quoted in ibid., 107.

65. Ibid.

66. Ibid., 106.

67. J. B. Webster, *The African Churches among the Yoruba, 1882–1922* (London: Clarendon Press, 1961).

68. See J. D. Y. Peel, *Aladura: A Religious Movement among the Yoruba* (London: Oxford University Press, 1968), 71.

69. Ibid., 183.

70. Ibid., 83.

71. Ibid., 108; emphasis added.

72. Ibid., 270.

73. Ibid., 108.

74. E. A. Ayandele, *The Missionary Impact on Modern Nigeria 1842–1914: A Political and Social Analysis* (London: Longmans, Green, and Co., 1966).

75. Webster, *African Churches*.

76. E. Bolaji Idowu, *Olodumare: God in Yoruba Belief* (London: Longman, 1962), 38.

77. J. O. Awolalu and P. A. Dopamu, *West African Traditional Religion* (Ìbàdàn: Onibonoje Press, 1979), 52.

78. Carol Christ, "Why Women Need the Goddess: Phenomenological, Psychological, and Political Reflections," in *Womanspirit Rising: A Feminist Reader*

in Religion, ed. C. P. Christ and J. Plaskow (San Francisco: Harper and Row, 1979), 275.

79. Hinderer, *Seventeen Years,* 60.

80. Fadipe, *Sociology of the Yoruba,* 169.

81. Johnson, *History of the Yorubas,* 96.

82. M. Lovett, "Gender Relations, Class Formation, and the Colonial State in Africa," in *Women and the State in Africa,* ed. Kathleen A. Staudt and Jane L. Parpar (Boulder, Colo.: Lynne Rienner Publishers, 1989), 25.

83. G. B. A. Coker, *Family Property among the Yoruba* (London: Sweet and Maxwell, 1958), 48.

84. P. C. Lloyd, *Yoruba Land Law* (New York: Oxford University Press, 1962), 80.

85. Coker, *Family Property.*

86. Ibid., 189–90; emphasis added.

87. Mann, *Marrying Well,* 19–20.

88. T. O. Elias, *Nigerian Land Law and Custom* (London: Routledge and Kegan Paul, 1951), 186.

89. Sara Berry, *Cocoa, Custom and Socio-economic Change in Rural Western Nigeria* (Oxford: Clarendon Press, 1975), 46–49.

90. Simi Afonja, "Land Control: A Critical Factor in Yoruba Gender Stratification," in *Women and Class in Africa,* ed. C. Robertson and I. Berger (New York: Africana Publishing, 1986).

91. Cited in ibid.

92. Gavin Kitching, *Class and Economic Change in Kenya: The Making of an African Petit Bourgeoisie* (New Haven, Conn.: Yale University Press, 1980), 285.

93. Fadipe, *Sociology of the Yoruba,* 171.

94. Simi Afonja, "Changing Modes of Production and the Sexual Division of Labor among the Yoruba," in *Women's Work, Development and Division of Labor by Gender,* ed. H. Safa and E. Leacock (South Hadley, Mass.: Bergin and Garvey, 1986), 131.

95. O. Adewoye, "Law and Social Change in Nigeria," *Journal of Historical Society of Nigeria* 3, no. 1 (December 1973): 150.

96. T. M. Aluko, *One Man, One Wife* (London: Heinemann, 1959), 40.

97. Cited in Mba, *Nigerian Women,* 40.

98. Chanock, *Making Customary Law,* 60.

99. Mba, *Nigerian Women,* 56; emphasis added.

100. Adewoye, "Law and Social Change," 156.

101. Coker, *Family Property,* 113.

102. Ibid., 162.

103. Ibid., 159; emphasis added.

104. W. Oyemakinde, "Railway Construction and Operation in Nigeria 1895–1911," *Journal of Historical Society of Nigeria* 7, no. 2 (1974): 305.

105. Ibid., 305.

106. Walter Rodney, *How Europe Underdeveloped Africa* (Washington, D.C.: Howard University Press, 1972), 227.

107. Oyemakinde, "Railway Construction," 312.

108. Dan Aronson, *The City Is Our Farm: Seven Migrant Yoruba Families* (Cambridge, Mass.: Schenkman Publishing Co., 1978), 128–29.

109. Fola Ighodalo, "Barriers to the Participation of Nigerian Women in the Modern Labor Force," in *Nigerian Women and Development,* ed. O. Ogunsheye et al. (Ìbàdàn: Ìbàdàn University Press, 1988), 363.

110. Ibid., 356.

111. Aluko, *One Man,* 42.

112. Memmi, *Colonizer.*

113. Fanon, *Wretched,* 41.

114. Callaway, *Gender,* 55.

115. Peter Ekeh, "Colonialism and the Two Publics: A Theoretical Statement," *Journal of Comparative Studies in Society and History* 17, no. 1 (1975): 91–112.

116. Ibid., 92.

117. R. S. Rattray, *The Ashanti* (reprint; Oxford: Clarendon Press, 1969), 84.

118. Denise Riley, *Am I That Name? Feminism and the Category of Women in History* (Minneapolis: University of Minnesota Press, 1988), 65.

Chapter 5: The Translation of Cultures

1. My chapter title uses the term "orature." About this term Micere Mugo has written: "Orature refers to creative compositions that manipulate language to produce verbal artistic expression. Ideally, such compositions should culminate in recitation, dramatization and other forms of artistic enactment. African Orature embraces myths, legends, stories, poems, epics, drama, music and dance, etc. It also incorporates history, religion, sociology, anthropology and education, to mention the most obvious connections. To study African Orature, therefore, is to engage in the exploration of a whole body of ethics and aesthetics that define the African world, using authentic and indigenous paradigms to do so" ("Orature in the Department of African American Studies," *Pan African Studies at Syracuse University: A Newsletter* 4 [spring 1994]).

2. Deborah Cameron, "Why Is Language a Feminist Issue?" introduction to *The Feminist Critique of Language* (New York: Routledge, 1990); Judith Orasanu, Mariam K. Slater, and Leonore Loeb Adler, *Language, Sex and Gender* (New York: The New York Academy of Sciences, 1979); Barrie Thorne, Cheris Kramarae, and Nancy Henley, eds., *Language, Gender, and Society* (Rowley, Mass.: Newbury Press, 1983); Dale Spender, *Man Made Language* (New York: Routledge and Kegan Paul, 1980).

3. Spender, *Man Made Language.*

4. Quoted in ibid., 145–46.

5. Henry Louis Gates Jr., *The Signifying Monkey* (New York: Oxford University Press, 1988), 30.

6. Ibid., 30.

7. Ayo Bamgbose, *A Short Yoruba Grammar of Yoruba* (Ìbàdàn: Heine-mann Educational Books, 1967), 2.

8. Ayo Bamgbose, *The Novels of D. O. Fagunwa* (Benin City: Ethiope Publishing, 1974), 61, 63.

9. Ibid., 63.

10. Ibid.

11. Karin Barber, *I Could Speak until Tomorrow: Oriki, Women, and the Past in a Yoruba Town* (Edinburgh: Edinburgh University Press, 1991).

12. Bolanle Awe, "Praise Poems as Historical Data: The Example of Yoruba Oriki," *Africa* (London) 44, no. 4 (1974): 331–49.

13. Today, *iyàwó* has become synonymous with *aya* and is the dominant word used to denote "wife." In the past, *iyàwó* denoted "bride."

14. Bamgbose, *Novels of D. O. Fagunwa,* 61.

15. Ibid., 62.

16. Olakunle George, "The Predicament of D. O. Fagunwa" (paper presented at the Institute for Advanced Study and Research in the African Humanities, Northwestern University, Evanston, Ill., January 27, 1993).

17. Ibid.

18. See Adeleke Adeeko, "The Language of Head-calling: A Review Essay on Yoruba Metalanguage," *Research in African Literatures* 23, no. 1 (spring 1992): 197–201.

19. Ibid., 199.

20. Ulli Beier, *Yoruba Poetry: An Anthology of Traditional Poems* (London: Cambridge University Press, 1970), 11.

21. Adebisi Salami, "Vowel and Consonant Harmony and Vowel Restriction in Assimilated English Loan Words in Yoruba," in *Yoruba Language and Literature,* ed. Adebisi Ofolayan (Ife: University of Ife Press, 1982).

22. For an extended discussion of Yorùbá/English borrowings, see Olusola Ajolore, "Lexical Borrowing in Yoruba," in *Yoruba Language and Literature,* ed. Adebisi Afolayan (Ile Ife, Nigeria: University of Ife Press, 1982).

23. Compare, for example, the praise poetry of Oko lineage in which reference is made to Àare Alakẹ, their female founder (see S. O. Babayemi, *Content Analysis of Oriki Orile,* n.p., n.d.).

24. Oyekan Owomoyela, *A Ki i: Yoruba Proscriptive and Prescriptive Proverbs* (Lanham, Md.: University Press of America, 1988), ix.

25. Olatunde O. Olatunji, "The Yoruba Oral Poet and His Society," *Research in African Literatures* 10, no. 2 (fall 1979): 178.

26. Ibid., 203.

27. Oludare Olajubu, "Book Reviews," *Research in African Literatures* 14, no. 4 (winter 1983): 541.

28. Isola Akinwumi, "The African Writer's Tongue," in *Research in African Literatures* 23, no. 1 (spring 1992): 18.

29. Olabiyi Yai, "Issues in Oral Poetry: Criticism, Teaching, and Translation," in *Discourse and Its Disguises,* ed. Karin Barber and P. F. de Moraes

Farias, Birmingham University African Studies Series 1 (Birmingham, England: Centre of West African Studies, 1989), 59.

30. Deborah Tannen, *You Just Don't Understand* (New York: Ballantine Books, 1990).

31. Joel Sherzer, "A Diversity of Voices: Men's and Women's Speech in Ethnographic Perspective," in *Language, Gender, and Sex in Comparative Perspective,* ed. Susan Phillips (Cambridge: Cambridge University Press, 1987), 99.

32. Sherzer, "Diversity of Voices," 98, 99.

33. Bade Ajuwon, *Funeral Dirges of Yoruba Hunters* (New York: Nok Publishers International, 1982); Wande Abimbola, *Ifa: An Exposition of Ifa Literary Corpus* (Ìbàdàn: Oxford University Press, 1976); Wande Abimbola, *Yoruba Oral Tradition* (Ìbàdàn: Oxford University Press, 1975); Adeboye Babalola, *Awon Oriki Borokinni* (Ìbàdàn: Rosprint Industrial Press Limited, 1981); Oyekan Owomoyela, "Tortoise Tales and Yoruba Ethos," *Research in African Literatures* 20, no. 2 (summer 1989); S. O. Bada, *Owe Yoruba Ati Isedale Won* (Ìbàdàn: University Press Limited, 1970); J. O. Ajibola, *Owe Yoruba* (Ìbàdàn: University Press Limited, 1979); Ulli Beier, *Yoruba Myths* (New York: Cambridge University Press, 1980).

34. Sherzer, "Diversity of Voices," 112–13.

35. Oludare Olajubu, "Composition and Performance Technics in Iwi Egungun," in *Yoruba Oral Tradition: Poetry in Music, Dance, and Drama,* ed. Wande Abimbola (Ìbàdàn: Ìbàdàn University Press, 1975), 877.

36. Barber, *I Could Speak,* 10.

37. Ibid.

38. Ayodele Ogundipe, "Esu Elegbara: The Yoruba God of Chance and Uncertainty: A Study in Yoruba Mythology" (Ph.D. diss., Indiana University, 1978), 21.

39. Ibid., 22.

40. Ibid.

41. J. D. Y. Peel, *Aladura: A Religious Movement among the Yoruba* (London: Oxford University Press, 1968), 183.

42. Ogundipe, "Esu Elegbara," 81.

43. Ibid., 83.

44. Ibid., 75.

45. Ibid., 97.

46. Ibid., 95–96.

47. Ibid., 85.

48. Ibid., 86; emphasis added.

49. Ibid., 91.

50. Ibid.

51. Ibid., 86

52. Ibid., 15–16

53. Ibid., 91.

54. Ibid., 90.

55. Maria Black and Rosalind Coward, "Linguistics, Social and Sexual

Relations: A Review of Dale Spender's 'Man Made Language,' " in *The Feminist Critique of Language,* ed. Deborah Cameron (New York: Routledge, 1990), 129.

56. Knowledge of English in Nigeria is a sign of class privilege and social mobility.

57. Ogundipe, "Esu Elegbara," 164.

58. Ibid., 158.

59. Ibid., 172–73; emphasis added.

60. Ibid., 173.

61. Karin Barber, *I Could Speak,* 277.

62. Judith Gleason, *Oya: In Praise of an African Goddess* (San Francisco: Harper, 1987), 2.

63. Barber, *I Could Speak,* 277.

64. Douglas R. Hofstadter, "A Person Paper on Purity in Language," in *The Feminist Critique of Language,* 195.

65. Troy Duster, "Purpose and Bias," *Transaction, Social Science and Modern Society* 24, no. 2 (1987), helped to further clarify my thinking on this issue.

66. Sue Ellen Charlton, *Women in Third World Development* (Boulder, Colo.: Westview Press, 1984), 23.

67. Cited in Elaine Sciolino, "800 Women Look to the Future of the Decade for Women," *New York Times,* October 20, 1986.

68. Aline K. Wong, "Comments on Turner's Feminist View of Copenhagen," *Signs* 6, no. 4 (summer 1981).

69. Linda Nicholson, "Interpreting Gender," in *Signs* (autumn 1994): 103.

Bibliography

Abimbola, Wande. *Ifa: An Exposition of the Ifa Literary Corpus.* Ìbàdàn: Oxford University Press, 1976.

———. "Ifa as a Body of Knowledge and as an Academic Discipline." *Journal of Cultures and Ideas* 1, no. 1 (1983): 1–11.

———. *Yoruba Oral Tradition.* Ìbàdàn: Oxford University Press, 1975.

Abiodun, Rowland. "Verbal and Visual Metaphors: Mythical Allusions in Yoruba Ritualistic Art of Ori." *Word and Image* 3, no. 3 (1987): 252.

Ade Ajayi, J. F. "Samuel Johnson: Historian of the Yoruba." In *Pioneer, Patriot, and Patriarchy: Samuel Johnson and the Yoruba People,* edited by Toyin Falola. Madison: African Studies Program, University of Wisconsin, 1993.

Ade Ajayi, J. F., and Robert Smith. *Yoruba Warfare in the Nineteenth Century.* Ìbàdàn: Ìbàdàn University Press, 1971.

Adeeko, Adeleke. "The Language of Head-calling: A Review Essay on Yoruba Metalanguage." *Research in African Literatures* 23, no. 1 (1992): 197–201.

Adeney, Bernard T. "Polygamy: How Many Wives in the Kingdom of God?" *Transformation: An International Evangelical Dialogue on Missions and Ethics* 12, no. 1 (1995): 5.

Adepegba, C. O. *Yoruba Metal Sculpture.* Ìbàdàn: Ìbàdàn University Press, 1991.

Adepoju, Aderanti. "Rationality and Fertility in the Traditional Yoruba Society, South-West Nigeria." In *The Persistence of High Fertility: Population Prospects in the Third World,* edited by John C. Caldwell. Canberra: Department of Demography, Australian National University, 1977.

Afolayan, Funso. "Women and Warfare in Yorubaland during the Nineteenth Century." In *Warfare and Diplomacy in Precolonial Nigeria,* edited by Toyin Falola and Robin Law. Madison: African Studies Program, University of Wisconsin, 1992.

Afonja, Simi. "Changing Modes of Production and the Sexual Division of Labor among the Yoruba." In *Women's Work, Development and Division of Labor by Gender,* edited by H. Safa and E. Leacock. South Hadley, Mass.: Bergin and Garvey, 1986.

———. "Land Control: A Critical Factor in Yoruba Gender Stratification." In *Women and Class in Africa,* edited by C. Robertson and I. Berger. New York: Africana Publishing, 1988.

Agiri, B. A. "Early Oyo History Reconsidered." *History in Africa* 2 (1975): 1–16.

Agiri, B. A., and T. Ogboni. "Among the Oyo-Yoruba." *Lagos Notes and Records* 3 (1972): 53.

Ajayi, J. F. Ade. *Christian Missions in Nigeria, 1841–1891.* Evanston, Ill.: Northwestern University Press, 1965.

Ajibola, J. O. *Owe Yoruba.* Ìbàdàn: University Press Limited, 1979.

Ajolore, Olusola. "Lexical Borrowing in Yoruba." In *Yoruba Language and Literature,* edited by Adebisi Afolayan. Ile Ife, Nigeria: University of Ife Press, 1982.

Ajuwon, Bade. *Funeral Dirges of Yoruba Hunters.* New York: Nok Publishers International, 1982.

Aluko, T. M. *One Man, One Wife.* London: Heinemann, 1959.

Amadiume, Ifi. *Male Daughters, Female Husbands: Gender and Sex in an African Society.* London: Zed Books, 1987.

Amos, Valerie, and Pratibha Parma. "Challenging Imperial Feminism." *Feminist Review* 17 (1984): 3–20.

Appadurai, Arjun. "The Past as a Scarce Resource." *Man* 16 (1981): 201–81.

Appiah, Kwame Anthony. *In My Father's House: African in the Philosophy of Culture.* New York: Oxford University Press, 1992.

———. "Out of Africa: Topologies of Nativism." *Yale Journal of Criticism* 12, no. 1 (1988): 153–78.

Apter, Andrew. *Black Critics and Kings: The Hermeneutics of Power in Yoruba Society.* Chicago: University of Chicago Press, 1993.

Asiwaju, A. I. "Dynamics of Yoruba Studies." In *Studies in Yoruba History and Culture,* edited by G. O. Olusanya. Ìbàdàn: University Press Limited, 1983.

———. "Political Motivation and Oral Historical Traditions in Africa: The Case of Yoruba Crowns." *Africa* (London) 46, no. 2 (1976): 113–47.

Atanda, J. A. *The New Oyo Empire: Indirect Rule and Change in Western Nigeria, 1894–1934.* Bristol, England: Longman, 1973.

———. "The Yoruba Ogboni Cult: Did It Exist in Old Oyo?" *Journal of the Historical Society of Nigeria* 6, no. 4 (1973): 371.

Atkins, Keletso. *The Moon Is Dead! Give Us Our Money! The Cultural Origins of an African Work Ethic, Natal, South Africa 1843–1900.* London: Heinemann, 1993.

Austin, John Langshaw. *Philosophical Papers.* Oxford: Oxford University Press, 1961.

Awe, Bolanle. "The Iyalode in the Traditional Yoruba Political System." In *Sexual Stratification: A Cross-cultural View,* edited by Alice Schlegel. New York: Columbia University Press, 1977.

———. *Nigerian Women in Historical Perspective.* Lagos: Sankore, 1992.

———. "Praise Poems as Historical Data: The Example of Yoruba Oriki." *Africa* (London) 44, no. 4 (1974): 331–49.

———. "The Rise of Ìbàdàn as a Yoruba Power." Ph.D. diss., Oxford University, 1964.

———. "Writing Women into History: The Nigerian Experience." In *Writing Women's History: International Perspectives,* edited by Karen Offen, et al. London: Macmillan Academic and Professional Press, 1991.

Awolalu, J. O., and P. A. Dopamu. *West African Traditional Religion.* Ìbàdàn: Onibonoje Press and Book Industries, 1979.

Ayandele, E. A. *The Missionary Impact on Modern Nigeria 1842–1914: A Political and Social Analysis.* London: Longmans, Green, and Co., 1966.

Babalola, Adeboye. *Awon Oriki Borokinni.* Ìbàdàn: Rosprint Industrial Press Limited, 1981.

Babayemi, S. O. *Content Analysis of Oriki Orile.* N.p., n.d.

———. "The Rise and Fall of Oyo c. 1760–1905: A Study in the Traditional Culture of an African Polity." Ph.D. diss., Center for West African Studies, University of Birmingham, England, 1979.

———. "The Role of Women in Politics and Religion in Oyo." Paper presented at the Institute of African Studies, University of Ìbàdàn, seminar entitled "Women's Studies: The State of the Arts Now in Nigeria," November 1987.

———. *Topics on Oyo History.* Ìbàdàn: Lichfield, 1991.

Bada, S. O. *Owe Yoruba ati Isedale Won.* Ìbàdàn: University Press Limited, 1970.

Bamgbose, Ayo. *The Novels of D. O. Fagunwa.* Benin: Ethiope Publishing Corp., 1974.

———. *A Short Yoruba Grammar of Yoruba.* Ìbàdàn: Heinemann Educational Books, 1967.

Barber, Karin. "Documenting Social and Ideological Change through Yoruba Personal Oriki: A Stylistic Analysis." *Journal of the Historical Society of Nigeria* 10, no. 4 (1981).

———. *I Could Speak until Tomorrow: Oriki, Women, and the Past in a Yoruba Town.* Edinburgh: Edinburgh University Press, 1991.

Barnes, Sandra T. "Women, Property, and Power." In *Beyond the Second Sex: New Directions in the Anthropology of Gender,* edited by Peggy Reeves Sanday and Ruth Gallagher Goodenough. Philadelphia: University of Pennsylvania Press, 1990.

Barrett, Michele. *Women's Oppression Today.* London: New Left Books, 1980.

Bascom, William. *The Yoruba of Southwestern Nigeria.* Prospect Heights, Ill.: Waveland Press, 1969.

Bates, Robert, V. Y. Mudimbe, and Jean O'Barr, eds. *Africa and the Disciplines.* Chicago: University of Chicago Press, 1993.

Beauvoir, Simone de. *The Second Sex.* New York: Vintage Books, 1952.

Beier, Ulli. *Yoruba Myths.* New York: Cambridge University Press, 1980.

———. *Yoruba Poetry: An Anthology of Traditional Poems.* London: Cambridge University Press, 1970.

Belasco, B. *The Entrepreneur as Cultural Hero: Preadaptations in Nigerian Economic Development.* New York: Praeger, 1980.

Berry, Sara. *Cocoa, Custom and Socio-economic Change in Rural Western Nigeria.* Oxford: Clarendon Press, 1975.

Biobaku, Saburi. "The Problem of Traditional History with Special Reference to Yoruba Traditions." *Journal of the Historical Society of Nigeria* (1956).

Black, Maria, and Rosalind Coward. "Linguistics, Social and Sexual Relations: A Review of Dale Spender's 'Man Made Language.'" In *The Feminist Critique of Language: A Reader,* edited by Deborah Cameron. New York: Routledge, 1990.

Bloch, Marc. *The Historian's Craft,* New York: Knopf, 1954.

Bodunrin, P. O., ed. *Philosophy in Africa: Trends and Perspectives.* Ile-Ife, Nigeria: University of Ife Press, 1985.

Bowen, T. J. *Central Africa.* Charleston: Southern Baptist Publication Society, 1857.

Brown, Judith. "A Note on the Division of Labor by Sex." *American Anthropologist* 72, no. 5 (1970): 1073–78.

Butler, Judith. *Gender Trouble: Feminism and the Subversion of Identity.* New York: Routledge, 1990.

Callaway, Helen. *Gender, Culture, Empire: European Women in Colonial Nigeria.* Oxford: MacMillan Press in association with St. Anthony's College, 1987.

Cameron, Deborah. "Why Is Language a Feminist Issue?" Introduction to *The Feminist Critique of Language: A Reader,* edited by Deborah Cameron. New York: Routledge, 1990.

Chamberlain, J. Edward, and Sander Gilman. *Degeneration: The Darker Side of Progress.* New York: Columbia University Press, 1985.

Chanock, Martin. "Making Customary Law: Men, Women and the Courts in Colonial Rhodesia." In *African Women and the Law: Historical Perspectives,* edited by Margaret J. Hay and Marcia Wright. Boston University Papers on Africa, no. 7. Boston: African Studies Center, Boston University, 1982.

Charlton, Sue Ellen. *Women in Third World Development.* Boulder, Colo.: Westview Press, 1984.

Chodorow, Nancy. *Femininities, Masculinities, Sexualities: Freud and Beyond.* Lexington: University of Kentucky Press, 1994.

———. *Feminism and Psychoanalytic Theory.* New Haven: Yale University Press, 1989.

Christ, Carol. "Why Women Need the Goddess: Phenomenological, Psychological, and Political Reflections." In *Womanspirit Rising: A Feminist Reader in Religion,* edited by C. P. Christ and J. Plaskow. San Francisco: Harper and Row, 1979.

Clapperton, Hugh. *Journal of the 2nd Expedition into the Interior of Africa.* Philadelphia: Carey, Lea, and Carey, 1829.

Clark, Gracia. *Onions Are My Husband: Accumulation by West African Market Women.* Chicago: University of Chicago Press, 1994.

Coker, G. B. A. *Family Property among the Yoruba.* London: Sweet and Maxwell, 1958.

Coles, Catherine, and Beverly Mack, eds. *Hausa Women in the Twentieth Century*. Madison: University of Wisconsin Press, 1991.

Collier, Jane F., and Sylvia J. Yanagisako, eds. *Gender and Kinship: Essays toward a Unified Analysis*. Stanford, Calif.: Stanford University Press, 1987.

Connell, R. W. *Masculinities*. Cambridge: Polity Press, 1995.

Crowder, M., and O. Ikime, eds. *West African Chiefs: Their Changing Status under Colonial Rule and Independence*. Ife: University of Ife Press, 1970.

De Coulanges, Fustel. *The Ancient City: A Study on the Religion, Laws and Institutions of Greece and Rome*. N.p., 1983 (1987).

De Moraes Farias, P. F. "History and Consolation: Royal Yoruba Bards Comment on Their Craft." *History in Africa* 19 (1992): 263–97.

Denzer, Laray. "Yoruba Women: A Historiographical Study." *International Journal of African Historical Studies* 27, no. 1 (1994): 1–38.

Devor, Holly. *Gender Blending: Confronting the Limits of Duality*. Bloomington: Indiana University Press, 1989.

Diop, Cheikh Anta. *Precolonial Black Africa*. Trenton, N.J.: Africa World Press, 1987.

Diop, Samba. "The Oral History and Literature of Waalo, Northern Senegal: The Master of the Word in Wolof Tradition." Ph.D. diss., University of California–Berkeley, 1993.

Drewal, Margaret T., and Henry J. Drewal. "Composing Time and Space in Yoruba Art." *Word and Image: A Journal of Verbal/Visual Enquiry* 3 (1987): 225.

Duster, Troy. *Backdoor to Eugenics*. New York: Routledge, 1990.

———. "Purpose and Bias." *Transaction, Social Science and Modern Society* 24, no. 2 (1987).

Eades, J. S. *The Yoruba Today*. New York: Cambridge University Press, 1980.

Edholm, Felicity, Olivia Harris, and Kate Young. "Conceptualizing Women." *Critique of Anthropology* 3, nos. 9 and 10 (1978): 101–30.

Ekeh, Peter. "Colonialism and the Two Publics: A Theoretical Statement." *Comparative Studies in Society and History* 17, no. 1 (1975): 91–112.

Ekejiuba, Felicia. "Contemporary Households and Major Socioeconomic Transitions in Eastern Nigeria." Paper presented at a meeting entitled "Workshop on Conceptualizing the Household: Issues of Theory, Method, and Application," Boston University, 1994.

Elberg-Schwartz, Howard, ed. *People of the Body: Jews and Judaism from an Embodied Perspective*. Albany: State University of New York Press, 1992.

Elias, T. O. *Nigerian Land Law and Custom*. London: Routledge and Kegan Paul, 1951.

Errington, Shelly. "Recasting Sex, Gender, and Power." In *Power and Difference: Gender in Island Southeast Asia*, edited by Jane Atkinson and Shelly Errington. Stanford, Calif.: Stanford University Press, 1990.

Fabian, Johannes. *Time and the Other: How Anthropology Makes Its Object*. New York: Columbia University Press, 1983.

Fadipe, N. A. *The Sociology of the Yoruba.* Ìbàdàn: Ìbàdàn University Press, 1970.

Fajana, A. *Education in Nigeria 1939–1942: An Historical Analysis.* Ìbàdàn: Longman, 1978.

Falola, Toyin. "Gender, Business, and Space Control: Yoruba Market Women and Power." In *African Market Women's Economic Power: The Role of Women in African Economic Development,* edited by Bessie House-Midamba and Flix K. Ekechi. Westport, Conn.: Greenwood Press, 1995.

Falola, Toyin, ed. *Yoruba Historiography.* Madison: University of Wisconsin Press, 1991.

Faniyi, Dejo. "Ekun Iyawo: A Traditional Yoruba Nuptial Chant." In *Ifa: An Exposition of the Ifa Literary Corpus,* edited by Wande Abimbola. Ìbàdàn: Oxford University Press, 1976.

Fanon, Frantz. *The Wretched of the Earth.* New York: Grove Weidenfeld, 1963.

Ferguson, Kathy. *The Man Question: Visions of Subjectivity in Feminist Theory.* Berkeley: University of California Press, 1993.

Foucault, Michel. *The History of Sexuality.* Vol. 1, *An Introduction.* New York: Random House, 1990.

Fox Keller, Evelyn, and Christine Grontkowski. "The Mind's Eye." In *Discovering Reality: Feminist Perspectives on Epistemology, Metaphysics, Methodology, and Philosophy of Science,* ed. Sandra Harding and Merrill B. Hintikka. Boston: Reidel, 1983.

Freierman, Steven. "African Histories and the Dissolution of World History." In *Africa and the Disciplines,* edited by Robert Bates, V. Y. Mudimbe, and Jean O'Barr. Chicago: University of Chicago Press, 1993.

Freund, Bill. *The Making of Contemporary Africa.* Bloomington: Indiana University Press, 1984.

Frye, Marilyn. *The Politics of Reality.* Trumansburg, N.Y.: Crossing Press, 1983.

Fuss, Diana. *Essentially Speaking: Feminism and the Nature of Difference.* New York: Routledge, 1989.

Gates, Henry Louis, Jr. *Loose Canons: Notes on the Culture Wars.* New York: Oxford University Press, 1992.

———. *The Signifying Monkey: A Theory of Afro-American Literary Criticism.* New York: Oxford University Press, 1988.

Gbadamosi, Bakare, and Ulli Beier. *Not Even God Is Ripe Enough: Yoruba Stories.* London: Heinemann Educational Books, 1968.

George, Olakunle. "The Predicament of D. O. Fagunwa." Paper presented at the Institute for Advanced Study and Research in the African Humanities, Northwestern University, Evanston, Ill., January 27, 1993.

Gilman, Sander. "Black Bodies, White Bodies." In *Race, Writing, and Difference,* edited by Henry Louis Gates Jr. Chicago: University of Chicago Press, 1988.

———. *On Blackness without Blacks: Essays on the Image of the Black in Germany.* Boston: G. K. Hall, 1982.

———. *The Case of Sigmund Freud: Medicine and Identity.* Baltimore: Johns Hopkins University Press, 1993.

———. *Difference and Pathology: Stereotypes of Sexuality, Race, and Madness.* Ithaca, N.Y.: Cornell University Press, 1985.

———. *Jewish Self-Hatred: Anti-Semitism and the Hidden Language of the Jews.* Baltimore: Johns Hopkins University Press, 1986.

Gleason, Judith. *Oya: In Praise of an African Goddess.* San Francisco: Harper, 1987.

Gordon, Rebecca. "Delusions of Gender." *Women's Review of Books* 12, no. 2 (1994): 18–19.

Gould, Stephen. *The Mismeasure of Man.* New York: Norton, 1981.

Grosz, Elizabeth. "Bodies and Knowledges: Feminism and the Crisis of Reason." In *Feminist Epistemologies,* edited by Linda Alcoff and Elizabeth Potter. New York: Routledge, 1993.

———. *Volatile Bodies: Toward a Corporeal Feminism.* Bloomington: Indiana University Press, 1994.

Guyer, Jane. *Family and Farm in Southern Cameroon.* Boston: Boston University, African Studies Center, 1984.

———. "Food, Cocoa, and the Division of Labour by Sex in Two West African Societies." *Comparative Studies in Society and History* 22, no. 3 (1980): 355–73.

Hallgren, Roland. *The Good Things in Life: A Study of the Traditional Religious Culture of the Yoruba People.* Loberod: Plus Ultra, 1988.

Hampate Ba, Amadou. "Approaching Africa." In *African Films: The Context of Production,* edited by Angela Martin. London: British Film Institute, 1982.

Haraway, Donna J., ed. *Primate Visions: Gender, Race, and Nature in the World of Modern Science.* New York: Routledge, 1989.

Harding, Sandra. *The Science Question in Feminism.* Ithaca, N.Y.: Cornell University Press, 1986.

Harding, Sandra, ed. *The Racial Economy of Science.* Bloomington: Indiana University Press, 1993.

Hartmann, Heidi. "The Unhappy Marriage of Marxism and Feminism: Towards a More Progressive Union." In *Women and Revolution: A Discussion of the Unhappy Marriage of Marxism and Feminism,* edited by Lydia Sargent. Boston: South End Press, 1981.

Henige, David. "The Problem of Feed Back in Oral Tradition: Four Examples from the Fante Coastlands." *Journal of African History* 14, no. 2 (1973): 223–25.

Herskovitz, Melville J. "A Note on 'Woman Marriage' in Dahomey." *Africa* 10 (1937): 335–41.

Hinderer, Anna. *Seventeen Years in the Yoruba Country: Memorials of Anna Hinderer.* London: Seeley, Jackson and Halliday, 1877.

Hobsbawn, Eric, and Terence Ranger, eds. *The Invention of Tradition.* Cambridge: Cambridge University Press, 1983.

Hodder, B. W. *Markets in West Africa: Studies in Markets and Trade among the Yoruba and Ibo.* Ìbàdàn: Ìbàdàn University Press, 1969.

Hofstadter, Douglas R. "A Person Paper on Purity in Language." In *The Feminist Critique of Language,* edited by Deborah Cameron. New York: Routledge, 1990.

Hountondji, Paulin J. *African Philosophy: Myth and Reality.* London: Hutchinson, 1983.

House-Midamba, Bessie, and Felix K. Ekechi, eds. *African Market Women and Economic Power: The Role of Women in African Economic Development.* Westport, Conn.: Greenwood Press, 1995.

Idowu, E. Bolaji. *Olodumare: God in Yoruba Belief.* London: Longman, 1962.

Ighodalo, Fola. "Barriers to the Participation of Nigerian Women in the Modern Labor Force." In *Nigerian Women and Development,* edited by O. Ogunsheye et al. Ìbàdàn: Ìbàdàn University Press, 1988.

Ilesanmi, T. M. "The Yoruba Worldview on Women and Warfare." In *Warfare and Diplomacy in Precolonial Nigeria,* edited by Toyin Falola and Robin Law. Madison: University of Wisconsin, African Studies Program, 1992.

Irele, Abiola. "In Praise of Alienation." In *The Surreptitious Speech: Presence Africaine and the Politics of Otherness, 1947–1987,* edited by V. Y. Mudimbe. Chicago: University of Chicago Press, 1992.

Isola, Akinwumi. "The African Writer's Tongue." *Research in African Literatures* 23, no. 1 (1992): 17–26.

Johnson, Samuel. *The History of the Yorubas.* New York: Routledge and Kegan Paul, 1921.

Jonas, Hans. *The Phenomenon of Life.* New York: Harper and Row, 1966.

Kessler, Suzanne J., and Wendy McKenna. *Gender: An Ethnomethodological Approach.* New York: John Wiley and Sons, 1978.

Kitching, Gavin. *Class and Economic Change in Kenya: The Making of an African Petit Bourgeoisie.* New Haven: Yale University Press, 1980.

Kopytoff, Igor. "Women's Roles and Existential Identities." In *Beyond the Second Sex: New Directions in the Anthropology of Gender,* edited by Peggy Reeves Sanday and Ruth Gallagher Goodenough. Philadelphia: University of Pennsylvania Press, 1990.

Kopytoff, Jean. *A Preface to Modern Nigeria: Sierra Leonians in Yoruba 1830–1890.* Madison: University of Wisconsin Press, 1965.

Krapf-Askari, E. *Yoruba Towns and Cities: An Inquiry into the Nature of Urban Social Phenomena.* Oxford: Clarendon, 1969.

Kwame, Gyekye. *An Essay on African Philosophical Thought.* Philadelphia: Temple University Press, 1995.

Laqueur, Thomas. *Making Sex: Body and Gender from the Greeks to Freud.* Cambridge, Mass.: Harvard University Press, 1990.

Law, Robin. "How Truly Traditional Is Our Traditional History? The Case of Samuel Johnson and the Recording of Yoruba Oral Tradition." *History in Africa* 11 (1984): 195–221.

———. *The Oyo Empire c. 1600–c. 1836.* Oxford: Clarendon Press, 1977.

Lazreg, Marnia. *The Eloquence of Silence: Algerian Women in Question*. New York: Routledge, 1994.

Lévi-Strauss, Claude. *Elementary Structures of Kinship*. Boston: Beacon Press, 1969.

Lloyd, Peter C. "Craft Organization in Yoruba Towns." *Africa* (London) 23, no. 1 (1953): 30–44.

———. "Divorce among the Yoruba." *American Anthropologist* 70, no. 1 (1968): 67–81.

———. *Yoruba Land Law*. New York: Oxford University Press, 1962.

———. "The Yoruba Lineage." *Africa* (London) 25, no. 3 (1995): 235–51.

Lorber, Judith. *Paradoxes of Gender*. New Haven: Yale University Press, 1994.

Lovett, M. "Gender Relations, Class Formation, and the Colonial State in Africa." In *Women and the State in Africa*, edited by Jane L. Parpart and Kathleen A. Staudt. Boulder, Colo.: Lynne Rienner Publishers, 1989.

Lowe, David M. *History of Bourgeois Perception*. Chicago: University of Chicago Press, 1982.

Mabogunje, Akin. *Urbanization in Nigeria*. London: University of London Press, 1968.

Mann, Kristin. *Marrying Well: Marriage, Status, and Social Change among the Educated Elite in Colonial Lagos*. Cambridge: Cambridge University Press, 1985.

Mannheim, Karl. *Ideology or Utopia?* London: Routledge and Kegan Paul, 1936.

Marks, Elaine, and Isabelle de Courtivron, eds. *New French Feminisms: An Anthology*. Amherst, Mass.: University of Massachusetts Press, 1980.

Matory, James. "Sex and the Empire That Is No More: A Ritual History of Women's Power among the Oyo-Yoruba." Ph.D. diss., University of Chicago, 1991.

Mazrui, Ali A. *The Africans: A Triple Heritage*. New York: Little Brown and Co., 1986.

Mba, Nina. *Nigerian Women Mobilized: Women's Political Activity in Southern Nigeria, 1900–1965*. Berkeley: University of California, Institute of International Studies, 1982.

Memmi, Albert. *The Colonizer and the Colonized*. Boston: Beacon Press, 1965.

Miller, Christopher. *Theories of Africans: Francophone Literature and Anthropology in Africa*. Chicago: University of Chicago Press, 1990.

Mohammed, Abdul Jan. "The Economy of Manichean Allegory: The Function of Racial Difference in Colonialist Literature." In *Race, Writing, and Difference*, edited by Henry Louis Gates Jr. Chicago: University of Chicago Press, 1986.

Morgan, Kemi. *Akinyele's Outline History of Ìbàdàn*. Ìbàdàn: Caxton Press, n.d.

Morton-Williams, Peter. "An Outline of the Cosmology and Cult Organization of the Oyo Yoruba." *Africa* 34, no. 3 (1964): 243–61.

Mudimbe, V. Y. *Parables and Fables: Exegesis, Textuality, and Politics in Central Africa.* Madison: University of Wisconsin Press, 1991.

———. *The Invention of Africa: Gnosis, Philosophy, and the Order of Knowledge.* Bloomington: Indiana University Press, 1988.

Mugo, Micere. "Orature in the Department of African American Studies." *Pan African Studies at Syracuse University: A Newsletter* 4 (spring 1994).

Nanda, Serena. "Neither Man nor Woman: The Hijras of India." In *Gender in Cross-cultural Perspective,* edited by Caroline Brettell and Carolyn Sargent. Englewood Cliffs, N.Y.: Prentice Hall, 1993.

Nandy, Ashis. *The Intimate Enemy: Loss and Recovery of Self under Colonialism.* Delhi: Oxford University Press, 1983.

Nicholson, Linda. "Feminism and Marx." In *Feminism as Critique: On the Politics of Gender,* edited by Seyla Benhabib and Drucilla Cornell. Minneapolis: University of Minnesota Press, 1986.

———. "Interpreting Gender." *Signs* 20 (1994): 79–104.

Nzegwu, Nkiru. "Gender Equality in a Dual-Sex System: The Case of Onitsha." *Canadian Journal of Law and Jurisprudence* 7, no. 1 (1994): 88, 91.

———. "O Africa: Gender Imperialism in Academia." In *African Women and Feminism: Reflecting on the Politics of Sisterhood,* ed. Oyèrónké Oyěwùmí. Trenton, N.J.: African World Press, forthcoming.

Ogbu, John U. "African Bride Wealth and Women's Status." *American Ethnologist* 5, no. 2 (1978): 241–62.

Ogundipe, Ayodele. "Esu Elegbara: The Yoruba God of Chance and Uncertainty: A Study in Yoruba Mythology." Ph.D. diss., Indiana University, 1978.

Ogundipe-Leslie, Molara. *Re-creating Ourselves: African Women and Critical Transformations.* Trenton, N.J.: Africa World Press, 1994.

Ogunkoya, T. *St. Andrews College, Oyo: History of the Premier Institution in Nigeria.* New York: Oxford University Press, 1979.

Ojo, G. J. Afolabi. *Yoruba Culture.* London: University of London Press, 1966.

Okin, Susan. *Justice, Gender, the Family.* New York: Basic Books, 1989.

———. *Women in Western Political Thought.* Princeton, N.J.: Princeton University Press, 1979.

Olajubu, Oludare. Book review in *Research in African Literatures* 14, no. 4 (1983): 538–43.

———. "Composition and Performance Technics in Iwi Egungun." In *Yoruba Oral Tradition: Poetry in Music, Dance, and Drama,* edited by Wande Abimbola. Ìbàdàn: Ìbàdàn University Press, 1975.

Olatunji, Olatunde O. "The Yoruba Oral Poet and His Society." *Research in African Literatures* 10, no. 2 (1979): 179–207.

Olupona, Jacob K., ed. *African Traditional Religions in Contemporary Society.* New York: Paragon House, 1991.

Omi, Michael, and Howard Winant. *Racial Formation in the United States from the 1960s to the 1980s.* New York: Routledge, 1986.

Ong, Walter. *Orality and Literacy: The Technologizing of the Word.* New York: Methuen, 1982.

Orasanu, Judith, Mariam K. Slater, and Leonore Loeb Adler, eds. *Language, Sex and Gender.* New York: New York Academy of Sciences, 1979.

Oroge, E. Adeniyi. "The Institution of Slavery in Yorubaland with Particular Reference to the Nineteenth Century." Ph.D. diss., University of Birmingham, England, 1971.

Oruboloye, I. O. *Abstinence as a Method of Birth Control.* Canberra: Australian National University, Department of Demography, 1981.

Owomoyela, Oyekan. "Africa and the Imperative of Philosophy: A Skeptical Consideration." In *African Philosophy: The Essential Readings,* edited by Tsenay Sreberequan. New York: Paragon House, 1991.

———. *A Ki i: Yoruba Proscriptive and Prescriptive Proverbs.* Lanham, Md.: University Press of America, 1988.

———. "Tortoise Tales and Yoruba Ethos." *Research in African Literatures* 20, no. 2 (1989): 165–80.

———. *Visions and Revisions: Essays on African Literatures and Criticism.* New York: Peter Lang, 1991.

Oyemakinde, Wade. "Railway Construction and Operation in Nigeria 1895–1911." *Journal of Historical Society of Nigeria* 7, no. 2 (1974): 305.

Pearce, Tola. "Importing the New Reproductive Technologies: The Impact of Underlying Models of Family, Females and Women's Bodies in Nigeria." Paper presented at the World Institute for Development Economics Research Conference, "Women, Equality and Reproductive Technology," Helsinki, August 3–6, 1992.

Pedler, F. J. *Economic Geography of West Africa.* London: Green, 1955.

Peel, J. D. Y. *Aladura: A Religious Movement among the Yoruba.* London: Oxford University Press, 1968.

———. "Kings, Titles, and Quarters: A Conjectural History of Llesha I: The Traditions Reviewed in History." *Africa* 6 (1979): 109–52.

———. "Making History: The Past in the Ijesha Present." *Man* 19 (1984): 111–32.

Pemberton, John. "The Oyo Empire." In *Yoruba: Nine Centuries of Art and Thought,* edited by Henry Drewal et al. New York: Harry N. Abrams, Inc., 1989.

Rattray, R. S. *The Ashanti.* Reprint. Oxford: Clarendon Press, 1969.

Riley, Denise. *Am I That Name? Feminism and the Category of Women in History.* Minneapolis: University of Minnesota Press, 1988.

Robertson, Claire. *Sharing the Same Bowl: A Socioeconomic History of Women and Class in Accra, Ghana.* Bloomington: Indiana University Press, 1984.

Robinson, Cedric. "Race, Capitalism and the Anti-Democracy." Paper presented at the Inter-disciplinary Humanities Center, University of California–Santa Barbara, 1994.

Rodney, Walter. *How Europe Underdeveloped Africa.* Washington, D.C.: Howard University Press, 1972.

Rosaldo, Michelle, and Louise Lamphere, eds. *Women, Culture, and Society*. Stanford, Calif.: Stanford University Press, 1974.

Rose, Hillary. "Hand, Brain, and Heart: A Feminist Epistemology for the Natural Sciences." *Signs* 9, no. 1 (1983): 73–90.

Rossi, Alice. "Gender and Parenthood." *American Sociological Review* 49, no. 1 (1984): 1–19.

Rubin, Gayle. "The Traffic in Women." In *Toward an Anthropology of Women*, edited by Rayna R. Reiter. New York: Monthly Review Press, 1975.

Sacks, Karen. *Sisters and Wives: The Past and Future of Sexual Equality*. Urbana: University of Illinois Press, 1982.

Salami, Adebisi. "Vowel and Consonant Harmony and Vowel Restriction in Assimilated English Loan Words in Yoruba." In *Yoruba Language and Literature*, edited by Adebisi Ofolayan. Ife: University of Ife Press, 1982.

Scheman, Naomi. *Engenderings: Constructions of Knowledge, Authority, and Privilege*. New York: Routledge, 1993.

Scheper-Hughes, Nancy, and Margaret Lock. "The Mindful Body: A Prolegomenon to Future Work in Medical Anthropology." *Medical Anthropology Quarterly* (1987).

Schiebinger, Londa. *The Mind Has No Sex? Women in the Origins of Modern Science*. Cambridge, Mass.: Harvard University Press, 1989.

Schmidt, Elizabeth. *Peasants, Traders, and Wives: Shona Women in the History of Zimbabwe, 1870–1939*. Portsmouth, N.H.: Heinemann Educational Books, 1992.

Sciolino, Elaine. "800 Women Look to the Future of the Decade for Women." *New York Times*, October 20, 1986.

Serequeberhan, Tsenay, ed. *African Philosophy: The Essential Readings*. New York: Paragon House, 1991.

Sherzer, Joel. "A Diversity of Voices: Men's and Women's Speech in Ethnographic Perspective." In *Language, Gender, and Sex in Comparative Perspective*, edited by Susan Phillips. Cambridge: Cambridge University Press, 1987.

Shorter, Edward. *A History of Women's Bodies*. New York: Basic Books, 1982.

———. *The Making of the Modern Family*. New York: Vintage Books, 1983.

Smith, Dorothy E. *The Everyday World as Problematic: A Feminist Sociology*. Boston: Northeastern University Press, 1987.

Smith, Robert S. "Alafin in Exile: A Study of the Igboho Period in Oyo History," *Journal of African History* 1 (1965): 57–77

———. *Kingdoms of the Yoruba*. Madison: University of Wisconsin Press, 1969.

Solarin, Tai. *To Mother with Love: An Experiment in Auto-biography*. Ìbàdàn: Board Publications Ltd., 1987.

Spelman, Elizabeth. *Inessential Woman: Problems of Exclusion in Feminist Thought*. Boston: Beacon Press, 1988.

Spender, Dale. *Man Made Language*. New York: Routledge and Kegan Paul, 1980.

Stevens, Phillips, Jr. *Stone Images of Esie, Nigeria.* New York: Africana Publishing Co., 1978.

Sudarkasa, Niara. *The Strength of Our Mothers.* Trenton, N.J.: African World Press, 1996.

———. "In a World of Women: Fieldwork in a Yoruba Community." In *The Strength of Our Mothers*, 191–220. N.p., 1996.

———. *Where Women Work: A Study of Yoruba Women in the Market Place and at Home.* Museum of Anthropology Anthropological Papers, no. 53. Ann Arbor: University of Michigan Press, 1973.

Sulloway, Frank. *Born to Rebel: Birth Order, Family Dynamics, and Creative Lives.* New York: Pantheon Books, 1996.

Tannen, Deborah. *You Just Don't Understand: Women and Men in Conversation.* New York: Ballantine Books, 1990.

Tcherkézoff, Serge. "The Illusion of Dualism in Samoa." In *Gender Anthropology*, edited by Teresa del Valle. New York: Routledge, 1989.

Temu, Arnold, and Bonaventure Swai. *Historians and Africanist History: A Critique.* London: Zed Press, 1981.

Thiong'o, Ngugi Wa. *Decolonising the Mind: The Politics of Language in African Literature.* London: James Currey, 1981.

Thorne, Barrie, Cheris Kramarae, and Nancy Henley, eds. *Language, Gender, and Society.* Rowley, Mass.: Newbury Press, 1983.

Turner, Bryan. *The Body and Society: Explorations in Social Theory.* Oxford: Blackwell, 1984.

Tutuola, Amos. *The Brave African Huntress.* New York: Little Brown and Co., 1958.

Urdang, Stephanie. *Fighting Two Colonialisms: Women in Guinea-Bissau.* London: Zed Press, 1979.

Wamba-Dia-Wamba, E. "Philosophy in Africa: Challenges of the Philosopher." In *African Philosophy: The Essential Readings*, edited by Tsenay Serequeberhan. New York: Paragon House, 1991.

Webster, J. B. *The African Churches among the Yoruba, 1882–1922.* London: Clarendon Press, 1961.

Wertheim, Margaret. *Pythagoras' Trousers: God Physics and the Gender Wars.* New York: Random House, 1995.

West, Candace, and Don Zimmerman. "Doing Gender." In *The Social Construction of Gender*, edited by Judith Lorber and Susan A. Farrell. Newbury Park, Calif.: Sage, 1991.

West, Cornel. *Race Matters.* New York: Vantage, 1993.

Wiredu, Kwasi. *Philosophy and an African Culture.* New York: Cambridge University Press, 1980.

Wong, Aline K. "Comments on Turner's Feminist View of Copenhagen." *Signs* 6, no. 4 (summer 1981).

Yai, Olabiyi. "In Praise of Metonymy: The Concepts of Tradition and Creativity in the Transmission of Yoruba Artistry over Space and Time." In *The

Yoruba Artist: New Theoretical Perspectives on African Arts, edited by Rowland Abiodun, H. J. Drewal, and J. Pemberton III. N.p., 1994.

————. "Issues in Oral Poetry: Criticism, Teaching, and Translation." In *Discourse and Its Disguises: The Interpretation of African Oral Texts,* edited by Karin Barber and P. F. de Moraes Farias. African Studies Series, no. 1. Birmingham, England: Birmingham University, Centre of West African Studies, 1989.

Yemitan, Oladipo. *Madame Tinubu: Merchant and King-Maker.* Ìbàdàn: University Press Limited, 1987.

Zachernuk, Phillip. "Samuel Johnson and the Victorian Image of the Yoruba." In *Pioneer, Patriot and Patriarchy: Samuel Johnson and the Yoruba People,* edited by Toyin Falola. Madison: University of Wisconsin, African Studies Program, 1993.

Index

Oyèrónké Oyěwùmí is assistant professor in the Department of Black Studies at the University of California, Santa Barbara. She has been a Rockefeller Humanist-in-Residence at the Center for Advanced Feminist Studies, University of Minnesota, and also held a Rockefeller fellowship at the Institute for the Study of Gender in Africa at the University of California, Los Angeles. Oyěwùmí's research interests are in critical social theory, Western culture, and African societies and cultures in their local and global dimensions.